Exploring
THE BIBLE

D1646216

1 and 2
Thessalonians

A practical commentary

Stanley Jebb

DayOne

© Day One Publications 2011
First printed 2011

ISBN 978–1–84625–287–7

Unless otherwise indicated, Scripture quotations are from the **New King James Version (NKJV)**®. Copyright © 1982 by Thomas Nelson, Inc. Used by permission. All rights reserved.

British Library Cataloguing in Publication Data available

Published by Day One Publications
Ryelands Road, Leominster, HR6 8NZ
☎ 01568 613 740 FAX 01568 611 473
email—sales@dayone.co.uk
web site—www.dayone.co.uk
North America—email—usasales@dayone.co.uk

Cover design by Wayne McMaster
Printed by Orchard Press (Cheltenham) Ltd.

This is a timely book. The coming 'day of the Lord' (1 Thes. 5:2) should put believers on the tiptoe of expectancy and create a passion for holiness. Unfortunately, happiness rather than holiness has become the prevailing concern in many modern evangelical churches. Trials are regarded as threats to our welfare instead of instruments in God's hand to promote our spiritual good. Stanley Jebb effectively demonstrates that Paul's burden for the Thessalonian Christians was that they should become living examples of the holy power of the gospel. We are to live in the light of the coming judgement, and Dr Jebb's book will help us to do this.

Paul E. G. Cook, author and retired evangelical pastor and preacher, Breaston, Derbyshire, UK

Paul's letters to the Thessalonians have a personal quality, a freshness and a vitality that make them always exciting to study. Stanley Jebb's vigorous and straightforward style is admirably suited to them. His commentary is exegetically enlightening without being ponderous, and is clear and heart-warming, practical and pastoral throughout. Its simplicity disguises, without concealing, the thorough labour behind it. This book could be recommended equally for personal Bible study and to the minister looking for help in preaching.

Stanley Jebb wrote this book because he was invited to do so; we may hope for more such invitations.

Mostyn Roberts, pastor of Welwyn Evangelical Church and lecturer in Systematic Theology at London Theological Seminary, UK

I have known Dr Jebb for three decades. He has been my only pastor. I myself pastored two churches for twenty-five years, and I received Dr Jebb's insight throughout. He taught me to reason and argue my case from the Bible, and this approach comes out clearly in this commentary, emphasizing the action to take rather than the words alone. A book reflects the heart of the writer, and this book's author is devoted to Christ and studies the Bible with a view to loving Christ better and making a difference to his

Appreciations

personal life, his family's life, 'his' church, and those he trains and mentors. This is a commentary looking for godly change in the reader.

David Fortune, director of Ministry for Christian Prison Resources, UK

The Thessalonian epistles handle issues requiring pastoral wisdom coupled with the firmness needed to help young Christians striving to be faithful to God in a hostile world. These very characteristics that marked Dr Jebb's years of ministry as a wise and widely respected pastor qualify him admirably to expound what are possibly the earliest of Paul's letters. Dr Jebb's unfailing pastoral touch means that even some of the most difficult passages in the New Testament are handled with a freshness and simplicity that show how up to date is the message of the Bible. Concise yet profound, the exposition sidesteps no problem.

Graham Harrison, minister in Newport, South Wales, and former lecturer at London Theological Seminary and director of the Evangelical Movement of Wales Theological Training Course, UK

This volume combines flawless exposition with far-reaching application. Drawing from a wealth of pastoral experience and with no sacrifice of scholarship, Stanley Jebb has given ordinary Christians a highly readable commentary. The shafts of insight and wisdom will also concentrate the minds of preachers, who would do well to use them in their own preaching. I unreservedly recommend this work. It would make an excellent gift for any pastor from a grateful parishioner!

Tony Sargent, emeritus principal of International Christian College, Glasgow, and adjunct professor of pastoral theology at Olivet University, San Francisco, USA

Contents

Foreword

I am grateful to Stanley Jebb for his kind invitation to write a Foreword for this book because I have much enjoyed reading what he has written and know that others will also benefit from it

These epistles contain doctrine as, of course, all the other epistles do, but they are also strongly ethical, and this comes through in what Dr Jebb has written. He writes as a deeply concerned, experienced and wise pastor who has contemplated both the contemporary world and the contemporary church and has found much to trouble him in both.

My first thought after reading this work was that I hoped it would be read by many in our churches; my second, which is no denial of the first, was that it is particularly needed by those in the pulpit. This is because, alongside clear and unambiguous teaching on justification by grace through faith and faith alone, there is great need for teaching on Christian ethics, and this must come chiefly from our pulpits.

In recent decades, there has been a seismic shift in our culture so that those who have been converted to Christ from non-Christian backgrounds usually have no clear understanding of the ethics of the Bible, and also because the values of the world make a constant assault on Christians through the media, even if they exercise caution as to what they watch and read. There are undisclosed presuppositions of a non-Christian or often an anti-Christian sort in so much with which we come into contact as Christians today. The antidote to this is the growth of a Christian mind through good teaching which is faithful to the text and to the overall theology of Scripture, and which is wisely and relevantly applied to the life of Christians who are called to live in today's real world. This is exactly what Dr Jebb has provided here.

One further point: we value Paul's letters because of their theology and because of their ethics, but I have increasingly come to value them because of the attitude Paul shows to others in them. The epistles to Timothy and Titus are usually called the Pastoral Epistles, but in a very real sense every Pauline epistle is pastoral, and every Christian writer who would act responsibly needs to emulate Paul by considering the influence of his or her book on others. Will it minister to their real needs? This was true of these two letters of Paul's in the first century, and, because of the way he has absorbed them and communicated their truth, it is also true of Stanley Jebb's writing in the twenty-first century.

Sound theology? Challenging ethics? Faithful pastoring? Yes—all true, of both Paul's letters and Stanley Jebb's commentary!

Geoffrey Grogan
Glasgow

Preface

It has been a rewarding experience to work through Paul's two epistles to the Thessalonians. I am grateful to my wife, Shirley, for her tolerance of the hours I spent two floors up in my loft-conversion study. She has been my helpmeet for over fifty years in Christian ministry. When someone once asked her what it was like now that her husband was 'retired' from the pastorate, she smilingly replied, 'I haven't noticed any difference.' What she meant was that we are both still busy in the Lord's work, though we now have more leisure time and a more flexible schedule.

There is a difference, though. I can now say 'No' to invitations (though I rarely do) and the buck no longer stops with me. I have always admired those men who can hold down a pastorate and write books. For me, pastoring a church and training men for the ministry at the same time was all I could manage.

So this commentary, apart from a succession of small booklets, leaflets, leadership training notes and church magazines, is a first. I offer it somewhat diffidently, aware of the vast amount of excellent material already available on these lovely epistles, some of which is mentioned in the Bibliography. I wrote this commentary only because I was invited to do so by the publishers.

I am deeply grateful to Dr Geoffrey Grogan for consenting to read the manuscript and for making a number of valuable comments. Needless to say, how I have interpreted his comments is my responsibility, as also are any errors that may remain in the rest of the book. Dr Grogan was the resident tutor at the Bible Training Institute, Glasgow, where I started my training, an institution of which he later became the much-loved Principal. I benefited from his teaching then as I have done since through some of his many books. Little did I suspect, when I graduated, that he would still be reading and commenting on my work over fifty years later!

My thanks are also due to Jim Holmes of Day One Publications, who has patiently guided me through the process of preparing a manuscript for publication. I am also extremely grateful to Suzanne Mitchell, whose meticulous editing and helpful comments have brought clarity to obscure places and saved me from many a blunder. As mentioned above, any remaining errors are my own.

If this book helps someone to walk the Christian pathway in a more biblical way, my wife and I will be well rewarded.

Stanley Jebb
Truro

Part 1

The First Epistle of Paul to the Thessalonians

Introduction

Author

The status of Paul the apostle as author of this epistle has never been effectively challenged. The author identifies himself as Paul in 1:1 and 2:18. Those who question the authenticity of Paul's letters on the grounds of slight differences in vocabulary, style or content do so on the unwarranted assumption that anyone who writes letters must always do so in the same style, about the same subjects and using the same vocabulary!

Paul, also known as Saul, was born in Tarsus, chief city of the Roman province of Cilicia, now known as Tersous in south-east Turkey. The date of his birth is unknown but is likely to have been within a few years of that of Jesus. He died, apparently as a martyr in Rome, in the mid to late 60s AD. He was educated in Jerusalem under the notable rabbi Gamaliel (Acts 22:3; 26:4–5).

Saul of Tarsus became a self-righteous and bigoted Pharisee who sought with all his might to destroy the church (Acts 9:1–2; 22:4–5; 26:9–11; Phil. 3:4–6). He was dramatically converted through a direct encounter with the risen Christ (Acts 9:3–7; 22:6–16; 26:12–18). After his conversion he spent a few years in various locations as a disciple and in thinking through the implications of his new-found faith (Gal. 1:15–21). He was commissioned by the Lord to be an apostle (Gal. 1:11–2:10; Acts 9:15; 22:6–16; 26:12–18). He was then sent out by the church in Antioch, along with Barnabas, to fulfil the commission already given them by the Lord (Acts 13:1–3). Part of Paul's ministry, from which succeeding generations have benefited, was writing powerful letters, of which thirteen are extant.

Historical background to the epistle

Paul's first letter to the Thessalonians is one of the most heart-warming

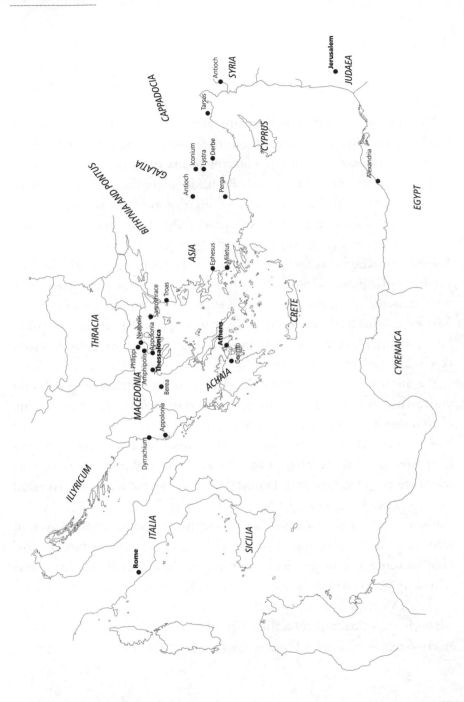

letters in the New Testament. The apostle was obviously delighted with the success of the gospel in Thessalonica and wrote to encourage and instruct the believers there. There is much we can learn from this letter for our own lives.

Have you ever had a powerful dream that has left its impression on you? The apostle Paul had such a dream, but it was more than a dream; it was a vision from God, and was confirmed as such by both circumstances and subsequent events. He received this vision while he was on his second missionary journey. We read about it in Acts 16:6–10.

Paul's vision proved to be of God, and it was because of this vision that the apostle, accompanied by Silas, Timothy and Luke, crossed over into Macedonia, the first entry of the gospel into Europe.

They sailed from Troas via Samothrace and Neapolis, eventually arriving at Philippi, the leading city in that part of Macedonia. Paul's ministry was effective. A businesswoman named Lydia and her household were converted, and a demonized slave-girl was delivered. But this success led to suffering and imprisonment (Acts 16:16–24).

We are apt to think that spiritual success and effectiveness should produce tranquillity, but in Paul's case it led to torture. Yet the suffering church has often proved to be the successful church.

After an earthquake, the jailor and his household heard the Word and were also converted. This raises the question whether we would be willing to be beaten and imprisoned if it led to someone else's conversion (Acts 16:23–34).

Philippi was a Roman colony, which meant that it enjoyed certain privileges, such as exemption from tax. Roman justice was supposed to prevail everywhere in the empire, but especially in its colonies. Paul and Silas had been unjustly beaten and imprisoned without trial, so Paul exercised his right as a free-born Roman citizen to extract an apology from the authorities. Paul did not want to delay his journey by having the incident investigated, so he and his companions, Silas and Timothy, went on.

Paul's visit to Thessalonica

They passed through two towns, Amphipolis and Appolonia, and arrived at Thessalonica, still with the marks of the lictors' rods, which had been inflicted illegally in Philippi, on his and Silas's backs. In spite of that suffering, Philippi held fond memories for him.

Paul's evangelistic ministry in Thessalonica is very briefly described by Luke in Acts. The city had a community of Jews and therefore a synagogue, so as Paul usually began his ministry among the Jews, on the Sabbath he made his way to the synagogue. There he dialogued, or reasoned, for three Sabbaths, expounding the Old Testament prophetic announcements, showing that the Messiah they all expected must die and rise from the dead. Once the Jews had been persuaded that this interpretation of the Law, the Prophets and the Psalms was correct, it was not difficult for them to believe that the Jesus whom Paul preached was the Messiah for whom they all hoped.

But while some of the Jews believed, the majority of the members of the Thessalonian church seem to have been Gentiles, as they had 'turned to God from idols' (1:9), and idolatry was no longer a common Jewish sin. Paul must have ministered among the Gentiles for some time since a large number of Gentiles were converted. The mention of three Sabbaths (Acts 17:2) should not mislead us into thinking that his time there lasted only two or three weeks. We are told in 2 Thessalonians 3:8 that he engaged 'night and day' in manual work there for a livelihood, which suggests a longer period; 'nor did we eat anyone's bread free of charge, but worked with labor and toil night and day, that we might not be a burden to any of you ...'

More significantly, we know from Philippians 4:16 that he received financial support more than once from the Philippians while at Thessalonica. 'For even in Thessalonica you sent aid once and again for my necessities.'

He was there long enough for the Thessalonian Christians to become acquainted with his conduct and character and for him to deal with them as a father does his children (2:11).

These facts, together with the large number of Gentile converts resulting from his ministry, strongly suggest that he was there for three or more months. We need to remember that the Acts of the Apostles is a condensed narrative, and considerable periods of time are sometimes packed into a small amount of text.

Again, however, as in Philippi, jealous Jews drove him out of Thessalonica and he went on to Berea, where at first he was received well. But once more he was driven out and he went on to Athens.

But now, having been forced to leave the new Christians of Thessalonica, he was anxious for news of their welfare. They were spiritual babes exposed to the opposition of his and their enemies, and therefore they needed his encouragement and support. He had himself been unable to pay a return visit, and so he chose to be left alone in Athens and sent Timothy to encourage them and to report back on their progress.

Why the Thessalonian authorities were alarmed by Paul

In order to understand why both the crowds and the authorities were so alarmed by the message preached by the apostles it is necessary to know something of the troubled history of Thessalonica. The charges were that they had 'turned the world upside down' and were 'acting contrary to the decrees of Caesar, saying there is another king ...' (Acts 17:6–7). A brief survey of the history of Thessalonica will explain why this was such a sensitive issue.[1]

Thessalonica was located in the ancient kingdom of Macedonia, which was, by the fourth century BC, for all practical purposes part of the Greek world.

The city of Thessalonica was founded c.315 BC by Cassander, the king of Macedonia. He named it after his wife, Thessalonica, the half-sister of

Alexander the Great. Built on the site of the ancient Therme and drawing into its embrace about twenty-four previously existing villages, the city was located at the head of the Gulf of Therme, on the best natural harbour of the Aegean Sea. This strategic location made Thessalonica the largest and most important city port for the whole of Macedonia in Roman times. It served also as the Roman provincial administrative centre during those periods when Macedonia was a separate province, as it was at the time of Paul's mission to Thessalonica.[2]

Alexander the Great used this Graeco-Macedonian territory as the jumping-off point for his conquest of Western Asia and Egypt. But when Alexander's empire was divided after his death (323 BC), Macedonia soon became a separate kingdom again. Approximately one hundred years later a series of three wars with Rome began. The third Macedonian War (171–168 BC), which took place when Perseus was king, ended with the Roman victory of Pydna, in which between 20,000 and 25,000 Macedonians were killed and 11,000 taken captive. The Romans made a further 150,000 Macedonians slaves and took so much booty that Roman citizens were exempt from direct taxation for a hundred years. So great was the degradation imposed on Macedonia that it became 'a region awaiting rebellion'.[3] The royal dynasty of Macedonia was abolished and the kingdom was divided by the Romans into four republics.

In 149 BC an insurrection took place under an adventurer named Andriscus, who claimed to be the son of Perseus. For a short time he reunited Macedonia under his rule. When his rebellion was suppressed in 148 BC the Romans decided to annex Macedonia as a province.

The four republics, set up twenty years before, remained as geographical divisions but had little political significance. Another rebellion took place after 148 BC under a young man named Euphanes, but this was quickly subdued.

In order to facilitate transport and consolidate their hold on the new province, the Romans built a new military highway, the Via Egnatia, from Apollonia and Dyrrachium on the Adriatic coast of Macedonia to Thessalonica. Before long it was extended eastwards to Philippi and the port of Neapolis, and, later still, to Byzantium. This highway became the main land route for both commerce and military movements between Asia Minor and the Adriatic port of Dyrrachium. Macedonia thus became a base for further extension of Roman power, and in 27 BC the Emperor Augustus handed it over to the control of the Roman Senate. In AD 15 Macedonia was combined with Achaia and Moesia to form one imperial province, but in AD 44 it was handed back to the Senate with Thessalonica as the seat of provincial administration.4

When Julius Caesar was murdered, civil war broke out in Rome. Thessalonica supported the Second Triumvirate, who were the eventual victors. As a reward, Marcus Antonius (Mark Anthony) made Thessalonica a free city in 42 BC. This had several important consequences.

First, the city was given a degree of local autonomy as well as the right to mint its own coins. Second, the city was promised freedom from military occupation and granted certain tax concessions. Third, Thessalonica did not become a Roman colony. This meant that Roman law, which would have replaced local legal institutions, was not imposed, and the city was relieved of the responsibility of absorbing a large settlement of demobilized Roman soldiers, as happened at Philippi, Cassandra and elsewhere. This left the local ruling elite in control of the city with its traditional institutions intact.

In the ancient world there was a close connection between religion and politics, so the authorities in Thessalonica sought to maintain a balance not only between local autonomy and subservience to Rome, but also between the worship of their own local deities and recognition of the Roman cult of emperor worship.

From the victory of Octavian (Augustus) over the forces of Marcus Antonius and Cleopatra at Actium in 31 BC until well after the time of

Paul, Thessalonica, like the other cities of Macedonia, entered a period of unparalleled peace and improving economic circumstances. It was in their interests to maintain this peace at all costs.

By the time of Paul the population of Thessalonica was quite cosmopolitan. Greek immigrants from the south had merged with the original Macedonian population, giving the city a distinctively Greek character. Also, after the battle of Actium, numbers of Latin-speaking people settled in Thessalonica, especially merchants and imperial administrators. From Acts 17 we learn that a significant Jewish community existed.

Although Paul began his mission among the Jews, as was his usual practice, the majority of his converts came from other religions (see 1 Thes. 1:9). Pagan religious cults were a normal part of Thessalonian daily life, as indicated by archaeological and inscriptional evidence. These mystery religions included the worship of Serapis, an Egyptian god, as well as the state-sponsored Dionysius, the god of wine and drunkenness, and Cabirian cults,[5] the last being the chief city religion. In addition there was the imperial religion in which Caesar was worshipped. These religions, especially the cult of Cabirus, were regarded as necessary for maintaining social unity and stability in Thessalonica.

The establishment of the imperial cult served to cement Thessalonian relations with Rome, and also to define the relation of power between the emperor and his subjects. In Greek tradition, power was represented as divine in origin. It is easy to see, therefore, how a missionary propagating a new religion, especially one regarding all others as false, would be a threat, both to the social order supported by the Cabirus cult and to the links with Rome via the imperial cult.

Paul's letter

When Timothy rejoined Paul, who had by now moved to Corinth, Timothy's favourable report on the Thessalonian church was encouraging, but it also had its graver aspects. This led Paul to write 1 Thessalonians, both to rejoice with the Thessalonians and to deal with the problems that had surfaced. This epistle is one of Paul's earliest, written about AD 51, within twenty-five years of the beginning of Jesus's ministry.

It seems that the believers in Thessalonica needed counsel. They were suffering persecution. Paul may have felt partially responsible for this, so he commended them for their faithfulness under trial (2:14; 3:1–4).

There also seems to have been some criticism or, at least, misunderstanding regarding Paul's ministry and motives. This had probably been instigated either by pagan opposition or by Jewish envy. Paul believed it right to seek to put the record straight (2:1–12).

It also appears that these new converts needed instruction and encouragement regarding moral standards in that pagan environment (4:1–8). In their new-found freedom in Christ and their expectation of his near return, some were tempted to neglect their daily work and needed warning about the evils of idleness (4:11; compare 2 Thes. 3:10–12). Moreover, some of the Christians had suffered bereavement and were concerned about the destiny of the deceased (1 Thes. 4:13–18).

At the end of his letter Paul added some short and succinct exhortations, mainly about worship (5:16–22).

Study questions

1. Read Acts 17:1–15. Why did Paul have to leave Thessalonica? What differences in attitude did he find in Berea?

2. Compare the greetings of all Paul's letters and note the differences. Can you suggest reasons for some of the variations?

3. Why do you think God used a vision to get Paul and his party into Europe (Acts 16:6–10; compare 10:9–17)?

4. Should Christians always move on when they are persecuted?

5. What kind of example do you expect from Christian leaders?

Notes

1 For a more comprehensive and detailed survey of the geography, history and religion of Thessalonica at that time, see **Gene L. Green,** *The Letters to the Thessalonians* (Grand Rapids, MI: Eerdmans / Leicester: Apollos, 2002), pp. 1–47.

2 **Charles A. Wanamaker,** *The Epistles to the Thessalonians* (NIGTC; Grand Rapids, MI: Eerdmans / Carlisle: Paternoster, 1990), p. 3.

3 **Green,** *Letters*, p. 14.

4 **F. F. Bruce,** *1 & 2 Thessalonians* (Word Biblical Commentary; Nashville: Thomas Nelson, 1982), pp. xx–xxi.

5 See **Green,** *Letters*, pp. 43ff., for details of the Cabirian religion.

The power of example (1 Thes. 1)

The greeting (v. 1)

Only in the Thessalonian epistles does Paul introduce himself simply by his name. In all his other letters he adds a description or qualification such as 'apostle', 'prisoner of Christ' or 'servant of Christ Jesus'. Evidently, this being one of the earliest of Paul's letters, his apostleship had not yet been challenged and the Thessalonians accepted him as he was, simply Paul. He follows the conventional form usual at the beginning of a letter of this period. It began with the name of the writer, followed by that of the addressee, and a greeting.

Paul includes Silvanus and Timothy in the greeting, mentioning Silvanus first as the older and more experienced fellow-labourer. It is generally agreed that Silvanus is the person who is named Silas elsewhere. Silas and Timothy were known to the Thessalonians as they had participated in the evangelization of the city (Acts 17:1–15).

WHO WAS SILVANUS?

Silvanus, or Silas, who is described in Acts as a prophet and one of the chief men among the brethren (Acts 15:22, 32), was a leading member of the church at Jerusalem. He was sent by the Jerusalem church, along with Judas Barsabas, to welcome into fellowship the Gentiles converted in Antioch (Acts 15:22–35).

When Paul and Barnabas, Paul's original travelling companion, had a strong disagreement over the advisability of taking on their travels John Mark, who had let them down once before, Barnabas took Mark and Paul chose Silas as his companion on the second missionary journey (Acts

15:36–41). As a senior member of the Jerusalem church Silas would have been a very useful companion, especially as he, like Paul, was a Roman citizen (Acts 16:37–39). He accompanied Paul through Syria, Asia Minor, Macedonia and Thessalonica. When Paul left for Athens Silas stayed behind in Berea, and then rejoined Paul at Corinth (Acts 16–18). Paul refers to Silas's work in Corinth in 2 Corinthians 1:19.

WHO WAS TIMOTHY?

Timothy was a native of a South Galatian city, probably Lystra, and the son of a mixed marriage, his father being a Greek and his mother a Jewess (Acts 16:1). When he became a Christian is not recorded, though it is probable that he was a convert from Paul's first missionary journey which included Lystra, because Paul refers to him as his 'son' (Acts 14; 1 Tim. 1:2; 2 Tim. 1:2). It seems that Timothy's grandmother, Lois, and his mother, Eunice, were converted before him, and that they gave him a good grounding in the Old Testament Scriptures (2 Tim. 1:5; 3:14–15).

Timothy had a good reputation among the Christians of Lystra and Iconium, and Paul recognized his qualities by adding him to his travelling party, probably as a substitute for John Mark (Acts 16:2–3). He had been equipped by the Lord for service and had been commissioned by the elders and Paul (1 Tim. 1:18; 4:14; 2 Tim. 1:6). Although he was of timid disposition (1 Cor. 4:17; 16:10–11; 2 Tim. 1:7), nevertheless Paul entrusted him with several important assignments (Acts 19:22; 20:4–5; 1 Cor. 4:17; 1 Thes. 3:2, 6; 1 Tim. 1:3), and he was Paul's constant and loyal companion (Rom. 16:21; 1 Cor. 16:10; Phil. 2:19–24; 2 Tim. 3:10–15), for which Paul warmly commended him. His name appears alongside Paul's in several of the latter's epistles (2 Cor. 1:1; Phil. 1:1; Philem. 1). He also appears to have suffered imprisonment for the faith (Heb. 13:23). The two letters to Timothy tell us much about the apostle Paul and his younger protégé.

Timothy had been instructed in the Old Testament Scriptures from childhood by a pious mother and grandmother. The effect of a godly upbringing is incalculable. Children of Christian parents are sinners like all other children. They do not need to be taught to lie, to steal, to lose their temper. The statement in 1 Corinthians 7:14 that the children of a believer are 'holy' must not be misunderstood. It does not mean that the child of a Christian parent is automatically a saint, any more than the unbelieving spouse is automatically made a believer by being married to a Christian. The context of that verse is the question whether a marriage remains a true marriage when one of the parents becomes a Christian. Should the believer leave the unbelieving spouse? No, says Paul. The marriage remains valid. The other party has been 'set apart' (sanctified) in marriage to the believer; the marriage is valid and the children are legitimate.

Children of Christian parents are dead in trespasses and sins until they are saved by God's grace. They cannot be regenerated by the faith of their parents. God has no grandchildren. Children cannot receive faith second-hand or by proxy. Baptism at any age and by any mode cannot regenerate them; it is not a saving rite. They need to be born again by the Spirit of God.

Is there no difference, then, between the children of Christians and those of unbelievers? Fundamentally, none at all. But believers have the promises of God and there are differences of context. This was the point that Paul was making when he referred to Timothy's mother and grandmother in 2 Timothy 1:5. Christians recognize their children as God's gifts. Therefore, not only are they thankful for them, but also they realize they have a responsibility for them. Their children are set in the context of spiritual potential; they are prayed for and with, and they hear the Word of God read and discussed in the home and taught and preached in the church.

Timothy's upbringing shines out in stark contrast to what happened during the period of the judges, as it is recorded in one of the saddest verses in the Bible: 'When all that generation had been gathered to their fathers, another generation arose after them who did not know the LORD nor the work which He had done for Israel' (Judg. 2:10). This verse implies the neglect of their duty by the Israelite parents. They could not force their children to 'know the LORD', but they could have ensured that they knew the record of his mighty deeds. Long before the time of the judges God had made clear the responsibilities of parents to teach their children (see Gen. 18:19; Exod. 12:26–27; 13:8–10; Deut. 6:4–9; 31:11–14), and he continued to press home that responsibility throughout Israel's history and into the new covenant era (Ps. 78:5; Prov. 22:6; Isa. 38:19; Joel 1:3; Eph. 6:4, etc.). In addition to teaching them, parents must set a good example to their children in their own behaviour and in their attitude to the Scriptures and to the local church. Parents cannot expect their children to love the Word of God if they themselves neglect it, nor can they expect their children to cultivate faithfulness in worship unless they set the standard. This will mean not only attending meetings regularly and punctually, but also being faithful in their private devotions and in family worship. If it ever becomes necessary for parents to discuss problems in the church or express criticisms of ministry, they should never, ever do so in front of their children, who take in far more from an early age than most parents realize.

Paul's greeting, however, was an innovation as this was perhaps the first time a letter had been written to a church (see 1 Thes. 5:27). As mentioned above, this letter was one of Paul's earliest epistles, if not the first (the other, perhaps more likely candidate for this honour being the letter to the Galatians). In Galatians Paul writes 'to the churches of Galatia' (1:2). He addresses 1 Thessalonians to 'the church of the Thessalonians in God the Father and the Lord Jesus Christ' (1:1). The word 'church' (*ekklesia*: congregation or assembly) was not, however, new.[1] The Greeks were familiar with it as it was the term used of the citizens of a Greek town assembled for public business. In fact, it is also used in the Greek Old Testament (Septuagint) to describe the children of Israel as the congregation of the Lord. This is why Stephen refers to the people of Israel during the wilderness wanderings as the *ekklesia* (Acts 7:38), which incidentally suggests a measure of continuity with the New Testament church. In the New Testament the word *ekklesia* can refer to the universal church (Eph. 1:22–23; Col. 1:18), the local church in a city or town (Rom. 16:23; 1 Cor. 1:2; 14:23), or even a portion of the local church meeting in a home (Rom. 16:5; 1 Cor. 16:19). So the Jews who met in the synagogue were an assembly or 'church', united in acknowledging the living God and observing his law. The citizens of Thessalonica were a 'church' or assembly when they met to discuss political affairs. But the assembly or church of the Thessalonians was distinct from either of them. Since the word *ekklesia* had no particular religious significance at that time the apostle needed to differentiate it from the secular assemblies with which the Thessalonians were familiar. How was this assembly different? The Thessalonian believers were bound together by their faith in the Lord Jesus Christ. They were no longer without God and without hope in the world. Though they were still *in* the world physically, they were not *of* it morally or spiritually. They were now in Christ Jesus, a new creation. The innovation is that this word was now applied to believers 'in God the Father and the Lord Jesus Christ'. The phrase 'in Christ' is one of Paul's favourite expressions and he uses it in greetings elsewhere (see Phil. 1:1; Col. 1:1), but to greet them as 'in God' is unique as a greeting in the New Testament, though the phrase does occur later in the text of both Ephesians and Colossians (Col. 3:3; compare Eph. 3:9). The word 'in' (Greek *en*) could possibly have instrumental force, thus pointing to the origin of the church which was brought into being by God the Father and the Lord Jesus Christ (see Acts 20:28). But the most natural meaning of the words is that God and Christ form 'the sphere in which the church exists'.[2]

The joining of God the Father and the Lord Jesus Christ under one preposition in the address indicates the exalted position of Christ in Paul's thought and points to his deity, as does his linking of them in the greeting (compare v. 3; 3:11–13; 5:18; 2 Thes. 1:1; 2:16–17; 3:5). The reference to the Holy Spirit in verse 5 completes the allusion to the Holy Trinity. Jesus taught his disciples to relate to God as Father (Matt. 6:9; Luke 11:2). Jesus is the human name of the Messiah, given to our Lord at the instruction of an angel (Matt. 1:21). It is derived, through Latin, from the Greek transliteration of the Hebrew 'Joshua', which itself is an abbreviation of 'Jehoshua', meaning 'Jehovah is salvation'. The title 'Lord', as applied to Jesus by Paul, is the regular translation in the Septuagint of the Hebrew 'Yahweh'. It is surely this source rather than Hellenistic sources that is behind Paul's usage of the title.

Paul wished the Thessalonians '[g]race' and 'peace'. This is the greeting in all his letters, except that in 1 and 2 Timothy and Titus the word 'mercy' is added. 'Grace' can refer to an attribute or quality of God or the Lord Jesus Christ, namely, kindness. Or it can mean the favour shown towards God's people which results in their deliverance from the guilt and punishment of sin, the transforming operation of the Holy Spirit in their hearts, and their entrance into glory. This is sovereign, unconditional and unmerited (Eph. 2:8).[3] Grace is the free, undeserved favour of God. It is manifested not only in the act of salvation (Rom. 3:24; 5:15; Eph. 2:8; 2 Thes. 2:16), but also in the ongoing supporting power by which God keeps and uses his saints to his glory (Acts 15:40; 2 Cor. 8:1, 7; Gal. 2:9). Peace is the result, the fruit, of the work of grace in a Christian's heart. The order is significant. There is no peace with God apart from the grace of God. It is only when the grace of God has worked in us that we can have peace with God. 'Therefore, having been justified by faith, we have peace with God through our Lord Jesus Christ' (Rom. 5:1).[4]

Although these Christians lived physically and spiritually in Thessalonica, their primary and more enduring location was a spiritual one. They lived in God and in Christ (1 Thes. 1:1). And that is where every believer lives. Are you aware of that? Jesus urged his disciples to 'abide', that is, 'continue to live', in him (John 15:4).

Paul's affection for them: the thanksgiving (vv. 2–8)

Paul and his companions express their affection by thanking God, and by assuring the Thessalonians that they regularly pray for them and constantly remember their excellent qualities, such as their 'work of faith, labor of love, and patience of hope'. The adverb translated 'without ceasing' (NKJV) or 'continually' (NIV) is usually found in connection with prayers or thanksgivings (Rom. 1:9; 1 Thes. 2:13; 5:17; 2 Tim. 1:3).[5] This should be understood as persistent, not non-stop, intercession (see Luke 18:1). The use of the plural ('we give thanks' and 'our prayers') implies the joint authorship of the letter, or, at the very least, that Silas and Timothy were united in sending their greetings. How does the trio's affection for the Thessalonians manifest itself?

THEY THANK GOD FOR THE THESSALONIAN CHRISTIANS (VV. 2–4)

Only in the epistle to the Galatians is this note of thanksgiving absent; the news Paul had received about the Galatians gave him nothing to give thanks about, as the false teaching the Galatians were beginning to embrace undermined the very gospel itself. Most of us, perhaps, pray for our fellow-church members from time to time, but how often do we actually thank God for them? It is easy to be thankful for those who are sweet and encouraging, but what about those who are a thorn in the flesh (2 Cor. 12:7–10)? If their effect is to cast us upon God in prayer, if they teach us to be tolerant, if by their attitude they cause us indirectly to grow in grace, is there not an oblique reason to thank God for them?

Before Paul begins to congratulate, teach, exhort or admonish, he thanks God for the signs of his grace in the Thessalonian believers. His thanksgiving is unreserved and unceasing. The three adverbial participles, 'making mention', 'remembering' and 'knowing', modify the main verb in verse 2, 'We give thanks'. The implication is that their thanksgiving was not an unconsidered or vague 'thank God for the Thessalonians', but was specific, based on remembered facts and clear knowledge. What do he and his fellow-workers thank God for especially? They thank God for the Thessalonians' work, labour, and patience or endurance. But these are not ordinary activities. The apostle links the famous triad of faith, love and hope with them (see also 5:8; Rom. 5:1–5; 1 Cor. 13:13; Gal. 5:5–6; 1 Peter 1:21–22; Heb. 10:21–24).

What a lesson there is here! How easy it is to have faith, love and hope in our hearts, but not to express them in our daily living! How easy to work and labour with an attitude of pride and superiority, or with resentment, and not to work with the inspiration of faith, the dynamic of love and the prospect of hope! The Thessalonians' faith issued in work. The modest word translated 'work' could refer to manual labour (2:9; 4:11; 2 Thes. 3:8–10; 1 Cor. 4:12; 9:6), to the ministry of church leaders (1 Thes. 5:12–13; Rom. 15:18 ('deed'); 16:3, 6, 9, 12, 21; 1 Cor. 3:13; 15:10; 16:9–10; 2 Cor. 6:5; Phil. 2:22; Col. 4:17), or to works of Christian charity (2 Thes. 1:11; 2 Cor. 9:8; Eph. 2:10; 4:12; Col. 1:10; 2 Tim. 2:21).[6] Their work was done in faith. It was based upon the sure foundation of 'the faith ... once for all delivered to the saints' (Jude 3). Their love moved them to 'labor'. The word indicates labour to the point of weariness, but it was not done in a self-pitying, martyrdom attitude of the 'poor me' syndrome. It sprang from love, manifested love and was performed in love. The chief objects of love were other Christians (4:9–10; 5:13; 2 Thes. 1:3), but they had learned from God through his love for them (1:4; 4:9; 2 Thes. 2:13, 16) that their love should also reach out to the unconverted (3:12).

Then there was also endurance, 'patience of hope': 'not a quiet passive resignation but an active constancy in the face of difficulties'.[7] This term indicates 'the ability to remain steadfast and to persevere in the face of suffering or temptation'[8] (Luke 21:19; Rom. 5:3–5; 2 Cor. 1:6; 6:4; Col. 1:11; 2 Thes. 1:4; 1 Tim. 6:11; Titus 2:2; Heb. 12:1; James 1:3–4; Rev. 2:2–3). It was inspired by hope because the source of this perseverance was not their own determination or 'stickability' but their hope in the Lord Jesus Christ (see Rom. 5:3–4; 8:25; 15:4). Hope in the New Testament is not a pious optimism, a vague 'hope so' attitude, but a fixed assurance that what God has promised will be fulfilled.[9] This hope enabled the Thessalonians to be patient in their tribulations and trials.

Sometimes in Paul's letters certain misgivings are implied, as in the case of the Corinthians, who manifested gifts rather than graces and possessed knowledge and utterance rather than love. Here, however, Paul thanks God for the marks of Christian character which are eminently spiritual: faith, love and hope. Faith rests on the past work of Christ, love is produced in the present by the Spirit of Christ, and hope looks to the future return of Christ. Nevertheless, all three graces affect the present, because they produce work, labour and patience. Unlike the figures in the Neo-Classical sculpture The Three Graces, which are lovely to look at but do not move, the Christian graces work, toil and endure, and produce a beauty of their own which is Christlikeness. It has been said that gifts can hang on a dead tree, but it is only a living tree that bears fruit.

For the Thessalonians, this lifestyle characterized by hard-working and patient faith, love and hope was not shaped by men's opinions, nor was it intended to produce men's applause. It was done in the sight of God, for his pleasure, according to his will and for his glory. Just as Elijah, when facing King Ahab, who was presumably dressed in all his regal finery, spoke of 'the LORD God of Israel ... before whom I stand', so we must give more honour to the Lord than to any dignitary whom we may meet (1 Kings 17:1). We are to work as in the presence of the King of kings and Lord of lords. Whatever we do, it must be done to the glory of God (1 Cor. 10:31).

Paul and his co-workers also thanked God for the Thessalonians' election (v. 4), as well they might, because God's election of the Thessalonians was not based upon their own merit or virtue (see 2 Thes. 2:13; Rom. 1:7; Jude 1; compare Deut. 4:37; 7:7–8; 10:15; Ps. 47:4; 78:68; Isa. 42:1; Matt. 12:18; Rom. 11:28; Eph. 1:4; Col. 3:12).[10] God is not like pagan deities, which have to be placated or bribed in order for the worshipper to receive blessings; God's love, as demonstrated by election, is unilateral, unmerited and unconditional (1 John 4:10, 19). Is it possible to know that one is chosen (elect)? Paul declares that it is, for he says his thanksgiving is made in the knowledge that the Thessalonians are elect. That means they were chosen in Christ from before the foundation of the world (Eph. 1:4). How did he know that? He tells them and us in verses 5 to 8.

THEY SEE IN THE THESSALONIANS THE MARKS OF ELECTION (VV. 5–8)
Paul recollects how their preaching in Thessalonica did not consist merely of words spoken: 'not … in word only, but also in power'. The phrase 'not … in word only' refers to 'speech unaccompanied by the convincing power of the Holy Spirit. Such speech, however eloquent and moving, would be ineffective in evoking faith from the hearers (cf. 1 Cor. 2:4–5).'[11] Paul does not contrast word and power, as though demonstrations of power are sufficient in themselves. It is noticeable that after the earthquake and the releasing of the prisoners in Acts 16 Paul 'spoke the word' to his hearers (Acts 16:32). Hendriksen draws attention to the way 'the concepts Spirit and power go together here, as so often'[12] (Rom. 1:4; 15:13, 19; 1 Cor. 2:4; Gal. 3:5; compare 2 Tim. 1:7–8). Notice how the apostle identifies himself and his colleagues with the 'gospel', which is elsewhere referred to as 'the gospel of God' (2:2, 8–9), 'the gospel of Christ' (3:2) and 'the gospel of our Lord Jesus' (2 Thes. 1:8). There was power present because the Holy Spirit was active among them. In the case of the apostles this reference to power may have included an allusion to

miracles, which were 'signs of an apostle' (2 Cor. 12:12; compare Mark 6:5; Acts 2:22; 1 Cor. 2:4; Heb. 2:4; contrast 2 Thes. 2:9). He reminds them of the character the apostles displayed (1 Thes. 1:5) and that the Thessalonians began to follow them and the Lord (v. 6). They received the message joyfully in spite of persecution and as a result became an example to other Christians. More than that, they themselves began to proclaim the gospel throughout Macedonia and Achaia (v. 7). 'This passage is a most forceful repudiation of the position of those who say that one can never really know whether he or whether anybody else is included in God's eternal decree of election.'[13]

What evidence was there to assure Paul of the Thessalonian believers' election?

Proofs that Paul and his companions experienced (v. 5)

The first reason why the apostles were sure of their election may seem strange to us, because it was subjective; it was in the preachers themselves.[14] They had the assurance and evidence within themselves that Paul's preaching had been effective. MacArthur writes, 'Paul knew the preaching at Thessalonica bore divine power because of the *full conviction* ... he had as he delivered it' (emphasis original).[15]

Leon Morris concurs:

Some scholars have felt that the assurance meant here is that which came to the converts when they put their trust in Christ, and this may not be out of the apostle's mind. But his primary meaning is the assurance that the Spirit gave to the preachers, for Paul is dealing with the way he and his companions came to know the election of the Thessalonians. They had the assurance in their own hearts that, as they were evangelizing, the power of God was at work.[16]

Though it is necessary to use words to preach, words alone are not enough. God must work. There was power or unction in Paul's preaching, and the sense that his words were going home into the hearers' hearts. This fire, this effectiveness, was not humanly generated passion. He was conscious that the Holy Spirit accompanied his words, producing the fire and penetrating the hearers' minds. The result was that he experienced a strong conviction, not only that the message was true for him, but also that the gospel was being received and was being made effective by the Holy Spirit in the lives of the hearers. And his companions shared that conviction. Nevertheless, words must be used. God has communicated his truth in words. This is propositional revelation.[17] The gospel cannot be communicated merely by feelings or impressions. Towards the end of his life Paul wrote to Timothy, 'If you instruct the brethren in these things, you will be a good minister of Jesus Christ, nourished in the words of faith and of the good doctrine which you have carefully followed' (1 Tim. 4:6).

Unfaithfulness in the life of a preacher undermines his own assurance. Paul's prayerfulness, penitence and obedience strengthened his own assurance and thus the conviction with which he preached. The remarkable conversions he had seen in Philippi of Lydia and the jailor had also strengthened his confidence. Even apostles were human, and Christian workers are always encouraged by observing blessing on their ministry.

Included in what Paul observed as signs of election was the fact that the Thessalonians could testify what kind of men the apostles had been among them (1 Thes. 1:5). There must be harmony between the message and the behaviour of missionaries, otherwise, no matter how powerful the preaching, the message will be contradicted. The drift of Paul's statement is surely this: the Thessalonians' election could not be doubted since God had sent such powerful and confident men among them, men on fire with the love and glory of God and whose message proved to be true by the effect it had on the hearers' lives. This leads to another strand of proof.

Proofs in the Thessalonians (vv. 6–10)

The manner, character and demeanour of the apostles was not, on its own, sufficient to prove the election of Paul's readers. So he turns from the subjective reasons for his assurance to the objective facts in the Thessalonian Christians themselves. He has already shown one clear proof that they were chosen in Christ from before the foundation of the world: namely, that faith, love and hope characterized their lives in the world. Now he gives seven additional signs of true conversion in verses 6 to 10.

1. THEY BECAME FOLLOWERS OF THE APOSTLES AND OF THE LORD (V. 6)

To become a Christian was not an easy choice. It meant becoming one of a despised and persecuted minority, as is the case in many countries today. This surely is the point behind Paul's statement that a man who aspires to be an overseer aspires to a good thing (1 Tim. 3:1). This is not mere ambition, which is nearly always bad;[18] in accepting a role of leadership in those days, and in certain lands today, a man was making himself a target for persecution and even martyrdom. Eldership was not a prestigious office, but a great responsibility with a heavy price to pay.

Paul occasionally links following himself with following the Lord (v. 6). Since the apostles were the channels of the infallible Word of God and were themselves faithfully following Christ, there was little danger in that mode of expression. In 1 Corinthians the apostle provides a safeguard with the words 'Imitate me, just as I also imitate Christ' (1 Cor. 11:1). Only as Paul faithfully followed the Lord could he be safely followed. This is the essence of discipleship. What Paul is saying, therefore, is that the Thessalonians became disciples. In the Great Commission of Matthew 28:19–20, the Lord commanded the apostles not to get decisions for Christ but to make disciples of Christ; not to make converts but to make disciples.[19] To be discipled or mentored, one needs a discipler or mentor. To disciple someone takes time, effort, patience and, in a Christian context, love. The Thessalonians were not those who had merely made an impulsive decision, nor was their conversion a mere intellectual assent to the gospel. They were disciples. A disciple is a disciplined follower, a learner, not a flash-in-the pan convert. This means the Thessalonians were brought into the context of fellowship (1 John 1:3).

2. THEY WELCOMED THE WORD 'IN MUCH AFFLICTION' (V. 6)

In other words, the severe persecution and intense opposition from their contemporaries (2:14; 3:3, 7; 2 Thes. 1:4, 6), which resulted from their becoming Christians, did not hinder them from accepting, believing and acting on the message preached. Opposition did not deter them in the pursuit of their chosen path.

Suffering is inevitable in one form or another. John Piper writes much about suffering in his books. For example, 'It is a biblical truth that the more earnest we become about being the salt of the earth and the light of the world, and the more devoted we become to reaching the unreached peoples of the world, and exposing the works of darkness, and loosing the bonds of sin and Satan, the more we will suffer.'[20] It is clear from the New Testament that suffering is a normal aspect of Christian discipleship (Matt. 8:18–22; 10:22–25; Mark 8:34; John 15:18–21; 16:33; Acts 9:15–16; 14:21–22). This was no 'easy-believism'. It was not decisionism, not a one-time decision that produced no lasting change in their lives. It was a thought-out conviction, a Holy Spirit-wrought conversion that could not be snuffed out by opposition.

3. THEY RECEIVED THE MESSAGE WITH PROFOUND JOY (V. 6)

The message was not grimly received with Stoic-like resignation. Morris quotes Lightfoot: 'The degree in which the believer is allowed to participate in the sufferings of his Lord should be the measure of his joy.'[21] The Lord Jesus Christ taught that Christians are to experience joy even in the midst of suffering (Matt. 5:11–12; Luke 6:22–23; 21:28). The knowledge that they shared the sufferings of Christ strengthened the apostles and other Christians (Acts 5:41; 16:25; Rom. 12:12; 2 Cor. 4:8–10; 7:4; Phil. 1:29; 2:17; Col. 1:24; James 1:2; 1 Peter 1:6; 4:13–14; compare 2 Cor. 8:2). This was no carnal, worked-up human excitement that could be paralleled in a pop concert. It was Holy Spirit-given supernatural joy, a joy that even suffering could not quench, a joy triumphant over all malignant opposition. Where Christians live in the midst of societies opposed to God and his cause, they will suffer; but suffering should not break their spirits, or make them bitter, or lead them to renounce the faith. God's grace will keep them trusting, humble and joyful through it all. Denney remarks that Paul knew the Thessalonians were elect because he saw in them that new power to rejoice in tribulations; a power which can only be seen in those who have the Spirit of God.[22]

4. THEY BECAME A MODEL TO ALL THE BELIEVERS IN MACEDONIA AND ACHAIA (V. 7)

This is the only occasion in the New Testament where a whole church is seen as a model for other churches.[23] The Holy Spirit regenerated them, opened their understanding and illuminated the Word to them. They received the Word, believed the Word and acted upon it. It was not a case of only hearing the Word, but the Holy Spirit worked through the Word so that their lives were radically changed, and this change became obvious to all.

5. THEY DID NOT MERELY LIVE THE LIFE, BUT THEY ALSO SPOKE IT (V. 8)

We have already noted the importance of words. Truth must be expressed in words. The gospel message rang out from them so that their reputation as genuine believers spread beyond the confines of their own Roman provinces. The Christian community far and wide came to know what a welcome the gospel had received in Thessalonica and what a change had occurred in the believers' lives. Because of their strategic location, not only could the members of the Thessalonian church reach out to the whole province, but also their reputation as remarkable Christians could easily spread.

This factor in witnessing is a constant. Today, Christians are observed, and their reactions to tragedy can have an enormous impact. I know of a case where the child of a Christian couple died after a prolonged and painful illness, and the way the parents bore their pain led to the conversion of another person.

The word translated 'sounded forth' or 'rang out' in verse 8 has affinities with our word 'echo', and it occurs only here in the New Testament.[24] In other ancient literature it is used to describe a clap of thunder, the loud roar of a crowd or a rumour that spreads everywhere.[25] The result of the lives and witness of the Thessalonian believers was that the apostolic team found it unnecessary to preach in certain places.

First Peter 3:15 says, 'But sanctify the Lord God in your hearts, and always be ready to give a defense to everyone who asks you a reason for the hope that is in you, with meekness and fear.' Do people ask us why we have hope? Are you different enough to cause people to ask you why you are a believer?

6. THEY REPUDIATED THEIR FORMER IDOLATRY (V. 9)

Bruce remarks,

It is plain that the community addressed in such terms as these consisted predominantly of converted pagans. From the record of Acts 17:1–9 the impression might be gained that the Thessalonian converts were mainly Jews and God-fearers; but evidently more evangelization was carried on in the city than Luke reports; the missionaries must have stayed longer than the two or three weeks during which they were granted the hospitality of the synagogue.[26]

Idolatry was commonplace, a normal social phenomenon in the ancient world. The fact that the Thessalonian believers repudiated this was noted by their neighbours as being, quite literally, remarkable. It was observed that the God they turned to was 'living and true'. This description of God contrasts sharply with idols, which are lifeless, helpless and false (Deut. 5:26; Josh. 3:10; 1 Sam 17:36; 1 Kings 17:1; 2 Kings 19:4; Ps. 42:2; Isa. 37:4, 17; Dan. 6:26; Acts 14:15; 2 Cor. 3:3; 6:16). They 'turned to God', not only to believe on him, but also to serve him (compare Acts 14:15).

God is the 'true' (*alēthinos*), or real, and living God, as contrasted with dumb idols, which are not real or genuine (2 Chr. 15:3; Isa. 65:16; Jer. 10:10; John 17:3; Rom. 3:4; 1 John 5:20). This is the only occurrence of *alēthinos* in Paul's letters, though a related word, *alēthēs*, occurs in Romans 3:4, meaning there that God 'always speaks the truth'.[27] To turn to God from idols could be as true of Jewish proselytes as of Christians, but that this refers to Christian conversion is made clear by verse 10. 'It is not easy to reject and eject gods which one has worshipped from the days of childhood, and which by one's ancestors ... have always been considered very real ... It amounts to nothing less than a religious revolution.'[28]

Idolatry was woven into the social fabric of the ancient world. To turn from it was a serious breach of social practice which could not be hidden. To become a Christian could be very costly, as it is still in many parts of the world today. How different were the Thessalonian believers from those who, in this modern age, profess to be Christians but live lives virtually indistinguishable from those of the modern pagans among whom they live! The Roman emperors would not have persecuted the early church if they had been content to keep their religious beliefs to themselves. It was because their Christian faith demanded a changed lifestyle, as well as vocal expression, and because they expected to change society, that they were persecuted.

Philip Graham Ryken writes that popular surveys reveal that Christians today often live the same way as everyone else. 'We have the same incidence of domestic violence, the same rate of divorce, the same selfish patterns of spending, and the same addictive behaviors as the general population.' He goes on to cite a ministry newsletter that reports, 'For every ten men in your church, nine will have kids who leave the church, eight will not find their jobs satisfying, six pay the monthly minimum on their credit card balances, five have a major problem with pornography, four will get divorced and only one has a biblical worldview.'[29]

One of the most serious errors of much modern Christianity is the idea that Christians must be as like the world as possible in order to win others to Christ. The apostle John dealt with this tendency in his first epistle:

Do not love the world or the things in the world. If anyone loves the world, the love of the Father is not in him. For all that is in the world—the lust of the flesh, the lust of the eyes, and the pride of life—is not of the Father but is of the world. And the world is passing away, and the lust of it; but he who does the will of God abides forever.

(1 John 2:15–17)

Here, of course, the term 'world' does not signify the world of nature, the created order, nor does it mean the world of people as people, such as God loves in John 3:16. In this context 'world' means mankind in organized opposition to God, the spirit of worldliness, which is characterized by lust, pride and materialism.[30]

7. THEY LOOKED FOR THE RETURN OF CHRIST (V. 10)

The Thessalonian Christians showed a healthy anticipation of the return of Jesus Christ. Clearly, the subject of Christ's return must have been prominent in the evangelization of Thessalonica as the Christians were familiar with the subject, and Paul now gives additional teaching on that doctrine in this letter and in the second epistle to the Thessalonians (see Appendix 3). Those who do wait for the return of Christ are not to neglect their daily work, as Paul makes clear later in the epistle (4:9–12). It is simply not true that those who look forward to the Second Coming of Christ are no earthly use. 'Serving God and holding fast to a strong eschatological expectation were not antithetical but complementary.'[31] Some of the greatest social benefactors, not to speak of all the famous Christian workers, have been those who lived in the light of Christ's promised return. Interpretations of eschatology that teach us to neglect society and not to seek to improve it are manifestly erroneous. Their argument is that we should not 'polish the brass on a sinking ship'. But the earth is the Lord's (Ps. 24:1) and we are to be salt and light in it (Matt. 5:13–14). Notice that nothing in Paul's statement suggests that there is to be any other eschatological event before the return of Christ.

In the light of these facts we can easily understand Paul's affection for the Thessalonian believers. If we go through the chapter again we can also see ...

The apostles' example (vv. 5–6)

In what way were Paul and his co-workers an example to the Thessalonians?

THEIR PREACHING WAS WITH POWER (V. 5A)

'Power' here does not mean noise or shouting; it means effectiveness. Paul preached the gospel effectively and powerfully. This was seen in the results in the lives of the Thessalonian believers. Power comes from the Word itself (Jer. 5:14; 23:29), but it is the Holy Spirit who applies it (Acts 1:8). Paul preached with conviction.

It is prayer that prepares the messenger (Gen. 32:28; Acts 4:23–31). E. M. Bounds wrote, 'What the Church needs today is not more machinery or better, not new organizations or more and novel methods, but men whom the Holy Ghost can use—men of prayer, men mighty in prayer. The Holy Ghost does not flow through methods, but through men. He does not anoint plans, but men—men of prayer.'[32]

THEIR LIVES MATCHED THEIR PREACHING (V. 5B)

Evidently part of the impact of the gospel upon the Thessalonians was the kind of men that Paul, Silas and Timothy were. They were hard-working, sacrificial, and faced their sufferings with joy. It is not only what we say that impacts people with the gospel; our lives must speak also. Someone once remarked to a person trying to witness, 'Your life speaks so loudly that I cannot hear what you say.'

THEY BECAME ROLE MODELS (V. 6)

The word translated 'followers' in the KJV and NKJV is translated 'imitators' in the RSV and the NIV. It comes from *mimētai*, from which we get the word 'mimic'. I recall that, in one of his books, Michael Griffiths writes about three churches in Japan, each of which prays in a different way because it mimics the missionary who planted it. In one church they whistle when they pray, because their missionary had false teeth and whistled when he spoke! In another they shout, because their missionary, who was deaf, shouted! Paul would not have countenanced such superficial mimicry. The Thessalonians were not mere mimics in a trivial sense. They were not like parrots. They truly were followers, disciples.

THEIR ASSURANCE ENCOURAGED ASSURANCE IN THEM (V. 6)

Christians who have doubts about their own beliefs are unlikely to encourage faith in others. Paul later wrote to Timothy, 'For this reason I also suffer these things; nevertheless I am not ashamed, for I know whom I have believed and am persuaded that He is able to keep what I have committed to Him until that Day' (2 Tim. 1:12). As a result of these positive examples, the Thessalonians began to copy the apostles. It is said that imitation is the sincerest form of flattery. But this was not mere flattery; it was conviction that the life manifested by Paul and his co-workers, the Christian life, was the only life worth living.

It is inevitable that new converts learn first from those who bring them to Christ. This is no problem so long as the mentor is following the Lord. A friend of mine once told how, when he was laying crazy paving in his garden, he leaned against the wall and crossed his legs while he looked at the task to see what to do next. Out of the corner of his eye he observed that his young son was adopting exactly the same physical posture in imitation! Children are great imitators, which is one important reason why parents must live godly lives. This is why the Lord, through Moses, first exhorted the Israelites to love the Lord with heart, soul and strength, before exhorting them to teach their children (Deut. 6:4–6). It is also why Paul exhorted the Ephesian elders to 'take heed' to themselves in order to be able to shepherd the flock of God (Acts 20:28; compare 1 Peter 5:3). Robert Murray McCheyne, the godly minister of the early nineteenth century in Dundee, is famously reported to have said that his people's greatest need was his own personal holiness.[33]

Sincere imitation of godliness is commendable. Note the following Scriptures:

- 1 Corinthians 4:16—'Therefore I urge you, imitate me.'
- 1 Corinthians 11:1—'Imitate me, just as I also imitate Christ.'
- 2 Timothy 3:10—'But you have carefully followed my doctrine, manner of life, purpose, faith, longsuffering, love, perseverance ...'
- Philippians 4:9—'The things which you learned and received and heard and saw in me, these do, and the God of peace will be with you.'
- Hebrews 6:12—'... that you do not become sluggish, but imitate those who through faith and patience inherit the promises.'

However, the Thessalonians were not merely imitators; they also became examples themselves.

The example the Thessalonians became (vv. 6–10)

'Example' is an interesting word. It comes from the Greek word from which we also get the English word 'type', referring to the older form of letterpress printing in which solid metal examples of the letters are inked and the paper pressed onto them, so that the image of the letter is reproduced on the paper. The lives of the Thessalonians made an impression on their neighbours, encouraging them to believe on the same Saviour and live the same kind of life. Notice that they were not just 'examples' to the pagans, but also to the believers throughout Macedonia and Achaia. That is much more demanding. The other believers observed them, admired their lives and copied them.

It is one thing to set a moral standard higher than that of pagan neighbours; it is quite another to set an example to fellow-believers. Their lives must have been a challenge to other Christians. Such an example is most effective when it is unselfconscious. We need to be like Moses, who was not aware that his face shone (Exod. 34:29). The Thessalonians, no doubt, did not set out to impress, but what they were in sincerity impressed itself upon others. So often Christians sink down to the standards of other Christians around them. We need men and women who will press on to know the Lord (Ps. 63:8; Hosea 6:3; Phil. 3:7–14). We need church members whose lives are a challenge and an encouragement to others, and to whom Christians can look up. The Thessalonians had become followers of the apostles and of the Lord, and now they became examples. 'One who is not an imitator cannot become an example.'[34]

In what way were they examples?

THEY RECEIVED THE WORD IN AFFLICTION (V. 6)

It is one thing to hear the Word; it is quite another to receive it (that is, accept it), believe it and act upon it. It is one thing to receive the Word in comfort; it is quite another to receive it when it means persecution. In one Islamic country a Muslim became a Christian, having carefully considered the gospel message over a period of time. He said to the Christian missionary who witnessed to him, 'I know this may cost me my life, but I know it is the truth.' Some of the Thessalonian believers would have lost their jobs; others would have suffered physically. All would have received insults, sneers, and criticism at the very least. But did they receive the Word in a glum, dogged, fearful way? No! We have already noted that:

THEY RECEIVED THE WORD JOYFULLY (V. 6)

This was the joy produced by the Holy Spirit. The apostle Paul speaks in Romans 14:17 of such joy: 'for the kingdom of God is not eating and drinking, but righteousness and peace and joy in the Holy Spirit.' Again in Romans 15:13 he writes, 'Now may the God of hope fill you with all joy and peace in believing, that you may abound in hope by the power of the Holy Spirit.' Peter likewise writes in his first epistle of 'joy inexpressible and full of glory' (1 Peter 1:8). That is to be the characteristic of robust Christianity. True spiritual joy should not be confused with the happiness that depends upon circumstances. Paul manifested joy even though he was imprisoned and in chains (Phil. 1:4, 25; 2:2, 17–18; 4:1).

THEY DEMONSTRATED A CLEAR WITNESS TO THOSE AROUND THEM (V. 8)

The Word of God sounded forth from them. And their witnessing was not limited to their immediate locality. It spread far and wide.

THEY TURNED TO GOD FROM IDOLS (V. 9)

This is not just the changing of opinions. It is a recognition that what used to come first in your life before you became a Christian was an idol.

Anything can become an idol. For the rich young ruler, it was money. It may be any material thing. It may be sport or a hobby. It may even be a girlfriend or boyfriend, a husband or wife. Things that are not wrong in themselves, if they replace God as the first thing in your life, become idols. This is a constant danger. In his first epistle, the apostle John expounds in great detail how we can be sure we are true Christians; when we might think he has exhausted the subject, he then concludes his letter with this solemn exhortation: 'Little children, keep yourselves from idols' (1 John 5:21).

THEY 'TURNED' (V. 9)

'Turning' implies repentance. The Greek word translated repentance (*metanoia*) means an inward change of mind resulting in an outward change of life and behaviour (see Mark 1:4, 15; Acts 2:38). There are superficial methods of evangelism and shallow evangelistic courses which soft-pedal sin and do not teach repentance. That is unbiblical, and, apart from the grace of God, such methods are bound to produce shallow Christians, if indeed they produce true Christians at all. The Thessalonians sincerely repented of their idolatry in their minds and turned from it in their lives, turning to God instead. They turned from false gods to the living God. He and he alone is the true God.

There are two points to note here. First, becoming a Christian involves repentance, that is, turning from sin to God (Prov. 28:13). This clearly implies a change of direction. Our lives must be headed in a different direction from that which ruled us before conversion. We used to sing,

What a wonderful change in my life has been wrought
Since Jesus came into my heart![35]

That change is a change of direction and, usually, of lifestyle. It certainly means a change of worldview, our outlook on life that determines how we live.

Second, we must turn to the true and living God. People can be converted to a false religion or to a political party. They can also be converted to a Jesus of their own making, rather than to the living Christ of the Bible. We need to be sure that we have turned to the only true God.

What an example! Is your life an example to other believers? Can you sing with sincerity, 'The dearest idol I have known, Whate'er that idol be, Help me to tear it from Thy throne, And worship only Thee'?[36]

THEY AWAITED THE LORD'S RETURN (V. 10)

They were looking forward to heaven and glory, above all, seeing their Saviour. Notice how the main elements of the gospel are wrapped up in verse 10. Jesus (his humanity) is God's Son (his deity). He is in heaven (his ascension and reign). He will return (his Second Coming). He was raised (resurrection) from the dead (crucifixion). He delivers us (redemption) from the wrath to come (judgement).

This chapter ends on a solemn note. The apostle, in mentioning the Lord's return, refers to one vital aspect of salvation. The Lord delivers us from 'the wrath to come', the divine judgment to be poured out on the wicked at the end of time (Matt. 3:7; Luke 3:7; Rom. 2:5, 16). Some commentators consider that the thought of God exercising wrath is unworthy of the Christian idea of God, and so the wrath must be an impersonal force.[37] But as Bruce rightly comments, '… to treat the wrath of God as an impersonal process of retribution operating in the universe does insufficient justice to Paul's thought. For Paul, God is personal, and his wrath must be as personal as his grace …'[38]

Two aspects of the wrath of God are described in the New Testament. One is a present-day wrath, like a slow-burning fuse, the settled indignation which because of our fallen nature rests on the sinner (Eph. 2:3). This is described in Romans 1:18–32, where we are told that God manifests his wrath by giving rebellious people up to their sin and depravity. The other aspect of wrath is a cataclysmic, sudden manifestation, as in the Judgement, which is the wrath referred to in 1 Thessalonians 1. This is described mainly in the Book of Revelation, but is anticipated in several other places, such as Matthew 3:7; Luke 3:7; Romans 2:5; 5:9. The wrath of God is very real. Are you delivered from it?

Study questions

1. 'Example' is an important theme in Paul's writings. Examine the following Scriptures and note down what you learn about 'example': 1 Timothy 4:12; Titus 2:7; Hebrews 13:7; James 5:10; 1 Peter 2:21; 5:3.

2. Either 1 Thessalonians or Galatians was Paul's earliest letter to a church. What differences do you notice in the attitude or manner of writing from the first chapter of each?

3. Think about those whose examples have helped you as a Christian. Are there any who have hindered you? How can you avoid hindering others and be an example yourself?

4. Read the following Scriptures and consider what effect knowledge of election should have on your life: John 15:16; Ephesians 1:4; 2:10; 2 Thessalonians 2:13.

Notes

1 The noun *ekklesia*, 'church, assembly', would not have any sacred associations in the minds of recent converts from paganism. Hence Paul qualifies it (**F. F. Bruce,** *1 & 2 Thessalonians* (Word Biblical Commentary; Nashville: Thomas Nelson, 1982), p. 7).

2 Ibid.

3 **William Hendriksen,** *1 & 2 Thessalonians* (London: Banner of Truth, 1972), p. 42.

4 **Hendriksen** discusses whether this greeting is an exclamation, a declaration or a mere wish. He concludes, from the evidence of Num. 6:24–26; Luke 10:5–6; and 2 John 3, that this is a declaration of what will actually happen to those who are ready to receive such blessings by faith (*1 & 2 Thessalonians*, pp. 43–45).

5 **Gene L. Green,** *The Letters to the Thessalonians* (Grand Rapids, MI: Eerdmans / Leicester: Apollos, 2002), p. 87.

6 Ibid. pp. 89f.

7 **Leon Morris,** *The First and Second Epistles to the Thessalonians* (NICNT; Grand Rapids, MI: Eerdmans, 1991), p. 42.

8 **Green,** *Letters*, pp. 90f.

9 For a discussion of 'hope' in the New Testament see **Walter A. Elwell, (ed.),** *Evangelical Dictionary of Biblical Theology* (Grand Rapids, MI: Baker / Carlisle: Paternoster, 1996), pp. 355ff.; and **Gerald F. Hawthorne, Ralph P. Martin, Daniel G. Reid, (eds.),** *Dictionary of Paul and His Letters* (Downers Grove, IL / Leicester: Inter-Varsity Press, 1993), pp. 415f.

10 'Election is not a device for sentencing people to eternal torment, but for rescuing them from it' (**Morris,** *First and Second Epistles*, pp. 43–44).

11 **F. F. Bruce,** *1 & 2 Thessalonians* (Word Biblical Commentary; Nashville: Thomas Nelson, 1982), p. 14.

12 **Hendriksen,** *1 & 2 Thessalonians*, p. 51.

13 Ibid. p. 48.

14 Ibid. p. 51. 'The reference here is (at least primarily) to the full assurance of the missionaries as they spoke the word.'

15 **John MacArthur, Jr.,** *1 & 2 Thessalonians* (MacArthur New Testament Commentary; Chicago: Moody, 2002), p. 22.

16 **Morris,** *First and Second Epistles*, p. 47.

17 'The defence of propositional revelation has always been a central tenet of evangelicalism and a primary plank in the debate over biblical inerrancy' (**Douglas Groothuis,** *Truth Decay: Defending Christianity against the Challenge of Postmodernism* (Downers Grove, IL: IVP, 2000), p. 112).

18 **J. Oswald Sanders** discusses this in the first chapter of his book *Spiritual Leadership* (London: Marshall, Morgan & Scott, 1967), p. 9.

19 In the Great Commission in Matthew 28:19–20 there is only one imperative verb—'make disciples'. The other verbs are participles which, in a sense, form a context for that primary command.

20 **John Piper,** *Future Grace* (Sisters, OR: Multnomah / Leicester: Inter-Varsity Press, 1995), p. 342.

21 **Morris,** *First and Second Epistles*, p. 49.

22 **James Denney,** *The Epistles to the Thessalonians* (London: Hodder & Stoughton, 1892), p. 46.

23 **Green,** *Letters*, p. 99.

24 Hendriksen, *1 & 2 Thessalonians*, p. 53.

25 Green, *Letters*, p. 101.

26 Bruce, *1 & 2 Thessalonians*, p. 18.

27 Ibid.

28 Hendriksen, *1 & 2 Thessalonians*, p. 56.

29 Philip Graham Ryken, *What Is the Christian Worldview?* (Phillipsburg, NJ: Presbyterian and Reformed, 2006), pp. 10f.

30 ' "The world" is not the fabric of the universe. Nor is he simply talking about earthly blessings or the structures of society … Here [the word 'world'] is a disposition, an outlook, a frame of mind. It is the anti-God mentality of the human race, the worldwide fondness for sin and self which causes men and women to sin and stumble into wickedness' (**Michael Eaton,** *1, 2, 3 John* (Focus on the Bible Series; Fearn: Christian Focus, 1996), p. 68).

31 Green, *Letters*, p. 109.

32 E. M. Bounds, *Power Through Prayer* (London: Marshall, Morgan & Scott, n.d., 13th impression), pp. 10f.

33 R. M. McCheyne, *From the Preacher's Heart* (Fearn: Christian Focus, 1993), p. 14.

34 Hendriksen, *1 & 2 Thessalonians*, p. 53.

35 Rufus H. McDaniel, 1914.

36 William Cowper, 'O For a Closer Walk with God', 1772.

37 For example, see **C. H. Dodd,** *The Epistle of Paul to the Romans* (London: Hodder & Stoughton, 1932), pp. 20–24. Compare **Leon Morris,** *The Apostolic Preaching of the Cross* (2nd edn.; London: Tyndale, 1960), pp. 125–183.

38 Bruce, *1 & 2 Thessalonians*, p. 20. **Leon Morris** discusses this matter thoroughly in his *Apostolic Preaching of the Cross*, chs 5–6. He also has a brief discussion in his commentary on the Thessalonian epistles, including the following: '… in the thought of the New Testament writers there is no place for an impersonal agency that can act in independence of God.' He continues, 'The wrath of God is no vindictive passion, and it does not imply lack of control, as human wrath does … God's wrath lacks the imperfections that are bound up with the purest of human righteous indignation' (**Morris,** *First and Second Epistles*, p. 55).

The model witness (1 Thes. 2)

In this chapter of 1 Thessalonians the apostle Paul describes how he and his companions proclaimed the gospel to the Thessalonians. He also gives details about their remarkable response to the message.

Paul's missionary visit was not fruitless (v. 1)

A careful reading of the passage will reveal that an element of self-defence is woven into Paul's writing. It seems that some of his opponents had been attacking his reputation, spreading false accusations about his character and methods. This experience was not new to the apostle. He had already suffered in this way earlier in his travels, and would do so to the end of his days on earth. The word translated 'in vain' (NKJV) or 'a failure' (NIV) has been variously understood. Some take it to mean 'fruitless' or 'barren of results'; others relate it to the character of the preaching. Another suggestion is that it indicates that Paul did not come to them empty-handed, but with something to give them. Leon Morris's preference is for something like 'hollow, empty, wanting in purpose and earnestness'. But even so, a church was founded in spite of the opposition. So Paul, by his emphatic 'you know', is affirming the well-known fact that his visit was not without purpose.[1]

Paul's suffering at Philippi did not dampen his zeal to preach (v. 2)

Even though they had been treated outrageously (*hubrizesthai*) in Philippi, by being stripped and publicly flogged, this caused them, not to utter a muted message in Thessalonica, but rather to be bold in God. The word translated 'we were bold' (NKJV) or 'we dared to tell' (NIV) is derived from a word (*parrēsia*) meaning freedom of speech but with the added idea of courage.[2] In one of his very last letters he warned that all who would seek to live a godly life 'will suffer persecution' (2 Tim. 3:12). So criticism is to be expected, yet in this letter Paul seeks to vindicate himself. Why did he do so? Surely the answer is that the truth was at stake. When the attacks are not merely upon us but upon the gospel or the work of Christ, we need to answer the accusations and show that they are false. But when we are suffering a merely personal attack it may be best not to reply in order to follow the example of our Lord, as the apostle Peter teaches: 'For to this you were called, because Christ also suffered for us, leaving us an example, that you should follow His steps: "Who committed no sin, nor was deceit found in His mouth"; who, when He was reviled, did not revile in return; when He suffered, He did not threaten, but committed Himself to Him who judges righteously' (1 Peter 2:21–23; compare Matt. 5:11–12). But when the truth of the gospel is involved we may find it necessary to put the record straight. Paul does this, and thereby demonstrates the model witness. In referring to the gospel as 'the gospel of God' (Greek, but NIV renders it 'his gospel') Paul turns the attention of the readers away from himself to God. Although he is ready at times to call the message 'my gospel' because he identifies with it, here, in answering criticism, he is showing that the message is from God and not from men.

It seems that his opponents had accused him of teaching false doctrine and of having wrong motives. They alleged that he was preaching only to advance his own position, and therefore he was insincere in his ministry. Paul refutes these charges by pointing out that he proclaimed the gospel in the midst of conflict. If he had been self-serving he would not have been willing to preach against such opposition.

His preaching was pure (v. 3)

The defiling elements of doctrinal error, impure motives and guile were completely absent from his teaching, which was orthodox, pure and sincere. No matter how eloquent a preacher may be, if he is guilty of doctrinal error, serious moral failure, financial impropriety or deliberate deception, he should not be listened to, no matter how entertaining his performance or what crowds he can gather. We all sin and fail in one way or another, 'For there is not a just man on earth who does good and does not sin' (Eccles. 7:20), therefore judging another, which has to be done sometimes (e.g. 1 Cor. 5:1–8), must be done in humility with a view to possible restoration to the Lord, if not to ministry (Gal. 6:1).

He was not a mere crowd-pleaser (v. 4)

Nor did Paul seek merely to please men; his constant aim was to please the God who had called him. He did not seek to win men over by flattery. Sometimes one hears people claim that they have a 'right' to preach and teach. No one has a 'right' to preach. It is a trust, a privilege, given to those who are called (Gal. 1:15; see also Heb. 5:4). But all Christians have a duty to witness. The difference may be likened to those found among people in a court of law. Some are specialists 'called to the bar' who are trained as barristers or advocates (see Eph. 4:11); theirs is the task to argue the case, to defend or prosecute. Almost anyone else who has evidence to give can be called upon to bear testimony as a witness to what he or she has seen or heard or knows from some other means. In the same way, some men are called to be pastors, teachers or evangelists. Not everyone is called to such a ministry. But all are called to be ready to witness (1 Peter 3:15).

His preaching did not hide an avaricious mentality (vv. 5–6)

He did not 'butter-up' his hearers with the aim of eliciting donations or increasing his personal wealth. In Mark 7:21–22 our Lord listed covetousness along with evil thoughts, adulteries, fornications, murders, thefts, wickedness, deceit, lewdness, an evil eye, blasphemy, pride and foolishness as evil things which come from within a person and cause defilement. F. F. Bruce describes covetousness as 'not merely the desire to possess more than one has, but to possess more than one ought to have, especially that which belongs to someone else'.[3]

It is a matter of public knowledge that some so-called preachers get wealthy by appealing for funds. One can hear such men brazenly claim in public that they have a right to be rich because Jesus was a wealthy man! After all, they claim, Jesus had a treasurer to look after his money—he had so much! However, our Lord Jesus, in the days of his flesh, testified that he had nowhere to lay his head (Matt. 8:20; Luke 9:58). The charge of covetousness laid against Paul was obviously false as he had laboured with his own hands to support himself, even though, as a genuine servant of God, he had a right to be supported (2 Thes. 3:7–9; 1 Cor. 9:3–18; 2 Cor. 11:7–11; 1 Tim. 5:17–18; see also 6:5–10; Mark 6:7–13; Matt. 10:5–15; Luke 9:1–6; 10:1–12). Nor was he seeking popularity, even though as an apostle he might be entitled to fame, or even special respect. He never sought glory from men.

He was as tender as a mother with her baby (v. 7)

As to his manner, he was gentle among them, rather than rough and insensitive. They had no reason to complain that his preaching or his counselling were abrasive. A nursing mother feeds, cares for and protects her baby, and that was how Paul dealt with these babes in Christ (see Gal. 4:19). When we are tired, for example, after preaching, or when we are in a hurry or very busy, it is easy to be abrupt or short with people. We need to ask God to help us to manifest the gentleness of Christ (2 Cor. 10:1; Gal. 5:22–23). However, gentleness does not rule out discipline. There are times when the mother who feeds the child has to be firm with the child, and to some extent feeding authorizes firmness.

His ministry was not limited to words; he gave himself (v. 8)

There was deep affection in Paul's heart for the Thessalonians. He gave *himself*, not just words, to the work and to them. When we share the gospel, our own possession, enjoyment or experience of its benefits is not diminished, but sharing our lives involves self-denial (see 2 Cor. 8:5; 12:15).4 Paul virtually laid down his life many times in the course of his ministry, and the Thessalonian work was no exception. Laying down our lives for others does not necessarily mean dying physically, though it will mean dying to self. It means being willing to sacrifice time, energy, privacy, sleep at times, and even money where necessary for the sake of the ones being cared for.

He worked long hours so that he would not be a financial burden to them (v. 9)

Paul does not refer to the financial support sent by the Philippians, which in any case was apparently not sufficient to remove completely the need for his own manual labour. Bruce suggests that perhaps he did not want to embarrass the Thessalonians or make them feel ashamed, as he did the Corinthians (2 Cor. 11:8–9).5 A minister's or a missionary's work is not a nine-to-five job, though it is essential that a servant of God does rest. Paul's example in the matter of self-support is unimpeachable. While a labourer is worthy of his hire, there are often times and situations when a minister may need to labour at some other employment in order to support himself and not be a burden on a small church. The difference between a minister and a layman is not whether or not he is paid to do the work but whether or not he has a genuine call. Where his support comes from is irrelevant. A missionary may have to do the same, first in order to gain access and respect in a foreign country, but also if he or she is not being supported from elsewhere. Paul never made lack of support a reason for not labouring in the gospel.

He and his team behaved in a holy, righteous and blameless manner (v. 10)

'Devoutly' refers to the spirituality of the team. 'Justly' indicates that they dealt impartially and fairly with all. 'Blamelessly' means that their personal lives were beyond reproach. What a standard! How easy it is to be lop-sided: for example, to be devout in personal life but unfair in dealings with others, or to be a 'really good guy' liked by all, but severely lacking in a personal devotional life and walk with the Lord.

His attitude towards them was father-like (v. 11)

Like a good father, he dealt with the Thessalonian converts by exhorting and encouraging. In this chapter Paul uses the analogy of both mother and father. When speaking of cherishing his converts, he uses the picture of a mother (v. 7), and when referring to teaching, he uses the picture of a father (compare 1 Cor. 4:14–15). In the Old Testament God is spoken of using pictures of both a father and a mother (Isa. 66:13; Ps. 103:13).

A good father can be strict, but he loves. He can command or charge, but he also encourages and comforts. He will teach his children how to behave and live, and he will seek to protect them from every form of harm, evil and danger, physical, mental or spiritual, because he cares for them.

His concern was that they might live lives that honoured the Lord (v. 12)

To 'walk' in this sense means to order one's life. Christians must always remember that the way they live reflects upon the Lord they love.

What a motive! What a standard! The purpose behind a Christian worker's exhorting, teaching, comforting and correcting is not his or her own reputation or satisfaction, but that other Christians should live in a way that brings glory to God (1 Cor. 6:20; 10:31). Christians are called into God's 'kingdom', not into a mere human government (Col. 1:13), though while on earth we are to respect and obey the legitimate government (Rom. 13:1–7; see also Matt. 22:15–22). The reign of Christ began at his resurrection and ascension (Eph. 1:20–23; Ps. 110:1; 1 Cor.

15:23–28) but the kingdom will be fully manifested when his glory is revealed and believers are resurrected at the end of time (see 2 Thes. 1:5–10). Their destiny is glory (Rom. 2:10; 1 Cor. 2:7; 15:43; Col. 1:27; 3:4).

It is only too easy to avoid criticism and persecution by merging into the world and not living a godly life. But Christians are expected by the Lord to be salt and light in the earth (Matt. 5:13–14). If we are ashamed of the Lord, he will be ashamed of us before God the Father (Mark 8:38). To live as true Christians we must be prepared to face the arrows of the enemy (Eph. 6:16). If we stand up for Christ we shall become targets of Satan, and he will use whomever he can to discredit us. But God will not allow us to be tempted above what we are able to bear (1 Cor. 10:13). And we have the armour of righteousness described in Ephesians 6:10–20. Paul was able to refute the false accusations by pointing to the facts to which the Thessalonian believers themselves could bear witness. Notice his repeated appeal to their testimony: 'you yourselves know' (v. 1), 'as you know' (v. 5), 'you remember' (v. 9), '[y]ou are witnesses' (v. 10), 'as you know' (v. 11). Clearly he was determined to set the record straight.

One lesson we should learn from this element of Paul's teaching is that we should be careful not to listen to gossip, nor should we pass it on to others. Paul cautioned Timothy, 'Do not receive an accusation against an elder except from two or three witnesses' (1 Tim. 5:19). 'Receiving' an accusation does not mean believing it straight away. The accusation is to be received with a view to investigation. This does not mean that we should be gullible. It means that we should take notice only of proven facts, not insinuations or malicious gossip. An old but useful test as to whether we should repeat something we have heard consists of three questions: Is it true? Is it kind? Is it necessary?

In dealing with these accusations the apostle teaches us what a model witness is to be like. He mentions both negative and positive factors. How are we to witness? Which factors are important? If we look over this part of the chapter again we can learn how to witness.

How not to be a witness

DO NOT DOUBT THE VALUE OF YOUR PERSONAL TESTIMONY (V. 1)

Paul's witness was not in vain. Neither is yours. Even though we may not see immediate and visible results, witnessing is never in vain. Why not? Because the Word of God will always accomplish the purpose for which God sends it forth:

So shall My word be that goes forth from My mouth;
It shall not return to Me void,
But it shall accomplish what I please,
And it shall prosper in the thing for which I sent it. (Isa. 55:11)

Even if the Word does not convert, it may convict, and it will be used as evidence on the Day of Judgement. The risen Lord, in his letter to the church at Pergamos, refers to Antipas as 'My faithful *martyr*' (Rev. 2:13, emphasis added). The Greek word *martus* means both witness and martyr. In the days of the early church, to be a witness frequently meant paying for it with one's life as a martyr. How weak, in comparison, is our witness in the West today! But elsewhere in the world, where the gospel is new to the population and challenges current idolatries, opposition often results in martyrdom. 'Therefore, my beloved brethren, be steadfast, immovable, always abounding in the work of the Lord, knowing that your labor is not in vain in the Lord' (1 Cor. 15:58).

Hendricksen writes, 'It was the message by means of which the missionaries, clothed with authority from God and with yearning sympathy, had pleaded with the hearers to forsake their wicked ways and to turn to God in Christ.'[6]

DO NOT USE DOUBTFUL METHODS (V. 3)

Paul did not employ deceit or guile, and his methods were free from impurity. This was in stark contrast to the pagan religions with their temple prostitutes. Even modern-day cults have been known to use so-called 'hookers for Jesus'. We should never employ deceitful tactics. Our methods must be above reproach. Some churches are tempted to use entertainment in order to attract hearers, to make worship services attractive to unbelievers, and to avoid mentioning anything challenging or embarrassing to non-Christians. But at some point, if they are to be faithful and preach the true gospel, they must introduce the fact of sin, the danger of judgement and the necessity of repentance and faith in the Saviour. If they do not, and simply offer a nice life for those who turn to Jesus, they are being false to the gospel. They could be accused of using the device of the huckster called 'bait and switch': offering something tempting and attractive, but then switching it for something else. This is deceit and guile.7 Of course, some unbelievers will criticize us because they do not like the message of the gospel. But we must be transparently honest in the ways we work. There is nothing new in that. Many rejected our Lord's teaching, but he did not change it. The rich young ruler seemed to have great potential, and Jesus loved him, but when the young man turned away Jesus did not pursue him (Mark 10:17–22; compare Matt. 19:16–22; Luke 18:18–27). It has been remarked that some churches would have run after him and made him a deacon! Likewise, many mocked Paul and turned away, but he did not attempt to make his message acceptable to pagans. On the contrary, he pronounced an 'anathema' against those who compromised the gospel (Gal. 1:6–9).

DO NOT BECOME MERE MEN-PLEASERS (V. 4B)

Paul's aim was to please God, not men. This must always be our motive. It is what God thinks of our work, not what other people think, that matters. However, sometimes God speaks to us through other Christians, so we should examine ourselves and our work carefully before God when other sincere and mature Christians express concern over what we are doing or teaching. This has implications for our worship, which should be glorifying to God and edifying to believers. There would seem to be no justification for shaping our worship in order to entertain the man in the street.

DO NOT EMPLOY FLATTERY IN ORDER TO WIN PEOPLE FOR CHRIST (V. 5A)

Paul did not do this, and neither did our Lord Jesus. Both the Lord and his servant Paul spoke straight to the point and never sought to flatter their hearers in an effort to gain a hearing. Paul did employ recognized patterns of court-room speech when on trial before Festus and Agrippa (Acts 24–26), but he did not tone down his message. To speak in modern idiom does not mean changing the message.

DO NOT SERVE MERELY FOR FINANCIAL GAIN (V. 5B)

Unlike some modern TV evangelists, Paul did not preach for his own financial enrichment. Three common snares for a Christian worker are money, sex and pride (or popularity). Christian workers are often poorly paid or inadequately supported, so the thought of the possible financial rewards a particular assignment may bring can be a source of temptation. Paul was entirely free from the love of money which brings a snare (1 Tim. 6:10). Of course, the worker is worthy of his hire (1 Tim. 5:17–18), and it is right that Christian workers should be properly supported financially. But that should not be the main motive for Christian service. Materialism can appear in many guises, for example, thinking that we must have this, that or the other latest gadget in order to function effectively. A dangerous phrase used in modern marketing is to describe some commodity as a 'must-have' object.

DO NOT GLORIFY YOURSELF (V. 6)

In witnessing, giving a testimony or preaching, we must be careful that we do not project ourselves. John the Baptist's words should summarize our aim: 'He must increase, but I must decrease' (John 3:30; compare 1:19–34). In a sense, we should be hidden and Christ glorified. I once heard someone say that we cannot at the same time show ourselves to be clever and our Lord to be glorious.

Paul did not expect the unconverted to support him, but he worked at his trade of tent-making to support himself (v. 9) and by doing so placed himself on the same level as the labourers of Thessalonica. Many workers today, especially on the mission field, use their skills or professions to support themselves. Today, many believe that a man should train for a secular job before training in theology as a minister or missionary. This is not only so that the man can support himself, but also so that he can gain experience of the world in which he and his future hearers live. All the apostles seem to have had experience and training in a secular trade before Jesus called them. To support oneself in ministry makes one immune to the financial squeeze that some churches have occasionally wickedly exerted upon ministers. It also enables men to plant churches where there is no immediate financial support.

Paul was, however, supported by other Christians, as we read in Philippians 4:15–18:

Now you Philippians know also that in the beginning of the gospel, when I departed from Macedonia, no church shared with me concerning giving and receiving but you only. For even in Thessalonica you sent aid once and again for my necessities. Not that I seek the gift, but I seek the fruit that abounds to your account. Indeed I have all and abound. I am full, having received from Epaphroditus the things sent from you, a sweet-smelling aroma, an acceptable sacrifice, well pleasing to God.

Those are the negative factors. Now we turn to the positive instruction in this chapter.

How to be a witness for Jesus

BE BOLD IN SPITE OF OPPOSITION (V. 2)

Paul had faced much opposition, both in Philippi and in Thessalonica. The temptation to mute our testimony will always be present when we face opposition. In Acts 4 the disciples prayed specifically for boldness (Acts 4:29). Perhaps that should be our prayer, too. Of course, boldness does not imply rudeness. We should always show the appropriate respect to all whom we address. As witnesses we have been entrusted with a wonderful message; we must be faithful to this trust (1 Thes. 2:4). We must not trim the gospel message to gain hearers, but faithfully present the whole message.

BE GENTLE IN YOUR DEALINGS (V. 7)

Compare 2 Timothy 2:24: 'And a servant of the Lord must not quarrel but be gentle to all, able to teach, patient ...' Verbal abuse and bad-tempered arguing must never be employed in our witnessing. As the apostle writes elsewhere, we should aim '... to speak evil of no one, to be peaceable, gentle, showing all humility to all men' (Titus 3:2).

BE WILLING TO PUT UP WITH INCONVENIENCE (V. 8A)

There is a cost in witnessing. The witness must be prepared to give not only the bare message, but also him- or herself. It is so easy to imagine that if we have presented a simple outline of the gospel message—such as 'All have sinned; the wages of sin is death; Jesus died to pay the price of sin; if we believe on him we shall be saved'—we have then done our duty. We can present such a message without inconveniencing ourselves in the slightest. But Christian witnesses should make themselves available to those they are witnessing to, and be ready to explain the message more fully, answer any questions, show concern and compassion and pray earnestly for them. This will involve time and inconvenience. To give ourselves to a task means that we are in earnest and are serious about it, making every effort to see that the job is done properly.

In Acts 6:4 we read that the apostles refused to be side-tracked from their calling into something that, however worthy, was not their task. Instead they said, '… we will give ourselves to prayer and to the ministry of the word.' Notice the order: prayer first, then ministry. Notice too the intensity of their prayer: they *gave* themselves. Prayer prepares the messenger as well as the message. It can also prepare the hearers. The witness will pray because the Holy Spirit has given him or her a love for the unsaved.

LOVE THOSE TO WHOM YOU WITNESS (V. 8B)
Like their Master, witnesses will have compassion on those who are like lost sheep, for the same Holy Spirit indwells them, and 'the fruit of the Spirit is love, joy, peace, longsuffering, kindness, goodness, faithfulness, gentleness, self-control. Against such there is no law' (Gal. 5:22–23).

BE CAREFUL AT ALL TIMES NOT TO BEHAVE IN A WAY
THAT WOULD COMPROMISE THE GOSPEL (V. 10)
We should endeavour, by God's grace, to be devout, just and blameless in our behaviour. Paul later wrote to the Corinthians, 'We give no offense in anything, that our ministry may not be blamed' (2 Cor. 6:3).

USE APPROPRIATE LANGUAGE IN YOUR COMMUNICATION (V. 11)
'How forceful are right words!' (Job 6:25). The careful choice of words is important for preachers and witnesses. They will exhort, encourage and even implore those to whom they speak (v. 11).

Their aim will not be to procure mere decisions but disciples, that is, those who continue faithfully to trust in Christ, and who grow in grace and knowledge (2 Peter 3:18) and seek to live lives pleasing to God. This is the clear emphasis in the New Testament. There are well over 200 references to 'disciples' in the New Testament. The word 'believers' occurs only twice, and 'Christians' only three times. From Acts 11:26 we see who were qualified to be called 'Christians': it was the *disciples*. A disciple is a disciplined follower of *someone*, not something. In the Great Commission in Matthew 28:19–20 there is only one imperative verb in the original Greek: 'make disciples'. The other verbs are participles that depend on that imperative. Making disciples for Christ involves not just a crisis but a process, as well as 'teaching them to observe' (that is, practise, obey, carry out) all that Jesus taught.

More light on conversion (vv. 13–16)

Paul now thanks God that the Thessalonians received his message as the Word of God and were willing to suffer just as the churches in Judea had suffered.

Before we proceed with the application of this passage there is a problem that needs to be faced. The difficulty concerns the sharp criticism of the Jews (or 'Judeans', as it is in the NKJV) in verses 14 to 16. Some scholars, noting the contrast in Paul's attitude between this passage and Romans 9–11, have tried to solve the problem by suggesting that this section was not written by Paul and is a later interpolation, even though there is no textual evidence to support this proposal. Another device, used by the NKJV, is to translate the word *Ioudaiōn* as 'Judeans' rather than 'Jews'.

But these suggestions are not at all necessary. In the first place, the Epistle to the Romans is a carefully considered doctrinal presentation of the gospel that was sent to a church Paul had never visited, while the First Epistle to the Thessalonians is a letter written in the heat of battle to a church the apostle knew well. We have already noted in the Introduction that there is no necessity for all Paul's letters to be written on the same subjects and in the same style.

Second, in Romans, Paul is making a doctrinal and practical statement about the place of Israel in the purposes of God; in 1 Thessalonians 2 he is encouraging Christians who have been and are being persecuted, comparing their experiences with those of the churches in Judea who also had been persecuted. In fact, even in the Romans passage, where he admits to having 'great sorrow and continual grief' for his fellow-countrymen (9:2), and could almost wish himself 'accursed from Christ' for them (9:3), he nevertheless charges them with not seeking righteousness by faith (9:32) and for having a zeal for God that is not according to knowledge; seeking to establish their own righteousness and not submitting to the righteousness of God (10:3–4); and not obeying the gospel (10:16). He also quotes Isaiah 65:2 to the effect that they are 'a disobedient and contrary people' (10:21; see also 11:3, 7–10).

Third, it is erroneous to imagine that the apostle Paul was incapable of using, or was unlikely to use, sharp language concerning his fellow-Jews. He certainly could do so, as, for example, when he 'withstood Peter' publicly because of his hypocrisy (Gal. 2:11–21). When Paul was before the Jewish Council he rebuked the high priest for commanding those who stood by to strike him on the mouth, saying, 'God will strike you, you whitewashed wall …' (Acts 23:1–3). In these 'politically correct' days we must be careful not to judge the behaviour of those of another era by what would be acceptable today. After all, John the Baptist cried out publicly to the Pharisees and Sadducees who were coming to (observe?) his baptism, 'Brood of vipers! Who warned you to flee from the wrath to come?' (Matt. 3:7; compare Luke 3:7, where the words are said to be addressed to the crowds). Moreover, some of the most scathing words given to Jews in the New Testament were uttered by the Lord Jesus, himself a Jew as far as his human birth was concerned (Matt. 23). He even charged them with the murder of Zechariah (v. 35).

Let us now look more closely at the text of verses 13 to 16. Paul begins a new thanksgiving with the words 'For this reason' or 'Therefore' (omitted by the NIV). This could refer either backwards or forwards, but in this case it refers to what follows, as the next clause begins with 'because'. The cause of his thankfulness is the way they received the gospel and also endured the suffering which resulted from their conversion. Paul and his companions were so grateful to God for the remarkable response to the gospel that they thanked God 'without ceasing' (v. 13; compare 1:2; 5:18; 1 Cor. 1:4; Eph. 5:20; 2 Thes. 1:3; 2:13; Philem. 4).

The Thessalonians not only received the gospel, but they also embraced it. The word translated 'received' (*paralabontes*, v. 13) was a technical term for receiving a tradition and is used in the New Testament of the transmission of the apostolic doctrine (1 Cor. 11:23; 15:1, 3; Gal. 1:9, 12; Phil. 4:9; Col. 2:6; 1 Thes. 4:1; 2 Thes. 3:6). 'In each case the message or instruction has an authoritative character because it comes from an authoritative source.'[8] The word translated 'welcomed' (*edexasthe*) strengthens the word 'received' in that it places more emphasis on personal appropriation. It is used of welcoming a guest, implying both acceptance and approval.[9] It 'indicates their own initiative in eagerly embracing it'.[10] They not only received the gospel message, but they also appropriated it for themselves.

They received the message, not as a merely human word but as 'the word of God' (compare Gal. 1:11–12). 'Paul's drive and forcefulness came not from some thought that he was abreast of contemporary trends in philosophy or religion or science, but from the deep-seated conviction that he was God's mouthpiece, and that what he spoke was the veritable word of God.'[11]

The confirmation that the apostles' preaching was truly the 'word of God' was seen in the way in which it was at work in the Thessalonians' lives. 'The word of human beings, however wise in substance or eloquent in expression, cannot produce spiritual life: this is the prerogative of the word of God, which works effectually (*energeitai*) in believers.'[12] It is important to be aware that there are anti-God forces at work that are real and not illusory. But as Os Guinness writes, 'Reality is not to be mistaken for legitimacy. In a day of contentless religious experiences, the appeal of powerful spiritual phenomena is far wider than their legitimacy.'[13]

The word 'believe' is in the present tense, conveying the idea of a continuous process of belief (rather than a single act of decision, which would more naturally be expressed by an aorist[14]).

IMITATORS OF THE JUDEAN CHURCHES (V. 14)

They became 'imitators' but not by deliberate copying, as though the Thessalonians sought persecution; their imitation was passive, not active, and came about by the same experience of persecution being reproduced in them. 'Persecution, according to the New Testament, is a natural concomitant of the Christian faith, and for the Thessalonian believers to undergo suffering for Christ's sake proves that they are fellow-members of the same body as the Judean churches.'[15]

'[Y]our own countrymen' could be understood to refer to those who lived in the same location, but the word in the Greek means 'fellow-tribesmen' and indicates more specifically than the English that the persecutors were Gentiles. Of course, the original trouble was fomented by the Jews in the local synagogue, but it spread to the Gentiles and their rulers (Acts 17:5). Which persecution of the Judean churches Paul had in mind is not clear. It is unlikely to be that which followed the death of Stephen (Acts 8:1–4; 9:1) as Paul (then called Saul) was himself involved in that (Gal. 1:22–23; 1 Tim. 1:13). A brief respite followed Saul's conversion (Acts 9:31), but persecution was renewed when Herod Antipas sought to gain the favour of the Jews (Acts 12:1–5). Apparently, another period of persecution took place under the Roman procurator Ventidius Cumanus (AD 48–52) and Paul may have had this in mind.

PAUL DIRECTLY CHARGES THE JEWS WITH KILLING THE LORD JESUS (VV. 15–16)

This is the only place in the New Testament where that charge is made directly.[16] Although the crucifixion of Jesus was carried out by the Romans, it was the Jewish community in Jerusalem, at the instigation of the religious authorities, that was ultimately responsible (Mark 3:6; 14:1; 15:14–15; John 5:18; 7:1; 8:59; 11:45–53; Acts 2:23, 36; 3:13–15; 4:10; 5:30; 7:52). Paul, himself a Jew, was not alone in drawing attention to the fact that the Jews had a history of killing their own prophets; Jesus himself made the same accusation (Matt. 23:29–37; Luke 11:47–51; 13:33–34; Acts 7:52; Rom. 11:3; compare 1 Kings 19:10, 14; Neh. 9:26). It was fanatical opposition to the plan of God to include the Gentiles in his salvific purpose (Acts 22:21–23; see also Gen. 12:3) that led the Jews to seek to expel Paul and his co-workers from city after city (Acts 9:23–25, 29; 13:45, 50; 14:2, 4–6, 19–20; 17:5; 18:6, 12–17; 19:9; see also 2 Cor. 11:24, 26).

The participle translated 'have persecuted' comes from a verb meaning 'to chase out' and so 'drove out' (NIV) is more accurate. When Paul adds that these men 'do not please God' (compare Rom. 8:8) and 'are contrary to all men', he is not joining in the common characterization that appears frequently in ancient authors,[17] but referring to the fact that they opposed God's purpose by trying to block the proclamation of the gospel to the Gentiles (Acts 13:48–51; 14:2, 19; 17:5–10). By hindering the apostles' preaching to the Gentiles they were blocking the way to the hope of salvation and thus were 'hostile to all men' (NIV; Matt. 23:13–14; see also Acts 7:51–53).

ADDING SIN TO SIN (V. 16)

The phrase 'fill up the measure of their sins' or 'heap up their sins to the limit' (NIV) points to a 'long history of sin':[18] throughout their history they have frequently resisted God's Word. This, incidentally, also draws attention to the longsuffering, patience and mercy of God. The idea of filling up a cup of guilt occurs several times in Scripture (see Gen. 15:16; 6:11–13; Dan. 8:23; Matt. 23:31–32). James Denney takes up this theme:

The cup of their iniquity was filling all the time. Every generation did something to raise the level within. The men who bade Amos be gone, and eat his bread at home, raised it a little; the men who sought Hosea's life raised it further; so did those who put Jeremiah in the dungeon, and those who murdered Zechariah between the temple and the altar. When Jesus was nailed to the cross, the cup was full to the brim. When those whom he left behind to be his witnesses, and to preach remission of sins to all men ... were expelled or put to death, it ran over.[19]

As a result of their continued opposition to the spread of the gospel, 'the wrath of God has come upon them to the uttermost' (or 'at last', NIV). This means that in some way the wrath of God has already come upon them. 'The wrath itself has come! The woes will follow.'[20] It is not unusual for the New Testament to express some impending event as though it has already arrived. This underlines the fact that the event is certain (see John 3:18; 5:24; Rom. 8:30). The wrath of God has already begun to be worked out in the present (Rom. 1:18–32), but the final outpouring of wrath is still in the future (2 Thes. 1:7–10).

In AD 49 the Jews suffered greatly and were expelled from Rome by the Emperor Claudius. During the Passover that year, thousands of Jews were massacred in the temple. Paul may have had such a past disaster in mind. However, it is not beyond the realms of possibility that the destruction of the temple (AD 70) could have been predicted by this general promise of doom. Not that Paul was specifically predicting that horrific event; but he may have realized, or even have been inspired to sense, that something really terrible was imminent. After all, the church possessed Christ's prediction that the temple was going to be destroyed before the generation that heard his words had passed away (Matt. 24; Mark 13; Luke 21:5–36).

This passage is not anti-Semitic. Nor should it ever be used for anti-Semitic purposes. The Word of God is not anti-Semitic but realistic and factual. The lesson here for all people is that, if God's chosen people,

Israel, because of their enduring rebellion, should come under the wrath of God, should Gentiles not expect the same end if we too do not repent and obey the gospel?

Back in chapter 1 the apostle set out certain clear marks of true conversion. Here in chapter 2 he throws more light on what a genuine Christian is like.

A true Christian ...

RECEIVES THE PREACHING OF THE BIBLE AS THE WORD OF GOD, NOT OF MEN (V. 13A)

One of Paul's reasons for thankfulness was that the Thessalonians received the apostolic teaching as the Word of God. Paul presented the gospel, not as a topic to be debated, but as the truth to be believed and responded to.

There is much teaching around in schools, colleges, universities and, alas, even in supposedly Christian churches which denigrates the Word of God and treats it as a mere human document. A true believer will be so enlightened by the Holy Spirit that he or she will instinctively recognize that the Bible is not merely the word of men (although men were the agents God used to write it and their personalities were not hidden), but the Word of God. God did indeed speak through men when he gave the Word (2 Peter 1:20–21), but the end result is the inspired Word of God (2 Tim. 3:16–17). The Thessalonians not only received the Word of God but they positively welcomed it. One of the signs of true converts is that they are, like newborn babies, eager for the milk of the Word (1 Peter 2:2–3).

IS RECOGNIZED BY HIS OR HER RESPONSIVENESS TO THE WORD OF GOD (V. 13B)

The Word of God works effectively in true believers. They seek to obey its clear commands. One definition of love for Christ is keeping his commandments (John 14:15; 1 John 2:3). Obedience to God's Word is a mark of a true believer. It is not legalism to obey God's commands. Legalism may be defined as the attempt to earn salvation by keeping God's commandments, or as keeping commands without the true motivation—in other words, in a purely mechanical manner; not really loving God but keeping commands for their own sake.[21] Day by day, as Christians read and meditate upon the Word, their lives are changed and their characters are made more Christlike (2 Cor. 3:18; Eph. 5:26–27). The Bible works within us as no other book can, because it is inspired by God (2 Tim. 3:16–17). It is living and active (Heb. 4:12), and, as the sword of the Holy Spirit, it is wielded by him (Eph. 6:17).

IS ALWAYS WILLING TO LEARN FROM OTHER MATURE BELIEVERS (V. 14A)

We have already encountered the word 'imitators' in chapter 1, where it is translated followers. As we saw earlier, it is the translation of a word from which the English word 'mimics' is formed. But the Greek word does not imply the shallowness of the English derivation. This was no mere mimicry, as we have seen.

We must remain willing to learn all our lives. It is a mark of pride to be unwilling to learn from others. Christians never graduate from the school of grace. A few years ago, I read in a newspaper about a parrot named Nelson. His owner spent over £100 in vet's fees trying to cure his persistent cough, but to no avail. Further investigation revealed that for a time he had been a pet in an old people's home and had learned to mimic a whole variety of coughs and groans. His best one was the hacking cough of a heavy smoker! He had no cough of his own at all. This is not the kind of imitation implied here! The idea rather is of a serious effort to learn important things from other Christians. In chapter 1, we read that the Thessalonians imitated Paul and his companions. Here it is other Christian churches which are doing the imitating. This is the only place in the New Testament where we read of a whole church becoming the model and being imitated.

We can learn from godly Christians who live around us, and we can also learn from the biographies of outstanding Christians of the past. A good place to start is with the role models in the Bible, which is completely frank about the failings as well as the successes of its characters. Only the Lord Jesus Christ was, and is, completely sinless. He is therefore our chief role model. He has given us an example that we should follow (1 Peter 2:21). But we can learn much, too, from other personalities in Scripture.

Noah's godliness, obedience and perseverance may be emulated (e.g. Gen. 6:9, 22), but his drunkenness should be avoided (Gen. 9:20–27). We can follow the faith and obedience of Abraham (e.g. Gen.12:4; 15:6), but should endeavour never to mislead others (Gen. 12:10–20; 20:1–13). We may admire Peter's boldness but not his impulsiveness—and so on. Similar lessons may be learned from outstanding Christians in church history.

IS LIKELY TO BE PERSECUTED (VV. 14B–15)
This persecution may range from simply being ridiculed, snubbed or ignored to more serious and sinister forms. It is not inevitable, and Christians should never deliberately draw persecution upon themselves by being offensive or obnoxious in their witnessing. But, on the other hand, neither should they be ashamed or afraid to witness boldly for their Lord (Mark 8:38; Rom. 1:16). The apostle Paul warned that 'all who desire to live godly in Christ Jesus will suffer persecution' (2 Tim. 3:12). This opposition may come from one's own family, friends or acquaintances, and may include attempts to stifle one's witness (1 Thes. 2:16). Those who oppose the gospel in this way will have to answer to God for their activities.

Paul's desire to see them (vv. 17–20)
The gospel has power to create love and affection between Christians. A

few months before he wrote this letter, Paul had not known a single person in Thessalonica. Now he had many friends there and loved them dearly. This illustrates the promise of Jesus that, if in order to follow him we give up worldly and unhelpful associations, we shall receive many more in this life (see Mark 10:29–30).

Christians have so much in common that is of eternal worth that they should be glad to see one another. The return in glory of our Lord Jesus Christ is one such joy that we share in anticipation. Obviously, we cannot be a close friend to every other Christian, but where close bonds of fellowship are formed there is always mutual delight. That joy will be even greater when we meet in the Lord's presence at his return (vv. 19–20).

True Christians are likely to be opposed by Satan (v. 18)

'Satan hindered us.' Paul is able to discern in the incidents of his life the presence and working of both the Lord and the enemy. In Acts 16:6–10 he discerns the Holy Spirit at work in preventing him from preaching in Asia or Bithynia. How he discerned this we do not know. It may have been a deep conviction, a pressure on his spirit. Whatever it was, it felt 'clean', it was benign; there was no sense of evil attached to it.

Here he recognizes Satan's work in preventing him from visiting the Thessalonians. Again, we do not know the details, only that the opposition was obviously evil. Perhaps it was an attempt upon his life, or the outbreak of a serious sin or scandal in the church at Corinth. At any rate, Paul recognized the work of the enemy who, though he can hinder, cannot ultimately overcome believers in Christ. The world is the scene of incessant spiritual conflict and we need to be discerning in every part of our daily lives.

This warning should not make us afraid. We must avoid unhealthy superstition that sees a demon in every negative situation. Some difficult incidents and unhelpful situations are simply the outworking of life in a fallen world and the result of living among sinful people. Nevertheless, evil events have an evil personality behind them, usually working through people under Satan's control (Eph. 2:2). However, our lives are hidden with Christ in God (Col. 3:3). The devil cannot touch us without God's permission, as the Book of Job indicates (Job 1:8–12; 2:3–7; compare Luke 22:31). Satan can, as it were, 'roar' at us in order to tempt us or frighten us, but we are told to 'submit to God'; then we shall be in a position to 'Resist the devil', and he will flee from us (James 4:7).

We should, however, be on the alert. Our adversary the devil 'walks about like a roaring lion, seeking whom he may devour' (1 Peter 5:8). But in Christ we are perfectly safe. Why, then, does Peter warn us about him? Because Christians can do foolish things and make themselves vulnerable to attack. We cannot treat the Lord's express prohibitions with impunity and expect to get away with it.

Consider these verses: Jesus said, '… the ruler of this world is coming, and he has nothing in Me' (John 14:30). In other words, Satan had no foothold, no point of entry, no 'landing strip' in the life of our Lord. Paul warned the Ephesians not to 'give place to the devil' (Eph. 4:27). In the context this means that sinful behaviour can give the devil a foothold in our lives. For example, if a Christian is foolish enough and disobedient enough to play with tarot cards, attend a spiritistic séance or watch pornographic films, he or she is trespassing on the devil's territory and giving the enemy a foothold which can lead to spiritual disaster. Those who realize they have done something very wrong like this should immediately repent and confess it to God and ask his forgiveness, so closing the door to Satan.

Some time ago, a lady moved into my area and began to attend my church. She had become a Christian in her previous church. She said that, when she tried to pray, swear-words came into her mind. I asked her if she had ever attended a spiritistic séance. She had. I asked her if she read horoscopes. She did. In fact, she said that she had a horoscope-casting kit at home! I pointed out that these things are forbidden in the Word of

God, and that she needed to repent of them, ask for God's forgiveness and burn the horoscope kit. She did so and was delivered from her problem (see Lev. 19:26b; 2 Kings 21:6; 2 Chr. 33:6; Acts 19:19).

Opposition from the devil is inevitable; defeat is certainly not (vv. 19–20)

What does Paul mean when he refers to the Thessalonian Christians as his 'hope, or joy, or crown of rejoicing' (v. 19)? Just as parents rejoice in the hope and expectation that their children will grow to maturity and have happy and successful lives, so Paul, in his mind's eye, sees the Thessalonians as presented before the Lord at his return. How easy it is to be self-centred in our hopes and expectations! It is a great and glorious thing for us to expect to be present with the Lord, but what extra joy, what a 'crown of rejoicing' we will have if even one extra person will be there because the Lord used us to bring that person to Christ!

Study questions

1. Use this chapter of 1 Thessalonians as a check-list against your own life and witness.

2. Study Psalm 91, which provides assurance of protection to the obedient (abiding) believer from every kind of attack.

3. There are times when we should not seek to defend ourselves. Sometimes our Lord Jesus, 'when He was reviled, did not revile in return' (1 Peter 2:23). On other occasions, however, he answered his attackers. What was the difference between these occasions, and how can we decide when to defend our actions?

4. What makes a testimony effective? What makes it unhelpful?

Notes

1 **Leon Morris,** *The First and Second Epistles to the Thessalonians* (NICNT; Grand Rapids, MI: Eerdmans, 1991), pp. 58–59.

2 **F. F. Bruce,** *1 & 2 Thessalonians* (Word Biblical Commentary; Nashville: Thomas Nelson, 1982), p. 25.

3 Ibid. p. 30.

4 Ibid. p. 32.

5 Ibid. p. 35.

6 **William Hendriksen,** *1 & 2 Thessalonians* (London: Banner of Truth, 1972), p. 62.

7 See **John F. MacArthur, Jr.,** *Ashamed of the Gospel: When the Church Becomes Like the World* (Wheaton, IL: Crossway, 1993) for a thorough refutation of this error.

8 **Charles A. Wanamaker,** *The Epistles to the Thessalonians* (NIGTC; Grand Rapids, MI: Eerdmans / Carlisle: Paternoster, 1990), p. 111.

9 **Morris,** *First and Second Epistles,* p. 81.

10 **Bruce,** *1 & 2 Thessalonians,* p. 45.

11 **Morris,** *First and Second Epistles,* p. 79.

12 **Bruce,** *1 & 2 Thessalonians,* p. 45. Compare Matt. 14:2; Mark 6:14; 1 Cor. 12:6, 11; Gal. 2:8; 3:5; Eph. 1:11, 20; Phil. 2:13; Col. 1:29; but contrast Eph. 2:2; 2 Thes. 2:7, where the same word describes 'supernatural activity not from God' (**Gene L. Green,** *The Letters to the Thessalonians* (Grand Rapids, MI: Eerdmans / Leicester: Apollos, 2002), p. 140), 'a force not human' (**Morris,** *First and Second Epistles,* p. 81).

13 **Os Guinness,** *The Dust of Death* (London: Inter-Varsity Press, 1973), p. 311.

14 **Morris,** *First and Second Epistles,* p. 81.

15 **Bruce,** *1 & 2 Thessalonians,* p. 45.

16 Ibid. p. 46.

17 **Green,** *Letters,* p. 145.

18 Ibid. p. 147.

19 **James Denney,** *The Epistles to the Thessalonians* (London: Hodder & Stoughton, 1892), pp. 90–91.

20 **Hendriksen,** *1 & 2 Thessalonians,* p. 73.

21 Another definition is a 'preoccupation with form at the expense of substance', **Walter A. Elwell, (ed.),** *The Evangelical Dictionary of Biblical Theology* (Grand Rapids, MI: Baker / Carlisle: Paternoster, 1996), p. 478. A more detailed explanation of legalism is given by **David Chilton** in *Productive Christians in an Age of Guilt Manipulators* (Tyler, TX: Institute for Christian Economics, 1981), pp. 22–24. He gives four examples of legalism: (1) justification by works, (2) the requirement of obedience to Old Testament laws, (3) the requirement of obedience to man-made regulations (Rom. 14; Col. 2), and (4) confusion of sins with civil crimes.

A lesson in caring (1 Thes. 3)

In this chapter, Paul is continuing his defence. It seems that the feeling among some in Thessalonica was that Paul did not care much about them; that he had run away when danger threatened and had not returned when it had passed, but had left them to face their persecutors. His long absence was interpreted as indicating his lack of concern for them, and also that, although he had brought them into difficulties through his preaching, he was reluctant to come and help them out. In certain countries today, people who become Christians through the preaching of missionaries often face great difficulties, such as loss of jobs, ostracism, verbal and physical abuse, imprisonment, and, in some instances, death. It could be thought by some that the missionaries have brought them into these difficulties.

Paul therefore reminds the Thessalonians of what he has done and openly states his feelings for them. He sent Timothy at great personal inconvenience when he could not travel to them himself (vv. 1–5). He was greatly moved and comforted by Timothy's report (vv. 6–8). He tells them how much he longs to see them, a desire which is the subject of much earnest prayer (vv. 9–11). And as a proof of his affection he expresses his fervent prayer that God will cause them to abound in love and will establish their hearts blameless in holiness (vv. 12–13).

Christians should be willing to care for others (vv. 1–5)

Is the 'we' in verse 1 stylistic or does it indicate that Silas (Silvanus) was with Paul? Most likely it is the latter, as Silvanus was included with Paul and Timothy in the greeting (1:1), had been shamefully treated with Paul at Philippi (2:2), and was with Paul and Timothy when they were expelled from Thessalonica. So 'we thought it good to be left alone' probably means 'Silvanus and I' were left alone.

Verse 2 is rendered in various ways, partly because of slight textual variants. The NKJV describes Timothy as 'our brother and minister of God, and our fellow laborer ...', while the NIV renders it 'our brother and God's fellow worker'. In fact, all of these various designations are true. Timothy was a 'brother' in Christ. He was Paul's fellow-worker and also a minister of God. Moreover, he shared the immense privilege of being a fellow-worker with God (compare 1 Cor. 3:9).

Here the gospel, which was previously called 'our gospel' (1:5) and 'the gospel of God' (2:2, 9) is called the 'gospel of Christ', as Christ is the sum and substance of the gospel. He came to bring it and he is at its centre (compare Rom. 15:19; 1 Cor. 9:12; 2 Cor. 2:12; 9:13; 10:14; Gal. 1:7; Phil. 1:27; 2 Thes. 1:8).

Although Paul needed the assistance of Timothy, he was willing to be left alone in the pagan city of Athens, with all its idolatry and false philosophy, so that the Thessalonians could be encouraged and established by Timothy's presence and instruction. Paul was willing to put up with loneliness in the middle of alien beliefs for the sake of other Christians. But there was more to Paul's concern than that. Paul feared his preaching might have been 'in vain'; he knew of that possibility only too well (v. 5; Gal. 2:2; 4:11), although he also knew that ultimately the preaching of the gospel will never be in vain (1 Cor. 15:58; Phil. 2:16). He had warned them about the inevitability of persecution (see Acts 14:22) and was desiring news that they were standing firm. He was only too aware of the activities of 'the tempter' (see 2:18; Matt. 4:3; 1 Cor. 7:5), who goes around 'like a roaring lion' (1 Peter 5:8).

F. F. Bruce observes that Timothy was able to return to Thessalonica while Paul could not and speculates that it may have been that, as a junior partner, Timothy may not have been as much in the public eye as his two senior colleagues. Unlike Paul and Silas, who were full Jews and recognized as such (Acts 16:20), Timothy, the son of a Greek father, perhaps looked like a Greek and would attract 'no special attention in a Greek city'.[1]

Timothy was sent with three goals in mind: to establish the believers, to encourage them, and to report back to Paul (v. 5, 'I sent to know your faith'). Every minister should similarly aim at these three targets: to establish believers in the faith, to encourage them in their trials, and to keep abreast with where they are spiritually. These cannot easily be accomplished simply through preaching. The Lord Jesus, in spite of having preached, also taught and healed the multitudes, and had compassion on them because they were as sheep without a shepherd (Matt. 9:35–38). Pastoral visitation, discussion, study groups, homework, feedback and personal discipling—in other words, personal contact—are all valuable in getting to know the condition of the flock (Prov. 27:23; compare John 10:14).

Matthew Henry comments on the character reference Paul gives of Timothy in these words:

We sent Timothy our brother. Elsewhere he calls him his son; here he calls him brother. Timothy was Paul's junior in age, his inferior in gifts and graces, and of a lower rank in the ministry; for Paul was an apostle, and Timothy but an evangelist; yet Paul calls him brother. This was an instance of the apostle's humility, and showed his desire to put honour upon Timothy and to recommend him to the esteem of the churches. He calls him also a minister of God ... Ministers of the gospel of Christ are ministers of God, to promote the kingdom of God among men. He calls him also his fellow-labourer in the gospel of Christ ... Ministers of the gospel must look upon themselves as labourers in the Lord's vineyard; they have an honourable office and hard work ...[2]

The fact that Paul calls Timothy a 'brother' shows that he did not send someone whose absence would be of no consequence to him; rather he sent one who was dear to him and would accurately convey his own concern for the Thessalonians.

Timothy was a minister of God, a man who not only would be of great usefulness to the apostle had he not gone to Thessalonica, but who also was fully qualified to teach the Thessalonians. Timothy was also a fellow-labourer with Paul, so not only would the apostle miss a valuable part of his working team, but also Timothy could be trusted to work hard in Thessalonica. He was well qualified to establish them in the faith and to comfort them in their trials.

We also should be willing to put up with inconvenience in order to establish others in the faith (vv. 1–2). This may be costly in terms of time, money and effort. As it did for Paul, it may mean being separated from a friend or loved one for a time in order to meet other people's needs. We need the discernment given by the Holy Spirit in order to distinguish those in need whom we could help from those who are merely time-wasters. We need to be aware that the enemy can put people in our way who will simply hinder us and take time from us that could be used more profitably on others.

Paul sent Timothy to Thessalonica to establish or strengthen the believers in their faith and to encourage them. They were relatively young in the faith and needed strengthening. They needed to know, understand and be established in the truth. Then they needed to be encouraged to live it out. It seems that the Thessalonian Christians were becoming unsettled by trials, either theirs or the apostle's (vv. 3–4). The intense persecution was likely to have shaken the faith of some, so part of Timothy's task was to strengthen them (v. 3). Paul reminds them of something they knew well: that Christians are appointed, or destined, to suffer. The New Testament is full of this warning (see John 16:33; Acts 9:16; 14:22; Rom. 5:3; 8:35–39; 12:12; 2 Cor. 1:4; 4:8, 16–17; 6:1–10; 7:4; 11:23–27; 12:7–10; 2 Tim. 3:12; etc.). It is true that, as William Hendriksen observed, afflictions that have been predicted, and that take place in accordance with that prediction, can serve to strengthen faith.[3]

People can be turned aside from the faith, not only by persecution or suffering, but also by more subtle pressures. One of the striking features of the New Testament in this connection is the frequency of references to deception and the variety of words used to describe it. (See Appendix 2 for a list of words referring to deception.)

In addition there are more general warnings, such as in Matthew 7:15–23; John 10:1, 8; Acts 10:28–31; 20:29–31; 1 Timothy 4:1; 2 Timothy 4:3–4; 2 Peter 2:1–3; 1 John 4:1. Along with these warnings go the exhortations to be discerning: Acts 17:11; 1 Corinthians 2:14; 6:5; Hebrews 5:14.

Do you know someone who is a bit shaky in the faith? Could you help him or her? It may require time spent in talking and prayer. It may mean writing a letter of encouragement. It may cost us to take him or her out for a meal or provide hospitality. Our inconvenience, however, is but for a short time; the other person's spiritual life is a matter of eternity. In this life we will often come across those who are in distress. We cannot meet all needs, nor can we solve all problems. But we should be especially willing to help fellow-Christians who are suffering. Paul's example teaches us that we should be ready and willing to comfort those who are distressed.

The Thessalonians had obviously suffered some afflictions. The apostle had previously taught them that suffering was inevitable and now he writes to remind them that this is to be expected. They are not suffering because they have sinned.

Is there someone within reach of your help who is being persecuted? Has someone you know suffered bereavement or had a deep disappointment in life? We may be able to help fellow-Christians in their trials, or put them in touch with others who can help.

Paul must have felt considerable frustration that he was so far from these new believers and could be of little or no practical help. They needed an experienced man on the spot. Timothy's presence would not only be a comfort, but also meant that he could be of practical assistance. Some years ago, in South Wales, my wife and I had the joy of leading a young woman to Christ. She had a friend who had just moved to Dundee but who was also interested in the gospel. Could we help her too? We knew a godly minister in the area and put her in touch with him, and he had the joy of leading her to Christ also.

Paul wanted to find out how the Thessalonian Christians stood: whether their faith was strong or not. He desired to know how they were coping with afflictions and persecution (v. 5). Some people are natural communicators; others are not. But if we are involved in ministry, it is important that we take the time and trouble to enquire after the needs of those for whom we have some responsibility, or in whose lives we have an interest.

Paul has already mentioned Satan's hindering tactics (2:18); now he refers to his strategy of temptation. If the Thessalonians yielded to temptation Paul's labours could prove to have been in vain. Note the words 'by some means'. Satan has many ways of seducing people from the truth. He is a master at producing counterfeit manifestations and false or distorted teaching. One way in which people are led astray is by excitement being raised about a new ministry. Unusual things are happening, crowds are gathering, some experienced and well-known Christians are being drawn to the movement, which may even be called a 'revival'. The questions to ask at such times are: Is what is happening true to Scripture? Does it agree with sound biblical doctrine? What is the lasting fruit of this excitement? Is it causing people to behave in godly ways, or are there bizarre manifestations? As far as the Thessalonians were concerned, they could have been drawn back into paganism by former friends, led astray into heresy by false teachers, or made to draw back in fear by the severity of the persecution. Satan is the great author of persecution and through it he endeavours to tempt people away from the truth in order to avoid suffering. He also, through affliction, tempts people to murmur or complain, to accuse God of lack of love or of severity. We should seek to strengthen other Christians whenever we perceive them to be facing temptation.

Paul writes to the Galatians, 'Brethren, if a man is overtaken in any trespass, you who are spiritual restore such a one in a spirit of gentleness, considering yourself lest you also be tempted. Bear one another's burdens, and so fulfill the law of Christ' (Gal. 6:1–2). If you know that someone is being tempted into sin or compromise in some way, your words, or even just your presence, may help strengthen that person's faith and pull him or her back from the brink of failure. When young Christians suffer persecution for their faith the temptation is to give up. Timothy would be able to strengthen the Thessalonians in their temptations. He would know from Paul's teaching that 'No temptation has overtaken you except such as is common to man; but God is faithful, who will not allow you to be tempted beyond what you are able [to bear], but with the temptation will also make the way of escape, that you may be able to bear it' (1 Cor. 10:13).

Christians should rejoice over the progress of others (vv. 6–8)

Timothy had returned and brought good news of the Thessalonian Christians' standing, their faith, and of their affection for Paul and his colleagues. He reported that they wanted to see the rest of the team, just as Paul and Silas wanted to see them (v. 6). So, in Paul and Silas's 'affliction and distress' (v. 7), they were greatly comforted. 'For now we live, if you stand fast in the Lord.' Satan is adept at causing believers to doubt (Gen. 3:1–6), and it is possible that Paul may have wondered, in view of the treatment they had received, whether they had, after all, been guided by God to Macedonia (Acts 16:10). Timothy's report would have cast such doubts to the wind.

Christian workers can easily be afflicted by doubts as to their calling or the effectiveness of their ministries. News of blessing through their ministries is always encouraging.

Paul was delighted to receive Timothy's report. The 'now' in verse 6 indicates that Paul was writing immediately on Timothy's return. To deal promptly with correspondence and other matters is not only efficient and business-like, but is also a Christian virtue. Tardiness or procrastination should not characterize a Christian.

Sometimes we need to think and pray about a letter before writing it. But more often than not, our fault is not haste but delay. Getting work done, assignments completed or essays out of the way relieves the pressure upon us. When we are writing letters of congratulations, sympathy or condolence, the quicker we are, the more effective they will be.

When Timothy returned from Thessalonica Paul was suffering from persecution and distress caused by the enemies of the gospel. So severe was this affliction that he even alluded to it, by implication, as death (v. 8). The news that Timothy brought, however, was like a healing ointment to Paul's soul. He felt alive again.

Do you ever write words of thanks, comfort or support to your minister or missionaries you know? Do you ever tell them what their ministries have meant to you, or assure them that you are praying for them (if indeed you are!)? We are very quick to complain about things we do not like, but not so ready to express thanks. Over forty years ago I heard a minister preach on the following words from Romans 1:21: 'nor were thankful, but ...' I have never forgotten that message. He pointed out that unthankfulness was the beginning of a downwards slide into apostasy, gross sin and evil behaviour, as the rest of that chapter shows.

When Christians hear of the faith of others, they will share in the joy of those who have come to Christ. When they hear of the outworking of their faith in practical love, their reaction will be to give thanks to God for his grace. It is only too easy to be self-centred and think only of ourselves. Worse still, we can be envious of the success or progress of others. We should be able to rejoice as Paul did. The sheer warmth of the mutual affection between Paul and the Thessalonians is a cause of rejoicing.

If we have been put to inconvenience or even suffering in order to bring others to Christ, the news of their progress makes our afflictions easier to bear. When we hear that they are steadily growing, to paraphrase Paul's words, their steadfastness helps us live! Real living is not selfish enjoyment and pursuing our own goals; it is seeing the progress of others in which we have had some small part to play.

How Christians should pray for others (vv. 9–13)

So joyful is Paul at the good news of the Thessalonian Christians' steadfastness that he is almost at a loss for words (v. 9). Although he seems to work 'night and day' (2:9), he nevertheless finds time to pray (3:10). The fervency of his praying is expressed by the use of an unusual adverb, translated 'exceedingly', which literally means 'quite beyond all measure (highest form of comparison imaginable)'. Along with this, the word he uses for prayer is not the more common word expressing devotion, but one that signifies a 'want' or 'lack'.[4]

In verse 10 Paul refers to 'what is lacking' in their faith. In spite of encouraging growth and successful evangelism the Thessalonians were not perfect. They needed more instruction and a deeper knowledge of God. There is perhaps nothing more dangerous to new Christians—or older ones, for that matter—than for them to think they 'know it all' and need no further instruction. There is always more to learn, more development to achieve, and more experience to gain until we see Christ and are changed into his likeness. We should never, ever think we have nothing more to learn (see Rev. 3:17; 2 Peter 3:18; 1 John 3:2–3).

Although there is so much to praise God for, it appears that Timothy has reported that there are still deficiencies in the faith of the Thessalonians. The word translated 'perfect' or 'supply' (*katartisai*, v. 10) is used elsewhere of mending nets (Matt. 4:21) and also of bringing the saints to perfection (Eph. 4:12). It means 'to put into unified and good working condition'.[5] The word translated 'what is lacking' means, basically, 'to come behind', and the fact that a plural form is used suggests that more than one matter needs attention. Paul is not only eager to see them, but also keen to adjust the shortcomings in their faith. All Christians need to continue growing and learning more of Christ (Heb. 5:12–14; 2 Peter 3:18).

In the prayer, or 'wish'[6] or benediction, that follows in verse 11, Paul links Father and Son so closely that he uses a singular verb, so emphasizing their unity. The pronoun 'Himself' is emphatic, stressing that it is God who must work to enable Paul to get to Thessalonica, and not merely the apostle's desire.

How should we pray for those whom we are seeking to help?

WITH THANKSGIVING AND REJOICING (V. 9)

How often, when we pray for others, we forget to thank God for them! Paul not only prayed for them, but he prayed 'exceedingly'. This is not just saying a few prayers; it suggests wrestling or striving in prayer. Such prayer is hard work. Think of how Jesus prayed in the Garden of Gethsemane (Luke 22:44).[7]

THAT WE MAY HAVE THE OPPORTUNITY FOR
MUTUALLY STRENGTHENING FELLOWSHIP (VV. 10–11)

Spending time together in prayer or in helpful discussion of spiritual things can be helpful both to our friends and to ourselves.

THAT WE MAY BE ABLE TO HELP THEM IN THEIR
UNDERSTANDING OF THE GOSPEL (V. 10)

This will also increase our own understanding.

THAT THEIR LOVE MIGHT GROW (V. 12)

Paul now expresses the desire that the love of the Thessalonians may 'increase and abound', or 'abound and exceed'.[8] The two verbs are very similar in meaning and serve to emphasize Paul's desire that the Thessalonians' love may be full to overflowing, both towards one another and towards others. All of us need to grow in the graces or fruit of the Holy Spirit. So, when we pray that others' love may grow, we should pray that we may grow also.

Jesus taught that his disciples are to love one another. He said that this is one way we prove to the world that we are Christians: 'A new commandment I give to you, that you love one another; as I have loved you, that you also love one another. By this all will know that you are My disciples, if you have love for one another' (John 13:34–35).

Many Christians get confused over this command to love one another and find it hard to love the unconverted, especially those who are obnoxious or hateful. How can we possibly love all Christians, let alone our enemies? The answer is very simple but not easily spotted.

Part of the problem is that we tend to identify love with emotion, which in most cases is quite correct and understandable. But that association is not always accurate, at least not in every circumstance and situation. Modern society tends to identify love with sex, which again is misleading as it is true only within certain contexts. An understanding of the various Greek words for love may help.

According to C. S. Lewis, the Greek language has four words for love. These may be considered diagrammatically as four concentric circles. The innermost and smallest circle represents the Greek word for sexual love (*eros*, from which we get 'erotic'). This word does not occur in the New Testament, perhaps because it had become rather debased in usage, much as the word 'love' has today. However, in its proper context it is a legitimate love; it refers to the physical love of desire that God intended we may have for one person of the opposite sex within the bonds of marriage, and for life.

The next circle, moving outwards, represents *storgē*, a word meaning 'family affection'. This is the love one feels for one's family, including one's spouse. We have a certain kind of love for our immediate family which is different from any affection we may have for others.

The next circle represents the word *philia*, meaning 'friendship love'. We may have friends all over the world and there is a certain kind of affection we have for them which is different from both sexual love and family affection, though, of course, our families come within that circle too.

Each of those three involves a certain amount of emotion which is spontaneous and natural. These forms of love come naturally and require little or no effort. Now comes a different love. The fourth circle moving outwards represents *agapē* love, the love that is spoken of most frequently in the New Testament. That is the word used in 1 Thessalonians 3:12. *Agapē* love does not *necessarily* involve any emotion, though it may be linked with affection, pity, compassion, sympathy, even fear or anger. It does not depend upon natural affection, though that is included in the case of family ties. It is a purposeful love, a decision of the will to act benevolently towards another person, to wish another well, to do what is for his or her good. It is a deliberate love. One can love any person in the *agapē* sense, in that one decides to do good to him or her. Therefore we can love even the unlovely with *agapē* love, which is the fruit of the Holy Spirit (Gal. 5:22–23).[9]

Recent scholarship has shown that in the New Testament the *philia* group of words is used quite broadly, and though these words are used nowhere near as much as the *agapē* group, they are, in some contexts, almost synonymous.[10] However, as William Hendriksen writes, 'Synonyms are hardly ever (if ever!) exactly alike in meaning in every context.'[11] In other words, at times they can be used interchangeably, as indeed *agapē* and *philia* sometimes are. For example, in John's Gospel we read in two places that the Father loves the Son. In John 3:35 *agapaō* is used, but in John 5:20 *phileō* is used. In fact, there is quite an overlap between these words. That should not surprise us as it is the nature of language to be flexible. How many of us always use words precisely? A classic example of this (possible) overlap is found in John 21. Here the Lord Jesus questions Peter about his love, and both *agapaō* and *phileō* are used. Some translators, such as The Twentieth Century New Testament, J. B. Phillips and Weymouth, make a distinction, but most mainstream translations do not. William Hendriksen, in his commentary on the Gospel of John, does make a distinction and has a seven-page-long note at the end of chapter 21 in which he discusses this matter thoroughly. He lists all the authorities, both ancient and modern, who make a distinction, and those who do not. He concludes,

For the reasons indicated we believe that *agapaō in this story* (and generally throughout the Gospels, though *with varying degrees of distinctness in meaning*) indicates love, deep-seated, thorough-going, intelligent and purposeful, a love in which the entire personality (not only the emotions, but also the mind and the will) plays a prominent part, which is based on esteem for the object loved or else on reasons which lie wholly outside of this object; while *phileō* indicates (or at least tends in the direction of) spontaneous natural affection, in which the emotions play a more prominent role than either the intellect or the will [emphasis original].[12]

So when Jesus commands us to love others, he does not necessarily mean that we must feel an emotion. We may, but that is not essential. He means that we must act in their best interests or at least in obedience to God's command. That is why we are able to express *agapē* love to those whom we would not otherwise be able to like or admire. We seek what is best for them. This means we should care for one another in practical ways. The apostle Paul demonstrates in his writings and actions what it means to care for someone spiritually; we may have the opportunity to care for someone practically as well.

It is quite right that scholars should examine words in detail and tell us whether or not they are synonymous in abstraction, that is, in terms of study, but when we are dealing pastorally with people there are two different situations in which it is helpful, if not essential, to spell out the difference: first, as has already been mentioned, when Christians wonder how they can love everyone, and especially in what way they should love everyone in distinction from their spouses, children or close friends. Even scholars who insist that there is no difference between *agapē* and *philia* will admit that the context makes a difference. If we take the English word 'affection', all such scholars would surely admit that this word, in different contexts, has differing connotations. 'He has affection for his wife / cat / tomato plants / books / grandma / music'—these all contain different nuances of meaning.

But, second, some well-meaning Christians, understanding that we are to love one another, have fallen into the trap of sexual immorality because they have seen no distinction in the meaning of 'love' in different contexts. This is especially the case when religious emotions are running high. 'Critics of revivalism have frequently pointed out the close connection between spirituality and sensuality; the excited state of mind that issues from heightened religious emotions and the inevitable lack of control are presumed to throw wide open the door for sexual licence.'[13] It is helpful and necessary that scholars should point out the fact that, in theory and in certain contexts, these words are synonymous, but in the context of Christian fellowship they are distinct. Gene L. Green's comments on 1 Thessalonians 4:6 are apposite: 'In the intimate meetings held in the tight confines of the home or homes of fellow believers, Christians of both sexes were thrown together in a close, interpersonal setting that could easily have given rise to relationships that were outside the lines of morality.'[14] Green has served as a missionary, and pastors and missionaries often see the practical outworking and application of biblical teaching which scholars may overlook.

THAT THEIR HEARTS WILL BE ESTABLISHED BLAMELESS BEFORE GOD (V. 13)

This verse introduces a helpful and inspiring thought. Many true Christians long to be more holy. Paul implies that, if our hearts overflow with love to other believers and also to those outside the fellowship, our hearts will be strengthened so that God will look on them as blameless in holiness when the Lord Jesus Christ returns. Concentrating upon ourselves does not help our growth in grace half as much as does pouring out our love on others. 'Paul seeks love for his converts as the means by which their hearts may be established unblameable in holiness. That is a notable direction for those in search of holiness. A selfish, loveless heart can never succeed in this quest. A cold heart is not unblameable, and never will be; it is either Pharisaical or foul, or both.'[15]

Another serious prayer is that they, and we, might be established in holiness (v. 13). That suggests that holiness is to be more than transient. Holiness is Christlikeness, and our Lord was holy at all times. Holiness is not something we put on for meetings; it is, or should be, our true Christian character. We are no more holy than we are when we are alone when only God can see us. Is that an impossible standard? To help see the possibility of this we must recognize that there are two aspects of holiness or sanctification. There is our standing in Christ, which means that we are clothed in God's sight with Christ's righteousness (1 Cor. 1:30; Rom. 8:29–30). This is perfection. It can never be greater than it is at our conversion. But then there is our present state. We are to press on towards perfection in practice (Phil. 3:12–14; 2 Cor. 6:14–7:1). This is our growth in grace. We are to grow in likeness to Christ (Rom. 8:29; 2 Peter 3:18). One of the main ways that this comes about is through the application of the Word of God to our lives. The Lord Jesus, in his prayer for his disciples (including us, see v. 20) in John 17, said, 'Sanctify them by Your truth. Your word is truth' (v. 17). Another major influence in sanctification is prayer. Paul's prayers in his epistles are full of golden truth about the growth in grace of those whom he addressed.

Perfection will not be reached before the *parousia* (the return of Christ)! 'The Thessalonians are to be blameless in holiness, not in the judgment of any human tribunal, but before our God and Father, at the coming of our Lord Jesus Christ with all his saints.'[16] We shall not be perfected before we see the Lord, but we are to 'press toward the goal for the prize of the upward call of God in Christ Jesus' (Phil. 3:14).

Study questions

1. Read through 1 Corinthians 13 substituting the name 'Jesus' for every occurrence of the word 'love'. Now read verses 4–7 of that chapter and see if you can substitute the personal pronoun 'I' for 'love'. Ask God to help you to be more loving and to be willing to be inconvenienced for others.

2. Study Paul's prayer in Ephesians 3:14–19 and from it list some things you could pray for others.

3. In what ways can you help strengthen the faith of others?

4. Discuss the difference between 'faith' (trust in God) and 'the faith', the body of Christian doctrine. How do they relate to each other?

Notes

1 **F. F. Bruce,** *1 & 2 Thessalonians* (Word Biblical Commentary; Nashville: Thomas Nelson, 1982), p. 64.

2 **Matthew Henry,** *Commentary on 1 Thessalonians,* in *Commentary on the Whole Bible* (PC Study Bible; Seattle, WA: Biblesoft, 2006).

3 **William Hendriksen,** *1 & 2 Thessalonians* (London: Banner of Truth, 1972), p. 85.

4 **Leon Morris,** *The First and Second Epistles to the Thessalonians* (NICNT; Grand Rapids, MI: Eerdmans, 1991), p. 105.

5 **Bailey,** cited by **Morris,** *First and Second Epistles,* p. 105, note.

6 **Hendriksen,** *1 & 2 Thessalonians,* p. 90.

7 I cannot commend too highly **E. M. Bounds** on prayer. If possible, get the one-volume edition of his complete works on prayer (*The Complete Works of E. M. Bounds on Prayer* (Grand Rapids, MI: Baker, 1990)) and read it, study it, and re-read it!

8 Literal English translation by **Reverend Alfred Marshall** in *The New International Version*

Interlinear Greek–English New Testament (Grand Rapids, MI: Zondervan, 1976), p. 808.

9 See the article 'Love', in **Sinclair B. Ferguson** and **David F. Wright, (eds.),** *New Dictionary of Theology* (Downers Grove, IL/Leicester: IVP, 1988), pp. 398–400) and also **C. S. Lewis,** *The Four Loves* (London: Collins Fontana, 1963).

10 See, for example, **W. Gunther,** 'Love', in **Colin Brown, (ed.),** *The New International Dictionary of New Testament Theology*, vol. 2 (Exeter: Paternoster, 1976), pp. 538ff. See also **Don Carson,** 'Love', in **T. D. Alexander, Brian Rosner, D. A. Carson** and **Graeme Goldsworthy,** *New Dictionary of Biblical Theology* (Leicester: IVP, 2000).

11 **William Hendriksen,** *The Gospel of John* (London: Banner of Truth, 1959), p. 500.

12 Ibid. pp. 494–501.

13 **Arthur Fawcett,** *The Cambuslang Revival* (London: Banner of Truth, 1971), p. 143.

14 **Gene L. Green,** *The Letters to the Thessalonians* (Grand Rapids, MI: Eerdmans / Leicester: Apollos, 2002), p. 197.

15 **James Denney,** *The Epistles to the Thessalonians* (London: Hodder & Stoughton, 1892), p. 129.

16 Ibid. p. 130.

How to live a clean life (1 Thes. 4)

At the end of chapter 3 Paul prayed for the Thessalonians' growth in love and their establishment in holiness (3:11–13). But he does not only pray for them to be holy; now he backs up that prayer to God with an exhortation to them, urging their co-operation in practical aspects of holy living. Christian teaching is not mere theory; it is essentially practical. It is meant to shape our lives. Sometimes God uses us in the fulfilment of our own prayers. When we have prayed for people, we may need to encourage or exhort them verbally.

A plea for purity (vv. 1–8)

What is the goal? To live ('walk') so as to please God. In order to live a clean life we must:

MAKE IT OUR AIM TO PLEASE GOD (V. 1)

Although he is only halfway through the epistle, Paul begins this section with 'Finally ...' He instructs the Thessalonians how they ought to live and please God. If our lives are God-centred, we will not seek to 'walk' (live) in the way that attains maximum satisfaction for ourselves, but in a way that pleases God. The Greek text uses *dei*, which means 'it is necessary', translated in the NKJV as 'ought'. The NIV does not translate this. 'Such conduct was not optional but obligatory since the source of the teaching was not simply human but divine.'[1] The verbs translated 'urge', or 'ask' (NIV), and 'exhort' are repeated later in the book (4:10; 5:11–12, 14). On its own, in some contexts, the first verb (*erōtaō*) can signify merely to ask, but in the context of an exhortation it acquires a stronger meaning. Combining it with the verb 'to exhort' (*parakaleō*) also makes Paul's words much stronger (see also Phil. 4:3; 2 Thes. 2:1; 3:12; 2 John 5).

On 10 November 1942, during the Second World War, Britain's Prime Minister Winston Churchill gave a memorable speech at the Lord Mayor's Luncheon in London. After a series of defeats, ranging from Dunkirk to Singapore, the Allies had at last won a victory. Generals Alexander and Montgomery turned back Rommel's forces in North Africa at El Alamein, thus winning what Churchill called 'the battle of Egypt'. 'Now this is not the end,' Churchill intoned. 'It is not even the beginning of the end. But it is, perhaps, the end of the beginning.'[2] This is very applicable to Paul's word 'Finally ...' here.

What does the word 'finally' tell us? It indicates that, having dealt with the main burden of his letter, namely, to bare his heart to the Thessalonian Christians and to vindicate his conduct against the slanders of his enemies, Paul is now beginning the final section of his letter. This final section is intended to give ethical instruction to the young church. In these days, when so much impurity presses upon us from the media and from contemporary behaviour, this plea is still vitally necessary. It is so easy to let the world 'squeeze you into its own mould', as J. B. Philips expresses part of Romans 12:1–2.

Here in 1 Thessalonians Paul makes his plea very powerful in several ways.

First, he 'urges' and 'exhorts' his readers. He addresses them as *adelphoi*, that is, brothers (and sisters). This term implies that they are a family. 'It served to link together people who often had no previous contact with one another.'[3] An exhortation of this sort is like a powerful sermon. Paul speaks directly to them about this important matter. The preaching of the Word is one of the chief means God uses to help us to grow spiritually. This should be one of the main criteria used in deciding which church to join: is the Word of God preached regularly and faithfully?

Second, Paul gives extra weight to his exhortation by adding the words 'in the Lord Jesus'. This exhortation is not just a matter of one Christian worker's opinion; it is the will of the Lord for our lives. Christians will consider the will of God to be the paramount motivation in their lives, as they are located, spiritually speaking, in Christ. Christ is their environment.

Third, Paul encourages them to 'abound more and more', that is, to go all out for the goal. How many Christians put more effort into their recreation than into their religion? As someone once put it, 'Don't let your diversions become your occupations.'

Often we want to please other people. That is all right so long as it does not conflict with what God requires of us. Sometimes we have the freedom to please ourselves so long as doing so does not violate other biblical principles. But at all times our aim should be to live to please God (see 2:4).

In challenging the Thessalonians to live pure lives Paul readily acknowledges their present obedience in the words 'as you do walk'.[4] (The NKJV omits this encouraging clause of Paul's—which recognizes that they are already seeking to 'walk', that is 'live', pure lives—as it is omitted from many manuscripts. But see the NIV: 'as in fact you are living'.) In spite of its failures the church at Thessalonica was living in a Christ-like way. So while he urges further improvement he does not fail to notice their progress. This is a wise procedure. If we ever have to correct or criticize we should normally acknowledge positive progress in those we seek to help. However, Paul wants them to make more progress. He wants them to put into practice what they already know, and be more diligent in working out in their lives their theoretical knowledge. Several times in this epistle Paul reminds them of what they already know (1:5; 2:1, 2, 5, 11; 3:3–4; 5:2). How we all need that reminder! If only we put into practice what we already know about godly living we would all, no doubt, be much further on in maturity than we are.

GET TO KNOW, AND SEEK TO LIVE OUT, OUR BIBLE (V. 2)

Paul reminds them of the commandments already delivered in the name of the Lord Jesus. 'There is an authoritative note about the word commandment *(parangelia)*. The apostolic tradition is not to be treated indifferently; it is to be accepted because it is the tradition of Christ, by whose authority the apostles deliver it. This is indicated by the following phrase ... "through the Lord Jesus."'[5]

These commandments 'were not mere guidelines that could be ignored', but orders from God. 'As such they should not be glibly put aside or ignored according to the whims of those in the church ... Therefore, when the Thessalonians accepted the apostolic proclamation as the word of God (2:13) they also came under obligation to obey the moral commandments that accompanied it.'[6] When we become Christians we do not have the choice as to whether we will serve God or not, for we are 'bought at a price' (1 Cor. 6:20). 'Christian service is not an optional extra for those who like that sort of thing. It is a compelling obligation that lies on each one of the redeemed.'[7] We know, or should know, what God has already commanded in his Word.

Paul had already taught them how to live and please God. Now he exhorts them to put the teaching into practice. Knowing without doing produces hypocrites, or, at least, nominal Christians. It is not merely hearing the Word of God that changes our lives, but actually obeying it (see Matt. 7:24–27 and James 1:22–25). They had the teaching and they had consciences, but Timothy's report, it seems, galvanized the apostle into an extra effort to stir their consciences. We are all apt to think that because we know the Bible's teaching and have active consciences, we have sufficient light to live pure lives. So it should be. But James Denney has a pertinent word to say about our consciences:

We have not been true to conscience; it is set in our human nature like the unprotected compass in the early iron ships: it is exposed to influences from other parts of our nature which bias and deflect it without our knowledge. It needs to be adjusted to the holy will of God, the unchangeable standard of right, and protected against disturbing forces.[8]

Notice the references to the Lord Jesus Christ in verses 1–2. Paul urges and exhorts them 'in the Lord Jesus'. Because they are in Christ they are suitable recipients of such exhortation. The apostle reminds them that he gave them commandments 'through the Lord Jesus'. This shows that Paul used the words and example of Christ as the basis of his moral teaching. 'The mind of Christ is the norm for the Christian conscience.'[9]

SEEK TO OBEY GOD'S WILL (V. 3)

Paul explains that God's will includes abstention from sexual immorality, a particularly relevant exhortation for Thessalonian society. Although the word translated 'sexual immorality' is sometimes understood as meaning only fornication, that is, sexual intercourse outside marriage, here it includes all kinds of immorality. The Greek word *porneia*, from which we get 'pornography', 'meant any kind of sexual relation outside of heterosexual marriage, whether it was fornication, adultery, homosexuality, incest, prostitution, or bestiality'.[10]

We may find it hard to grasp what a sudden and complete change this meant for the new believers in Thessalonica. The religious cults they were involved in prior to conversion did not merely permit sexual promiscuity, but they even encouraged it. And this was not just a private matter but a common social practice. To break from sexual licence meant not only changing their personal lifestyles but also breaking with the social practices of their friends and neighbours.

Abstention from sexual immorality is not just one of a list of ethical constraints: it is centred on God's will. We do not have a check-list that we can tick off as we obey the rules one by one. Rather, as Christians, we are constrained to obey God's will in whatever realm it is made known to us (see Matt. 7:21; 12:50; 21:31; Mark 3:35; Luke 12:47; John 7:17; 9:31; Acts 13:22; Rom. 12:1–2; Eph. 6:6; Heb. 10:36; 13:21; 1 John 2:17). Although Paul later makes it clear that it is God who works sanctification in us by his Holy Spirit, nevertheless, our part is to align our behaviour with the revealed will of God.

Once, after I had given an evangelistic address at a nurses' Christian Union meeting, a young nurse came to me for counsel. She asked me, 'If I become a Christian, will I have to give up such and such?' I replied that it was not a question of giving up this or that but of coming under the authority of Jesus Christ as Saviour and Lord. Then, if the Lord told her that this thing would have to go, it must go. Receiving Christ as Saviour includes obeying him as Lord.

Many Christians want to know God's will for their futures, but often they forget the most fundamental requirements: the will of God for the present. 'For this is the will of God, your sanctification' (v. 3). What serious words these are! 'The will of God'; no true believer will ever want to go against the will of God deliberately. Christians often express concern over knowing the will of God for their lives, and that is admirable. But much of the will of God for our lives is already laid out in the Bible. The rest he will reveal in due course if we sincerely ask him and intend to obey him. But let us be careful to obey what has already been revealed. Willingness to obey is a prerequisite for receiving guidance from God, and that willingness is demonstrated by obeying what God has already commanded.[11] 'If anyone wills to do His will, he shall know concerning the doctrine, whether it is from God or whether I speak on My own authority' (John 7:17).

It is surely significant that when Paul teaches on sanctification he begins with abstention from sexual immorality. The attitude of the world is that sexual promiscuity is normal. A television programme I watched recently covered a group of girls in the USA who had pledged to remain virgins and save themselves for their future husbands. The attitude of the interviewer ranged from incredulity to scorn. She suggested that this was an impossibility and that the girls were either mad or at least seriously in error. This is how the world views sexual purity. Beware of the influence of television! Psalm 101:3a is relevant: 'I will set nothing wicked before my eyes …' Those who feed upon the 'soaps' are likely to begin to think that sexual immorality is normal. Remember also that the Lord Jesus included the thought-life in his definition of adultery (Matt. 5:27–28; see also 15:19; Mark 7:21–22). 'Sexual immorality' means any form of illicit sexual behaviour: any sexual activity, including thoughts, that deviates from the monogamous relationship between husband and wife.

In view of the permissive culture in Thessalonica, Paul considered abstention from sexual immorality to be the first priority in the Thessalonians' devotion to sanctification … every imaginable sexual vice was rampant in and around Thessalonica; therefore Paul was especially concerned that the Thessalonians could easily fall back into their former habits. So he gave them the direct uncomplicated command to *abstain from sexual immorality*. *Abstain* means complete abstinence, in this case, staying away from any thought or behavior that violates the principles of God's Word and results in any act of sexual sin [emphasis original].[12]

The will of God is not only a law to be obeyed but also a motivation to inspire. It is not a dead law but a living power; it is God working in us to do his will for his glory. It is not something against us but on our side. It is not an opposing force we have to cope with but a power on which we can depend. It is like a fast-flowing river; we can either swim with the current or try to swim against it. This analogy can be applied in two ways. For the Christian, a person 'in Christ', the river represents God's will, and we should swim in the flow of God's will for us. It can, however, be a picture of the world's attitudes and moral standards. In that case we need God's strength to swim against the current of popular morality. If we pursue an unchristian life of sensuality, impurity, lust and carnality, God is against us. If, by God's grace, we seek to live a Christian life of purity, self-control and godliness, God is on our side. 'Sanctification is the one task which we can face confident that we are not left to our own resources. God is not the taskmaster we have to satisfy out of our own poor efforts, but the holy and loving Father who inspires and sustains us from first to last.'[13]

EXERCISE SELF-CONTROL (V. 4)

'[E]ach of you', writes Paul, 'should know how to possess his own vessel in sanctification and honor.' The word 'vessel' has provoked much discussion. Some contend that it means 'wife', on the basis that a man's wife is termed 'the weaker vessel' in 1 Peter 3:7 and the word 'possess' could be rendered 'acquire'. The meaning would then be something like this: every man should get his own wife to avoid sexual immorality. The other interpretation is that 'vessel' refers to a person's own body, and there are texts that would support that interpretation, such as Acts 9:15; 2 Corinthians 4:7; 2 Timothy 2:21 (compare 1 Sam. 21:4–5).

On the whole, this last interpretation is to be preferred: first, because it makes more sense of the phrase 'know how to possess'; second, because mere possession of a wife does not preclude immorality in and of itself as much as 'knowing how to possess one's own body' does; and third, this interpretation allows it to be applied to women also, as they also need this exhortation.

Having examined the evidence, Leon Morris concludes,

It is not easy to decide the point, but it does seem to me that it would not be very natural for a Greek writer to speak of a wife as a 'vessel'. And in this case it would be the less likely since Paul is inculcating a high view of marriage, whereas it is a very low view that sees the wife as no more than a vessel for gratifying the husband's sexual desires.

We should also bear in mind that this comes in a letter addressed to the whole church, women as well as men, and it is impossible for a woman (married or single) to acquire a wife. This ... inclines me to the view that 'body' is meant here.[14]

The preferred interpretation of the word 'vessel' in verse 4, then, is 'body'. The Word of God is urging us to personal sexual self-control and purity. The purpose of self-control is to enable us to live honourably, not dishonourably. To be explicit, losing one's virginity outside marriage in conformity to what others do is not honourable but dishonourable. Thank God that, for those who have fallen in this way, there is forgiveness upon confession and repentance. 'He who covers his sins will not prosper, but whoever confesses and forsakes them will have mercy' (Prov. 28:13; compare 1 John 1:9). However, once we have sinned, although we can be forgiven, we can never undo what has been done. 'No Christian should ever ask how far his or her moral behavior can depart from God's standard and still avoid sin. Rather believers should strive to be utterly separate from immorality so that they can honor their bodies, which belong to God, and use them to glorify Jesus Christ, the Head of the Church (Eph. 1:21–23; 2:20–21; 4:15–16; 5:23; Col. 1:18, 24; compare John 10:1–16, 27–28; Heb. 13:20; 1 Peter 2:25; 5:4).'[15]

RECOGNIZE THE DANGER OF LUST (V. 5)

This verse expresses the truth that one of the chief sins resulting from not knowing God is impurity, the 'passion of lust'. Those who do not know God often allow lust to control their bodies and their behaviour. A Christian's master is the Lord, not lust. The phrase 'Gentiles who do not know God' is to be taken in a spiritual sense as referring to non-Christians (see Rom. 1:18–32 for a detailed exposé of the results of rejecting God's truth, and compare Eph. 4:17–18). Paul teaches that a prime cause of immorality is ignorance of God. 'It is a solemn thought that those who reject the knowledge of God that has been afforded them thereby make it inevitable that they will be given over to evil passions.'[16] Christians, those who know God (John 17:3), should not copy those who do not know him. In other words, we are not to take current standards of behaviour—the way the world behaves—as our guideline. Just because a certain standard of behaviour is common or popular does not make it right or acceptable. God's Word is to be our standard of behaviour.

NOT HURT OTHER PEOPLE (V. 6)

Defrauding your brother means hurting others. Illegitimate sexual activity always costs. Somebody always has to pay the price. Sooner or later it hurts somebody, more often than not the two who engage in it, but often other people as well. Besides, it will not go unpunished, for it is a very serious matter, as revealed by the words 'the Lord is the avenger of all such', or 'The Lord will punish men for all such sins' (NIV; see 2 Cor. 5:10). This does not simply refer to revenge or settling a score, as if God has to get even with us, but to even-handed justice. Since it is God and not man who will dispense the justice, no one should imagine that he or she will escape the consequences of evil behaviour. This should cause us to tremble, and should also be a help in resisting such temptation. If you have been involved in such sins you need to repent, confess your sins to God and forsake such behaviour. '[T]hat is not really repentance which does not separate the soul from sin.'[17]

RECOGNIZE OUR SPECIAL CALLING (V. 7)

Several callings are mentioned in the New Testament. In the verse 'Let each one remain in the same calling in which he was called' (1 Cor. 7:20), the word 'calling' can refer to one's position in society or even to one's daily work. But there are also specifically spiritual callings. For example, we are called from darkness to light (1 Peter 2:9); to fellowship with Christ (1 Cor. 1:9); and to eternal life (1 Tim. 6:12). Here in 1 Thessalonians we are called to 'holiness'. This calling is utterly opposed to 'uncleanness' (v. 7). Sanctification is the process by which we grow in grace, and holiness is the goal. Only God is perfectly holy, but he desires that we should grow to be more like Christ in respect to moral purity.

James Denney pertinently remarks,

The idea of 'calling' is one which has been much degraded and impoverished in modern times. By a man's calling we usually understand his trade, profession, or business, whatever it may be; but our calling in Scripture is something quite different from this. It is our life considered, not as filling a certain place in the economy of society, but as satisfying a certain purpose in the mind and will of God. It is a calling in Christ Jesus; apart from Him it could not have existed.[18]

BE AWARE THAT THIS IS GOD'S COMMAND (V. 8)

If we sneer at or reject this command we are rejecting not man's opinion, but God (see also Luke 10:16). This is a very serious matter. Moreover, impurity, it is implied, is a sin against the Holy Spirit who indwells us (1 Cor. 6:18–20).

To obey God should be a Christian's constant aim. As we have noted already (at 2:13b), it is not legalism to obey God. We are not alone in this fight; God has given us his Holy Spirit to enable us to keep his commands and to walk in obedience (Rom. 8:4). So we have the Word of God to guide us and the Spirit of God to enable us to obey God.

An orderly life (vv. 9–12)

Having dealt with sexual purity, Paul now writes concerning brotherly love, leading a quiet life, and working not shirking. James Denney observes that purity and love were characteristics of the early Christians:

When the gospel first came abroad in the world, two characteristics of its adherents attracted general attention, namely, personal purity and brotherly love. Amid the gross sensuality of heathenism, the Christian stood out untainted by indulgence of the flesh; amid the utter heartlessness of pagan society, which made no provision for the poor, the sick, or the aged, the Church was conspicuous for the union of its members and their brotherly kindness to each other.[19]

Should not this be the case today, too? After quoting Tertullian's saying, 'Behold how these Christians love one another!' Leon Morris makes the sad but true remark that this 'is hardly the comment that springs spontaneously to the lips of the detached observer nowadays'.[20]

The term 'brotherly love' (*philadelphia*) is normally referred to as the love members of the same family have towards one another; in other words, it is used of a blood-relationship. Used of members of the church it stresses the idea of the church as a family. The term is used of both men and women and so may be rendered 'brotherly and sisterly love'.

The fact that Paul begins this section with the words 'But concerning brotherly love …' has suggested to some commentators that Paul was replying to a question either sent by letter or conveyed orally by Timothy to Paul. But the phrase 'brotherly love' expresses such a general topic that it seems unlikely that the Thessalonians had sent such an enquiry, unless they were simply asking how far they should go practically in manifesting brotherly love. This is actually a very practical question that may or may not arise in Christians' minds today. It is fairly straightforward when help is needed in some ways, such as gardening, shopping or decorating, especially in times of sickness. But should money be given straight away when a need arises? There are two considerations to be taken into account. First, is God seeking to teach the needy Christian a lesson in this situation? If we immediately meet a financial need, God's lesson may be cut short. Prayer and careful weighing up of the situation are necessary lest we should short-circuit God's plan. Second, when a serious financial need arises, it is wise for the elders to ask permission to look into the accounts of the needy person to find out why the situation has arisen. It would be wrong for the church to pour money into a bag with holes in it. I know of a case when, some years ago, a recently married young couple asked for financial help. Upon investigation it was discovered that they had filled their house with furniture bought on hire-purchase, the total payments for which came to £10 per month more than the husband was earning! After receiving counselling and advice that this was very unwise if not dishonest, the young couple agreed to send back some of the unnecessary furniture and cancel those parts of the debt. Then the elders agreed to help them.

Another example is the giving of hospitality. This is enjoined in the New Testament in several places, and is especially required of elders (Rom. 12:13; 1 Tim. 3:2; Titus 1:8; 1 Peter 4:9). But, again, wisdom has to be exercised. To take an extreme example, a family with young children would be almost criminally unwise to offer hospitality to a child-abuser just released from prison. Indeed, in the days of the early church, guidelines had to be issued to prevent Christians being taken advantage of by wandering prophets.[21]

If indeed the Thessalonians had asked a question, it may be that there is a mild but disguised rebuke in Paul's reply, as though he were saying, 'You really know what you should do in this situation. You must apply the knowledge you already have. After all, you are taught by God to love one another. Put it into practice.' However, in this context it is probably more likely that in spite of the progress made by these new Christians, some of the church members were falling short in their behaviour, and so the apostle decided to give some instruction on this matter. Not that they were completely lacking in this grace; on the contrary, they were already practising brotherly love, having been taught by God about this (vv. 9–10).

The phrase 'taught by God' is one word in the Greek and occurs only here in the New Testament.[22] It echoes the promise of Isaiah 54:13 that 'All your children shall be taught by the LORD' (compare John 6:45; 1 John 2:27).

God is a God of order, as is readily observed in creation (Gen. 1). The microscopic details of living things, the stately orbits of the planets, and the way God prescribed order in Israel's worship testify to that fact. This is why God commanded, 'Let all things be done decently and in order' (1 Cor. 14:40). Deliberately to create disorder in life is to rebel against God. It may pass unnoticed in society and be unacknowledged or unrealized by many, even by some Christians, but the deliberate introduction of disorder in some modern music, art,[23] certain clothing styles, hairstyles and so on, is an expression of an underlying rebellion against God. We should not unthinkingly copy such manifestations of rebellion.

Those who are 'taught by God' (v. 9) will exhibit brotherly love (*philadelphia*), which is a manifestation of order, not of hatred, which is one aspect of disorder. Progress from disorder to order, and from no love to some love—or from some to more love—needs to be actively and intelligently pursued (v. 10). It will not happen by chance. Sinful people, if left to themselves, will degenerate into disorder in morals and behaviour.

Paul's exhortation that they should 'aspire to lead a quiet life' is something of a paradox or an oxymoron, since ambition usually involves energetic action. It is almost as though Paul were to write, 'Get busy to be still.' The verb translated 'to lead a quiet life' is used of silence after speech (Luke 14:4), cessation of argument (Acts 21:14) and rest from labour (Luke 23:56). 'It denotes tranquility of life which of course does not mean inactivity.'[24]

It seems that some were agitated over something. What was it? The most likely answer in the context is the imminent return of the Lord; that either they were getting over-excited or they were giving up work in anticipation of the *parousia*. The apostles had set a good example by labouring with their own hands (2:9), so there was no excuse. This is very significant, as the typical Greek attitude to manual labour was that the slaves attended to it. To the freeman it was degrading. The Lord Jesus had already set an example in this matter (Mark 6:3), and the Christian message included the teaching that manual labour is good (Eph. 4:28) and should be done as a service to Christ (Col. 3:17) and to God's glory (1 Cor. 6:20; 10:31).

The idlers, indeed, were not only neglecting the things they ought to be doing; they were actively engaged in things they ought not to be doing, by officious interference with other people's business. There is a great difference between the Christian duty of putting the interests of others before one's own (Phil. 2:4) and the busybody's compulsive itch to put other people right.[25]

Leading a quiet life, minding one's own business and working diligently are manifestations of order and run contrary to much of modern life. The fourth commandment is not only a command to rest, but also to work. A recent cartoon in a national paper showed a schoolboy with his arm in a sling being interviewed by a careers master who is saying, 'So you want to be a benefits fraud?'[26] Far from wanting to defraud the state, a true Christian will work hard in order to support him- or herself.

The comfort of Christ's return (vv. 13–18)

THE DANGER OF IGNORANCE (V. 13)

Paul frequently expressed the wish that his readers should not remain in ignorance of certain facts (Rom. 1:13; 11:25; 1 Cor. 10:1; 12:1; 2 Cor. 1:8). 'Ignorance of spiritual realities is always bad for the believer.'[27]

It seems likely that the Thessalonians had misunderstood the apostle to mean that the return of Christ would take place within their lifetimes. So when some of their number died, they wondered what had happened to them and whether they had missed out.

Apparently, some of the Thessalonians were worried about friends and relatives who had 'fallen asleep' (v. 13) before Christ had returned. So Paul writes to clear up the misunderstanding and to comfort them. The death of believers is often referred to as 'sleep' (Matt. 27:52; John 11:11–13; Acts 7:60; 1 Cor.15:6, 18). A simple reason for this is the common appearance of the body in death: relaxed and with the eyes closed. But there is a much more important reason. For believers, death is rest from labour and is also the precursor of resurrection, that glorious 'morning' when they will awaken in Christ's presence. The analogy of sleep does not in any way indicate that the believer is unconscious. It does not support the heresy of 'soul sleep' held by some cults. On the contrary, to the dying thief Jesus said, '… today you will be with Me in Paradise' (Luke 23:43; compare 2 Cor. 5:8). During his ministry Jesus taught a parable in which a rich man was conscious in Hades (Luke 16:19–31). In the Book of Revelation several passages depict the dead as fully conscious (e.g. Rev. 7:15–17; 20:4).

Paul is not suggesting that Christians should never grieve. They experience sorrows as much as others. But their sorrows are tempered by hope. Nor is he counselling stoic resignation or callous indifference. He is reminding them that, in the light of Christ's victory over death, they should not despair, for those who have 'fallen asleep' in Jesus will awake with him. The phrase 'sleep in Jesus' (v. 14) encapsulates the lovely thought that those Christians who have died 'in Jesus' are not at any time separated from him.

THE RESURRECTION ASSURED (V. 14)

The resurrection of Christ is the guarantee that those believers who have died already will come with him when he returns. The same one (God) who raised Jesus from the dead will also raise those believers who have died.

This verse is, in effect, a brief version of the extended explanation that

Paul wrote a few years later in 1 Corinthians 15. Christians who have died are with Jesus in death and will be with him in resurrection.

THE ORDER OF PRECEDENCE AT THE RESURRECTION (V. 15)

Paul now affirms 'by the word of the Lord' that those 'who are alive and remain until the coming of the Lord will by no means precede those who are asleep'. In the Old Testament, the phrase 'the word of the Lord' usually referred to a prophetic announcement (Isa. 1:10; Jer. 1:4; Ezek. 1:3; Hosea 1:1; Joel 1:1; Amos 5:1; Micah 1:1). However, in the New Testament it is used of the preaching of the gospel (Acts 12:24; 13:49; 15:35–36; 19:10; 1 Thes. 1:8; 2 Thes. 3:1), or to teaching given by the Lord during his earthly ministry (Acts 20:35). That Paul should refer to our Lord's teaching in this way was not unusual, for in other epistles he either quotes or alludes to our Lord's teaching (1 Cor. 7:10, 25; 9:14; 11:23, 25). Nor should it concern us that a specific quotation from Jesus cannot be found, for as the apostle John indicates, there is much that Jesus did that is not recorded in writing (John 20:30).

Some people think that the teaching about the return of Christ is simply another way of referring to our death when we go to be with the Lord. These verses in 1 Thessalonians refute that view, for Paul makes a clear distinction between those who have died and those who remain alive when Christ returns. If the return of Christ were simply about our deaths, this would contradict the clear teaching that some will be alive when Christ returns. There will be Christians alive and well on planet Earth when Christ returns, and they will not precede those who have died.

Those 'who sleep in Jesus' (v. 14) and 'those who are asleep' (v. 15) are obviously the same people. They are 'the dead in Christ' (v. 16). William Hendriksen writes, 'Anyone can see at once that the apostle is not drawing a contrast between believers and unbelievers, as if, for example, believers would rise first, and unbelievers a thousand years later.'[28]

THE GLORIOUS RETURN (VV. 16–18)

The Bible does not give us many details about the 'last things'. We would love to have more information. But God knows what is best for us, for, as Leon Morris remarks, '... the Bible was not written to gratify our curiosity. Rather it is intended to help us in our Christian lives, and ... the important thing is that we should be ready when the Lord comes.'[29]

Nevertheless, there are some specific details given here. The Lord will descend from heaven. There will be a shout, the voice of an archangel and a trumpet sound. The dead in Christ will rise first. Then 'we who are alive and remain' will be 'caught up' or raptured. We shall meet the Lord in the air, and we shall be for ever with him.

It is the Lord himself, 'This same Jesus ...' (Acts 1:11), who will descend from heaven. The Bible indicates that the return of the Lord Jesus Christ will be personal (John 14:3), visible (Rev. 1:7) and sudden (1 Thes. 5:2). The word translated 'shout' in verse 16 occurs only here in the New Testament. It was 'originally the order which an officer shouts to his troops, a hunter to his dogs, a charioteer to his horses, or a ship-master to his rowers'.[30]

The context suggests that the shout is the command of the Lord for the dead to rise, as when he commanded Lazarus to come out of the tomb (John 11:43). Someone has remarked that had Jesus not specified Lazarus by name at that time, all the dead would have risen! Hendriksen suggests that the phrases 'with the voice of an archangel, and with the trumpet of God' mean that the archangel will blow the trumpet. Whether this is so, or whether there is both an angelic shout and a separate trumpet blast, is immaterial. The main point is that there will be a great, glorious, terrifying sound that will be heard throughout the whole earth. This will not be a secret event!

This passage and Jude 9 are the only two places in the New Testament where the word 'archangel' is mentioned. In Jude 9 the archangel is named Michael, who is mentioned in Daniel 10:13, 21 and 12:1. It is possible that there is more than one archangel, because in Daniel 12:13 Michael is called *one* of the chief princes. Perhaps Gabriel is another, as he stands in the presence of God (see Dan. 8:16, 9:21; Luke 1:19, 26).

The dead in Christ will rise first, then those 'who are alive and remain [on the earth] shall be caught up together with them in the clouds to meet the Lord in the air'. The verb translated 'caught up' (*harpazein*)

implies violent action, sometimes indeed for the benefit of its object, as when the Roman soldiers snatched Paul from the rioters in the Jerusalem council chamber (Acts 23:10) or when the male child in the apocalyptic vision was caught up to God to preserve him from the great red dragon (Rev. 12:5). It is used in Acts 8:39 for the Spirit's snatching Philip away after his interview with the Ethiopian chamberlain and (more germanely to the present passage) of Paul's being caught up to the third heaven or paradise (2 Cor. 12:2–3).[31]

Some see this action as referring to a secret 'rapture' when believers will be 'snatched up' before the 'great tribulation' (Rev. 7:14). However, this is the only passage in the New Testament that speaks unambiguously of a rapture of the saints, although once that theory is accepted then other passages may be brought into line with it. Moreover, the context of this passage suggests that the rapture will be anything but a quiet and secret event!

Gene L. Green summarizes the purpose of this section in a fine paragraph:

The … passage has suffered much ill as it has been mined to provide clues concerning the timing of the 'rapture' of the church. Will this great event occur before seven years of tribulation, in the middle of the period, or at the very end? In the haste to answer this question, the real purpose of 1 Thessalonians 4:13–18 is overlooked. This teaching was presented to comfort those in grief by connecting the confession of the creed ('Jesus died and rose again') with the reality of the resurrection of the dead in Christ. This is not the stuff of speculative prophecy or best-sellers on the end times ... The decidedly bizarre pictures of airplanes dropping out of the sky and cars careening out of control as the rapture happens detract from the hope that this passage is designed to teach.[32]

The souls of those who have died in Christ will leave heaven, be reunited with their resurrected bodies, and then in those glorified bodies rise to meet the Lord in the air. The living survivors will have been changed 'in a moment, in the twinkling of an eye' (1 Cor. 15:52) and will join the resurrected believers with the Lord in the air, and so will ever be with the Lord. The main point, however, is not the order of events, but the fact that at the return of Christ believers will be reunited. There is eminent comfort in these words (1 Thes. 4:18). When society seems to be crumbling, when evil abounds, believers should be comforted with these glorious prospects.

Study questions

1. Impurity has become pandemic in the world so that it is almost taken to be normal. The Bible teaches otherwise. Study the following Scriptures and check whether you need to make changes in your reading, recreation, hobbies or regular companions: Exodus 20:14; Psalm 24:3–5; Matthew 5:8; Acts 15:20; Romans 13:13; 1 Corinthians 6:15–18; Galatians 5:19–21; Ephesians 5:5–6; Philippians 4:8; Colossians 3:5; 1 Timothy 1:5; 2 Timothy 2:22; Revelation 21:8, 27; 22:11.
2. Imagine that you only had the First Epistle to the Thessalonians, rather than the whole Bible. Gather together all the teaching in this epistle about the Second Coming of Christ and see what you would know about it.
3. What can we do to avoid being influenced by the flood of impurity and immorality in the media?
4. Why are so many marriages breaking up today?
5. How can Christians bring more order into their personal lives, relationships and church lives?

Chapter 4

Notes

1 **Gene L. Green,** *The Letters to the Thessalonians* (Grand Rapids, MI: Eerdmans / Leicester: Apollos, 2002), pp. 184f.

2 Cited at: quotationspage.com/quote/24921.html.

3 **Charles A. Wanamaker,** *The Epistles to the Thessalonians* (NIGTC; Grand Rapids, MI: Eerdmans / Carlisle: Paternoster, 1990), p. 147.

4 **F. F. Bruce,** *1 & 2 Thessalonians* (Word Biblical Commentary; Nashville: Thomas Nelson, 1982), p. 79.

5 Ibid.

6 **Green,** *Letters*, p. 186.

7 **Leon Morris,** *The First and Second Epistles to the Thessalonians* (NICNT; Grand Rapids, MI: Eerdmans, 1991), p. 115.

8 **James Denney,** *The Epistles to the Thessalonians* (London: Hodder & Stoughton, 1892), p. 136.

9 Ibid.

10 **Green,** *Letters*, p. 190.

11 **John MacArthur, Jr.,** has published some excellent material on knowing God's will, first as a booklet entitled *Found: God's Will* (Colorado Springs: Chariot Victor, 1973), and later as a recorded message entitled *Taking the Mystery out of Knowing God's Will* (issued 2006 and available from Grace to You: www.gty.org.uk).

12 **John MacArthur, Jr.,** *1 & 2 Thessalonians* (The MacArthur New Testament Commentary; Chicago: Moody, 2002), p. 104.

13 **Denney,** *Epistles*, p. 140.

14 **Morris,** *First and Second Epistles*, p. 121.

15 **MacArthur,** *1 & 2 Thessalonians*, p. 108.

16 **Morris,** *First and Second Epistles*, p. 123.

17 **Denney,** *Epistles*, p. 144.

18 Ibid. p. 145.

19 Ibid. p. 151.

20 **Morris,** *First and Second Epistles*, p. 127.

21 For example, the Didache states that hospitality was to be offered for no longer than three days to such prophets. See **J. Stevenson,** *A New Eusebius* (London: SPCK, 1960), p. 128.

22 According to **Wanamaker,** this word, *theodidaktos*, 'appears to be a Pauline coinage since there are no known instances of the term prior to Paul, and outside Christian circles there are virtually none after him' (**Wanamaker,** *Epistles*, p. 160).

23 'Modern art in its more consistent forms puts a question-mark against all values and principles. Its anarchist aims of achieving complete human freedom turn all laws and norms into frustrating and deadening prison walls; the only way to deal with them is to destroy them' (**H. R. Rookmaaker,** *Modern Art and the Death of a Culture* (London: Inter-Varsity Press, 1970), p. 161).

24 **Morris,** *First and Second Epistles*, p. 131.

25 **Bruce,** *1 & 2 Thessalonians*, p. 92.

26 Matt cartoon, *Daily Telegraph*; date unknown.

27 **William Hendriksen,** *1 & 2 Thessalonians* (London: Banner of Truth, 1972), p. 109.

28 Ibid. p. 115.

29 **Morris,** *First and Second Epistles*, p. 142.

30 **Hendriksen,** *1 & 2 Thessalonians*, p. 116.

31 **Bruce,** *1 & 2 Thessalonians*, p. 102.

32 **Green,** *Letters*, p. 229.

Present preparation for the future *parousia* (1 Thes. 5)

The Day of the Lord (vv. 1–11)

Each chapter in this letter closes with a reference to the return of Christ. This chapter also begins with one. Paul starts this section with the words 'But concerning …' which suggests that he is responding to a question, or at least to a perceived need. Curiosity about the future, especially about the end times, is a perennial human concern and it is expressed several times in Scripture (Dan. 12:6; Matt. 24:3; Mark 13:3–4; Luke 17:20; Acts 1:6; 1 Peter 1:10–11). Consistently, however, the Scriptures supply no direct answer as to when promised events will transpire (Dan. 12:7–9; Matt. 24:36; Mark 13:32; Acts 1:7).

As we begin this chapter we are reminded how well informed the Thessalonians were. It is most remarkable that, in spite of the short time that Paul and his associates spent in Thessalonica, and given that much of Paul's time there was spent in working hard to support himself and that the Thessalonians themselves would have had their own regular occupations, nevertheless Paul managed to teach them a considerable amount of doctrine. Paul credits them 'with a clear understanding of the signs of the times and the approaching end of the age'.[1] The regular occurrence throughout the letter of the phrase 'you know' points to their informed status (1:4–5; 2:1–2, 5, 11; 3:3–4; 4:2; compare 2 Thes. 2:6; 3:7). This is a challenge to present-day ministers and missionaries. How long would it take us to bring our hearers to the level of the Thessalonians? This is all the more impressive when we consider that they came from totally pagan backgrounds with no commonly understood Christian tradition. Paul, however, needed to remind them of or enlarge upon his previous instruction, particularly to explain the connection between the *parousia* (literally 'presence'; used to refer to Christ's return) and the resurrection (4:13–18).

BE READY FOR CHRIST'S RETURN (VV. 1–2)

There is no need to try to distinguish between 'times' and 'seasons' (compare Acts 1:7). Although there was a distinction in Classical Greek, by the time Paul wrote, this phrase was in common use and the two words had become more or less synonymous, much as they have today when used in that phrase.[2] The words 'you yourselves' are emphatic, and 'know perfectly' emphasizes how well informed the Thessalonians were. Paul had already taught them about the suddenness of Christ's return. The term 'day of the Lord' would have already been known to the Jewish converts as it is used frequently in the Old Testament to indicate 'that eschatological event when the Lord comes to judge the inhabitants of the earth and to pour out his wrath because of sin'[3] (see Isa. 13:6, 9; Ezek. 13:5; 30:3; Joel 1:15; 2:1, 11; 3:14; Amos 5:18, 20; Zeph. 1:7, 14; Zech. 14:1; Mal. 4:5). For believers, however, that day will be a day of salvation (Joel 2:31–32; 3:18; Zech. 14:1–21; 1 Cor. 1:8; 2 Cor. 1:14; Phil. 1:6, 10; 2:16; 2 Thes. 1:6–10). In Amos 5:18–20, the prophet seeks to correct faulty ideas concerning the Day of the Lord, and it seems this will always be necessary until the Day dawns. These Old Testament texts form the background to a variety of ways the Day of Judgement is referred to in the New Testament. It is 'the last day' (John 6:39–40); 'the day of [God's] wrath' (Rom. 2:5); 'the day of the Lord' (2 Peter 3:10); 'the day of the Lord Jesus' (1 Cor. 5:5); 'the day of redemption' (Eph. 4:30); 'the day of Jesus Christ' (Phil. 1:6); 'the day of Christ' (Phil. 1:10; 2:16; 2 Thes. 2:2); 'that Day' (Luke 21:34; 2 Thes. 1:10); 'the day of judgment' (2 Peter 2:9); 'the day of God' (2 Peter 3:12); and 'the great day' (Jude 6). Sometimes it is referred to simply as 'the [or 'this'] day [or 'Day']', the context indicating that it is the Day of the Lord (1 Thes. 5:4; Rom. 13:12; 1 Cor. 3:13; Heb. 10:25). Scripture is quite clear that there is an inevitable Day of

Judgement (see Heb. 9:27; 2 Cor. 5:10). It is quite inescapable (1 Thes. 5:3).

In 1 Thessalonians 5:2, the use of the present tense in 'comes' implies 'certainty rather than immediacy'.4 The Thessalonians were evidently well informed about the suddenness of Christ's return, due, no doubt, to the apostle's earlier instruction. The reference to 'a thief in the night' points to its sudden and unexpected nature. This analogy is also found in the teaching of Christ (Matt. 24:33–34; Luke 12:39–40) and it became common currency in the church (2 Peter 3:10; Rev. 3:3; 16:15).

BE PREPARED FOR THE JUDGEMENT (VV. 3–4)

The unbelieving world will be saying 'Peace and safety!' right up to the moment of disaster. The word translated 'safety' means, basically, 'that cannot be shaken'. This 'is the height of folly and misapprehension'.5 Just as when a pregnant woman's labour pains begin properly there is no escape from the inevitable outcome, so there will be no escape from the sudden destruction that will come upon unrepentant sinners. The 'unredeemed world will have no thought of a cataclysmic end to the universe, and it will be rejoicing in a fancied security right up to the very moment of the disaster'.6 Burglars usually break in at night when they are least expected. But the Thessalonian believers were not in darkness, so the return of Christ should not take them unawares (v. 4). A parallel warning is seen in our Lord's teaching in Luke 21:34–36, the only other place in the New Testament where the classical adjective *aiphnidios*, translated 'sudden', is found.7

With Christ's return also comes judgement, and that is an appointment all must keep.

As we saw in chapter 1, two different manifestations of the wrath of God are described in the New Testament. One is an ongoing judgement, the kind of judgement that takes place in history, such as is described in Romans 1. The other is a sudden outpouring of wrath such as will take place on the Day of Judgement, though occasionally it takes place in time also (see Luke 13:1–9).

Recent natural disasters, such as the 2011 earthquake and tsunami in Japan, the 2004 tsunami in the Indian Ocean, and Hurricane Katrina in New Orleans in 2005, raise questions in our minds. Why do such things happen? The atheist and the agnostic have no answer. To them there is no purpose in the universe. All that happens in their eyes is the result of blind chance, and there is no hope and no comfort.

But the Bible gives a clear answer. Satan tempted Adam and Eve to disobey God. They fell, and as a result they were punished, they lost fellowship with God, and the earth was cursed by God. All the sicknesses and natural disasters are the result of Adam's fall and God's curse (see Gen. 3:1–19). This is confirmed by the apostle Paul in Romans 8:18–23, where we are told that the creation is groaning and looking forward to the deliverance which is to come.

The Bible tells us that salvation includes not only men and women: there is deliverance for the creation, too. We can be given eternal life and forgiveness of our sins if we repent and believe on Jesus Christ as Lord and Saviour. Jesus Christ is going to return, and when he comes he will restore creation to its original purity. There will be new heavens and a new earth in which righteousness will dwell (2 Peter 3:10–13). Whether this will be an absolutely new creation or the present earth renovated and renewed is not known for certain, but the end result will be the same: a new creation.

Many people today are in the dark about this unavoidable appointment. Paul's readers were not; they were enlightened. They knew that Christ would return and that his return would be sudden and unexpected.

BEHAVE AS CHILDREN OF LIGHT (VV. 4–5)

Paul excludes the Thessalonian believers from this impending doom because they are no longer 'in darkness'; if they had remained in darkness, the Day would 'overtake' them. They are now children 'of light' and 'of the day'. There is a subtle change from the second person plural ('you') to the first person plural ('we'), perhaps to soften the exhortation by showing that Paul and his associates are included in the need to live as in the light.

Paul uses the figures of light and day versus darkness and night to encourage appropriate behaviour. The night-time is often associated not only with sleep but also with partying and drunkenness (compare Rom. 13:13; Eph. 5:8–18; Prov. 23:29–35). Darkness characterizes the lives of unbelievers, in that they are under the dominion of sin (John 3:19; Rom. 13:12; 2 Cor. 6:14; Eph. 5:11) which has darkened their understanding (Rom. 1:21; Eph. 4:18). When people are converted the experience is often likened to light coming into their lives, or their eyes being opened (John 9:25; Acts 26:18; 2 Cor. 4:3–6; Eph. 5:8; Col. 1:13; 1 Peter 2:9; compare Heb. 6:4; 10:32). Christians, having left the darkness of sin, now walk in the light of Christ, who is the light of the world (John 8:12), and in turn they become lights in the world (Matt. 5:14).

STAY AWAKE AND KEEP SOBER (VV. 6–7)

Paul urges them to be alert. He warns them to stay awake and be watchful, and to live lives of sobriety. While 'sleep' is used as a metaphor for death in 4:13–14, it is here used differently to 'characterize the moral and spiritual indifference of those who are not converted'.[8]

Obviously, when Paul urges them to stay awake, he is not referring to literal insomnia; he is presenting the case for spiritual wakefulness and watchfulness. Jesus called on his disciples to be alert both for his coming (Matt. 24:42–44; 25:13; Mark 13:32–37; Luke 12:35–40; compare Rev. 3:2–3; 16:15) and in order to avoid temptation (Matt. 26:40–41; Mark 14:37–38; compare 1 Peter 5:8).

He cautions them to be 'sober' and encourages them to be prepared for

Christ's return. The verb translated 'be sober' means just that: refrain from drunkenness. However, in the New Testament it includes the idea of exercising self-control. In accepting this wider interpretation of moderation and self-restraint, however, we must not overlook the chief meaning of the verb. There are many warnings in Scripture about the dangers of becoming inebriated through drinking fermented beverages. Noah, although in many ways a righteous man, disgraced himself through drunkenness (Gen. 9:20–23). Lot's daughters used the drugging power of alcohol in order to commit incest with their father (Gen. 19:30–38). Fermented drink was never to be used in the tabernacle, nor were priests allowed to drink it while on duty (Lev. 10:9–11). Among the many warnings in Scripture, Proverbs 23:29–35 is one of the most striking. (See Appendix 4 for an extended discussion of this matter.)

BE PREPARED FOR BATTLE (V. 8)

Paul now resorts to a favourite illustration of his: that of armour. He uses it in several other places but varies the significance he attaches to each item (see Rom. 13:12; 2 Cor. 6:7; 10:4; Eph. 6:13–17; compare Isa. 59:17). Here he likens the famous triad of faith, love and hope to pieces of protective armour.

Warfare is a frequently used analogy for the Christian life, and Paul desires that his readers be spiritually well armed for the conflict. Genuine faith and true Christian love protect our hearts. The hope (firm expectation) of salvation protects our minds from the darts of unbelief hurled at us by the enemy, both in our thoughts and audibly by unbelievers.

KNOW THAT GOD'S WRATH IS NOT OUR DESTINY (VV. 9–10)

Verse 9 assures us that believers are not appointed 'to wrath'. The word 'appoint' draws attention to the fact that salvation depends on the divine initiative. The danger of wrath for those who reject Christ is real. 'For the wrath of God is revealed from heaven against all ungodliness and unrighteousness of men, who suppress the truth in unrighteousness' (Rom. 1:18; compare Rom. 2:5–6). Modern man does not like the idea of God's wrath. Leon Morris wisely comments, 'Although the modern world likes neither the term nor the idea it connotes, we can scarcely do without either. There is an implacable divine hostility to everything that is evil, and it is sheer folly to overlook this or try to explain it away.'[9] God has appointed for salvation those who put their trust in Christ and Christ alone to save them.

'Salvation' is a comprehensive term in the Bible; it has been described as 'the overriding theme of the entire Bible'.[10] It includes deliverance from the guilt, pollution and punishment of sin, as well as all the spiritual blessings that come to believers on the basis of Christ's work. And there is so much more.[11] 'But haven't we as Christians already received it?' someone may ask. The answer is that there are three tenses used with regard to salvation: the past—we *have been* saved from the penalty of sin (Eph. 2:8–9; 2 Tim. 1:9; Titus 3:5); the present—we *are being* saved daily from the power of sin in our lives (Rom. 6:1, 12–14; 1 Cor. 1:18); and the future—we *shall be* saved from the presence of sin when we are taken to be with the Lord and given glorified bodies adapted to eternal life in God's presence (Rom. 5:9–10; 1 Cor. 15:51–52; 1 John 3:2–3).

The only way to obtain salvation is 'through our Lord Jesus Christ' (v. 9), for he himself said, 'I am the way, the truth, and the life. No one comes to the Father except through Me' (John 14:6). The apostles emphasized this in their preaching (Acts 4:12).

Verse 10 again uses the analogies of waking and sleeping for life and death. This is one of the few places in the Thessalonian epistles where the death of Christ is mentioned, and the only place where the purpose of his death is stated, though in other epistles Paul several times states the purpose of Christ's death (Rom. 14:9; 2 Cor. 5:15, 21; Gal. 1:4). This should not, however, be taken as an indication that this subject did not loom large in Paul's thinking at this time, nor should it be surmised that his theology of the cross was not yet developed. The reason why it is not mentioned very much is because the Thessalonians had not asked about it, and because Paul had so thoroughly taught them (Acts 17:3). After all, he wrote this epistle from Corinth, and he later wrote to the Corinthians, 'And I, brethren, when I came to you [from Thessalonica via Berea], did not come with excellence of speech or of wisdom declaring to you the testimony of God. For I determined not to know anything among you except Jesus Christ and Him crucified' (1 Cor. 2:1–2; compare 1:18–25). The cross was absolutely central in Paul's teaching. Christ's death in our place upon the cross ensures that all believers, whether they are alive or have already died when Christ returns, will live for ever with him. These words of assurance should encourage and build us up.

SO COMFORT ONE ANOTHER (V. 11)

Paul now exhorts the Thessalonian believers to comfort one another as and when they need comforting, and also to edify one another. At the same time he tactfully acknowledges that this is what they are already doing.

Sometimes we need reminding of these things. We may be used to help others by reminding them of these encouraging words, and not only by comforting them, but also by building them up. We all need to help one other grow and progress in the Christian faith. This should be the aim of every church member (Rom. 14:19; 15:2; 1 Cor. 14:3–5, 12, 17, 26; Eph. 4:12, 29; Col. 2:7).

Concluding exhortations (vv. 12–22)

RESPECT YOUR LEADERS (VV. 12–13)

The leaders are described by their activities. They 'labor among' the believers, they take the lead and in that sense are 'over [them] in the Lord', and they 'admonish' or correct them. The word translated 'labor' (*kopiaō*) is used by Paul for both manual work (1 Cor. 4:12; Eph. 4:28; 2 Tim. 2:6; compare 1 Thes. 1:3; 2:9; 2 Thes. 3:8) and spiritual work (Rom. 16:12; 1 Cor. 15:10; Gal. 4:11; Phil. 2:16; 1 Tim. 4:10; 5:17). This word implies strenuous effort producing weariness. Although the word for 'elder' (*presbuteros*) is not used in 1 Thessalonians 5:12, it is likely that elders are being referred to here. All the first Christians, the apostles and those converted on the Day of Pentecost were Jews or Jewish proselytes, and the early churches seem to have been organized on the pattern of the synagogue (see James 2:2, where 'assembly' is a translation of *sunagōgēn*, the usual word for 'synagogue'). The recognition of elders, therefore, would have been a natural occurrence. Paul seems always to have appointed elders quite early on after planting churches; he did this on his first missionary journey (Acts 14:23) and instructed his colleagues to do the same (Titus 1:5).

It seems that some Christians in the Thessalonian church were not giving proper respect and recognition to their leaders. Disrespect and lack of love can lead to discord in the Body of Christ. Paul urges them to recognize those leaders who labour, lead and teach. These three areas of responsibility should characterize a servant of God. He is to work, watch and warn. A diligent Christian leader will indeed labour. It is a costly and time-consuming business to care for God's flock.

Elders are overseers. They are 'over' (1 Thes. 5:12) the people of God in that they lead, guide and, in a sense, rule them. This is, however, to be 'in the Lord': their appointment is made by the Lord, they serve as unto the Lord, and the extent of their authority is only as the Lord permits. They are also to admonish, rebuke, warn or instruct (1 Tim. 4:13; 5:20; 2 Tim. 4:2; Titus 1:13; 2:15). No one likes to be rebuked, but if a rebuke is accepted in the right spirit (i.e. submissively[12]) it will be for the believer's good (see Heb. 13:7, 17).

The Christians are not only to recognize their leaders but also to 'esteem them very highly ... for their work's sake' (v. 13). It is perfectly natural to be drawn to some people more than to others. A similar personality, common interests and frequent contact may cause Christians to esteem some leaders more than others. But we are to be careful to esteem leaders for their work's sake, not for their personalities' sake, thus avoiding favouritism. This esteeming is not to be merely dutiful and mechanical, but 'in love', which 'is not a matter of personal liking'[13] but wanting the best for them.

Church members and leaders are also exhorted to '[b]e at peace' among themselves, not arguing or stirring up trouble. Only in such an atmosphere can the leadership function effectively, for 'effective leadership in the church demands effective following'.[14]

SHORT EXHORTATIONS (VV. 14–15)
The unruly are to be warned, the faint-hearted comforted, the weak upheld, and patience exercised towards all.

The disorderly or insubordinate, the extremists (such as in 1 Thes. 2:14–15; 2 Thes. 2:1–3; 3:6) and busybodies, and the idle, are to be warned about their behaviour. Those who are faint-hearted, whether they are concerned about departed relatives (4:13–18) or their own state (5:4–5, 9), are to be encouraged. The weak, whether physically, morally or spiritually, are to be upheld. All this is to be carried out in patience. This leads naturally to the next instruction in verse 15, because it is often the impatient who retaliate.

Retaliation is to be cut out and what is good is to be pursued (v. 15; compare Matt. 5:44; Rom. 12:17, 19; 1 Cor. 4:12; 6:7; 1 Peter 3:9). The Christians are not to render evil for evil, but are always to seek the good of others as well as pursue goodness themselves (compare 3:12; Rom. 13:10; 1 Cor. 14:1).

OUR 'STANDING ORDERS' (VV. 16–18)
The will of God for Christians includes constant rejoicing, regular prayer and thankfulness in all things.

The exhortations in these three verses have been called the 'standing orders of the Christian Church'.[15] Whether we live in peaceful or troubled times, whether we are in sickness or in health, whether surrounded by friends or foes, whether the path is clear before us or we are perplexed as to what we should do, our duty is clear: we are to rejoice always, pray without ceasing and give thanks in everything.

Rejoice always (v. 16)

This is not a meaningless and foolish ignoring of current circumstances. It is rather a recognition that God is sovereign and all things are under his control. If Paul and Silas could rejoice in their prison chains when their backs were bleeding from the beating they had received (Acts 16:25), surely we can rejoice in our tribulations.

There are circumstances in which it is natural to rejoice. It requires no special grace, nor even conversion, to be glad in favourable circumstances. There would be no point in this command if that is all that is implied. Even unbelievers can do that. But as Christian we are to rejoice *always*, even when circumstances or people are against us.

The Thessalonians had suffered for their faith. Seasons of distress or grief are inevitable in this fallen world (Gen. 3:16–19; Rom. 8:19–25). Some of the Thessalonians had recently lost loved ones (4:13), yet they were still to rejoice. The love of God in Christ, and the good news of salvation, are such that even in the most dreadful circumstances there was cause for them to rejoice. Like a spring of fresh water that gushes up through the sand on the beach even when the salt waves of the sea wash over it,[16] the joy of Christians in their Lord rises up even when the waves of misfortune crash over them. This does not mean that there will never be sorrow or sadness. But it does mean that the underlying attitude of Christians will be joy. Also, a firm trust in the sovereignty of God will enable us to look up and say, even in trial, 'Your will be done.'

The gospel is good news. Those who believe it and preach it should be joyful people. A cold, austere, formal or dreary worship belies the truth of the gospel just as much as irreverent, flippant, shallow or disorderly worship does.

Pray without ceasing (v. 17)

This does not mean they were to forsake their other responsibilities and be on their knees all the time. Rather it is an exhortation not to give up or neglect the regular habit of prayer, but to be in constant touch with God, even praying as they went about their daily business.

Prayer is one mark of a true Christian. When Ananias was in doubt whether Saul of Tarsus was to be trusted, the one fact the Lord gave as a mark of Saul's conversion was 'behold, he is praying' (Acts 9:11). Obviously Saul had 'said prayers' before as a Pharisee, but now he really prayed from the heart to the Lord he knew. Constant prayer will replenish our joy, empower us for service and keep us close to the Lord. Paul frequently urged the churches to continue steadfastly in prayer (Eph. 6:18; Col. 4:2; Rom. 12:12). We learn best how to pray by doing it, just as we learn to ride a bicycle—but with more significant and lasting consequences!

Give thanks in everything (v. 18)

Yet again Paul emphasizes thanksgiving (1:2; 2:13; 3:9; compare 2 Thes. 1:3; 2:13). The necessity for thanksgiving is a frequent theme in Paul's letters (e.g. Rom. 1:8; 1 Cor. 1:4; Eph. 5:20; Phil. 1:3; 4:6; Col. 1:3; 2:7; 3:17). Now, having set before them his own example, he exhorts them directly to give thanks in everything.

Perhaps he had heard or sensed that this was a weakness in the lives of the Thessalonians so he kept referring to it. One of the weaknesses of many Christians is the failure to be thankful. Thanksgiving is often absent from our praying. If our prayers were received by God only when they included sincere thanksgiving, how many would be answered? It is considered good manners to express gratitude for favours received from our fellow-men and -women; how much more should we thank God for all the blessings he showers upon us! We are so ready to ask for things from God, but so neglectful in thanking him for what he has already given. A thankful heart is a happy heart.

These three activities (rejoicing, praying and giving thanks) are together 'the will of God' for us (the word 'this' is singular). If we really want to know God's will for our lives, these three attitudes are one aspect of it.

The presence of the Holy Spirit is pre-supposed in all that Paul has said. Only with the help of the indwelling Spirit of God can we hope to continually rejoice, pray and give thanks.

DO NOT QUENCH THE HOLY SPIRIT (V. 19)

This metaphor symbolizes the Holy Spirit as fire ('Do not put out the Spirit's fire', NIV; compare Matt. 3:11; Luke 3:16; Acts 2:3). In order to understand this command, consider first what it does *not* mean.

Resisting, rejecting or rebuking false teaching or ignoring shallow and inconsequential utterances, such as so-called prophecies, is *not* quenching the Spirit. Neither is holding back a contribution or comment to a more appropriate time. For example, someone might have a 'blessed thought' and offer to unload it in a public meeting, but having shared it first with an elder (a wise procedure) the latter may say that it is more appropriate for a small house-group but not for the main service; that is *not* quenching the Spirit. That is the elder guarding the flock and maintaining a good standard of teaching.

Quenching the Spirit does mean, for example:
- to reject the Spirit's conviction, as King David must have done when he took Bathsheba (2 Sam. 11:1), or as Judas must have done when he betrayed Christ, in spite of the warning (Matt. 26:20–25). The Holy Spirit arbitrates in our minds. He rings alarm bells. He gives us

an uneasy conscience when we are about to do or say something wrong. To reject his conviction is to quench the Spirit.

- to resent the Spirit's control. We know that God wants to do something in our lives, and for us to follow a certain course of action, and we resent the necessity of obeying his teaching through the Scriptures. We can be guilty of this by making a serious step without praying and asking for God's guidance. We can also be guilty of this if we use our gifts to glorify ourselves, or, like Korah in Numbers 16, 'burn false fire' by worshipping in an unscriptural way or ministering beyond our remit or gifting. We do not like God's instructions in his Word, so we disregard them.
- to resist the Spirit's commands. We may do this by turning a deaf ear to what his Word says, or even by deliberate procrastination. Saul's behaviour in 1 Samuel 15 is an example of this sin.
- to rebel against the Spirit's commission, as Jonah did. If God has given us clear instructions to serve him in a particular way, to then rebel against that commission is to quench the Holy Spirit's leading.
- to refuse the Spirit's companionship. The Lord desires our fellowship (John 4:23–24; 1 John 1:3), but if we neglect to have a time of personal devotions we are quenching that divine desire.

'Quenching' alludes to fire, which is a symbol of the Holy Spirit. We may quench a fire by suppression (covering it up), by neglect (putting no fuel on it) and by suffocation (putting on the wrong kind of fuel). Prayer, meditation on the Scriptures and obedience will cause the Spirit's flame to burn brightly in our hearts.

We need to find a balance in our worship between allowing for participation by church members at appropriate times and in suitable circumstances, and observing decency and order (1 Cor. 14:40). Open participation is more suitable for smaller gatherings such as home-groups. For one thing, in a large gathering only a small proportion of those present can participate meaningfully; for another, it is more difficult to maintain order, and, since most worship services are public, harder to keep out false doctrine or unhelpful teaching. Consequently, in most churches today contributions by the members in public worship are not expected.

Even in some nonconformist churches there has been a tendency to introduce liturgy, that is, a settled form of corporate worship, including read prayers and, often, congregational responses, which is taking control to an extreme degree. On this tendency James Denney comments sharply,

A liturgy may indeed be a defence against the coldness and incompetence of the one man to whom the whole conduct of public worship is at present left, but our true refuge is not this mechanical one, but the opening of the mouths of all Christian people. A liturgy, however beautiful, is a melancholy witness to the quenching of the Spirit: it may be better or worse than the prayers of one man; but it could never compare for fervour with the spontaneous prayers of a living church.[17]

Denney may well be right, but sometimes, carefully prepared prayers are preferable to extempore prayers if the minister or other worship leader tends to get in a verbal rut. In my later years of ministry I have sensed an anomaly in a minister's practice of carefully preparing what he says to the congregation, but leaving to the whim of the moment what he says to God on the congregation's behalf. I once heard Dr Arthur Dakin, former Principal of Bristol Baptist College, say at a ministers' fraternal in about 1958, 'Prepare your prayers carefully with the people in mind, then when you come to pray in the pulpit forget the people and think only of God.'

One of the dangers of a liturgical approach is that worshippers can come to depend upon the form of words and believe that, as long as the right words are used, worship has happened. But that can be dangerously near to what happens in pagan worship. Jonathan Skinner expresses this well:

One of the keynotes of pagan worship is a reliance on ritual. It is believed that through certain activities, words and chants, spiritual power can be unleashed. The New Testament, by contrast, reveals a non-ritualistic religion, which is simple and straightforward. Throughout the ages this has often been forgotten, and we end up with priests wearing ornate clothing, performing intricate rituals.[18]

The whole point, surely, is this: that our whole hearts and souls should be in our worship, and that it should be absolutely sincere, for both extempore prayer and liturgical prayers can be empty and insincere.

DO NOT DESPISE INFORMAL TEACHING BUT TEST ALL THINGS (VV. 20–21)

This simple command, whose application may have been quite clear to the Thessalonians, is fraught with difficulty for Christians today. It is not clear why the Thessalonians needed this exhortation. It may have been because of the occurrence of false prophecies, or because they despised impromptu utterances. The trouble was that in rejecting the chaff they were perhaps also throwing out the wheat.

The first question is, what is meant by 'prophecies'? One noted commentator, John Gill, understands this to refer to the Old Testament prophetic word. There is then good reason for the warning. Many Christians ignore, or at least neglect, the Old Testament, yet it is full of Christ, as the risen Lord himself made clear (see Luke 24:27, 44). Moreover, much of the New Testament, for example, Romans, Galatians and Hebrews, is unintelligible without the Old Testament background.

However, this understanding of the text seems to be unlikely. It is much more probable that occasional extempore utterances, claimed to be inspired by the Holy Spirit, were being despised or ignored by some. Consequently, the majority of commentators apply the word 'prophecy' in the New Testament to the spoken word in the church, whether it is studied exposition or extempore exhortation.

Paul cautions the Christians not to despise such, and then goes on to commend discernment between the false and the true, the unprofitable and the profitable.

Some commentators claim that there was nothing miraculous about New Testament prophecy. But William Hendriksen writes, '... we do not share this opinion. The Church in its infancy had no complete Bible (Old and New Testament) ... In that situation God graciously provided special supports or endowments, until the time would arrive when they were no longer needed. One of those gifts was prophesying.'[19] Leon Morris likewise states that 'the essence of prophecy as the early church understood it appears to have been that the Spirit of the Lord spoke to and through people'[20] (1 Cor. 12:10; 14:30).

In other words, Paul does not mean prediction of the future, but rather speaking forth the Word of the Lord sometimes by means of the interpretation of Scripture. A prophet, as the etymology of the word indicates, was a person who 'spoke forth' the Word of the Lord. Such words from a genuine prophet expressed the mind and will of God. A prophet, therefore, was a man (but see 2 Kings 22:14; 2 Chr. 34:22; Acts 21:9; 1 Cor. 11:5) whose rational and moral nature had been quickened by the Spirit of God and who possessed in an uncommon degree the ability of speaking words of edification, exhortation and comfort. In other words, some would claim, he was a Christian preacher, an interpreter of the will of God; in 1 Corinthians 14:3 prophets speak for the purpose of edification (building up), exhortation (encouragement), and comfort (consolation). However, sometimes a prophet would foretell the future (Acts 11:27–28; 21:10–11).

Whatever the exact meaning of 'prophecies' in 1 Thessalonians 5:20, we next ask, does this question have any relevance for us today? Opinions are still divided over whether 'prophecies' means preaching or implies a miraculous gift. Is the spiritual gift of prophecy still in operation today?

There are at least four views:

1. that prophecy, along with other miraculous gifts, is no longer available today. The charismatic gifts have ceased. That is the cessationist position.
2. that all the charismatic gifts are still available and are being exercised today. That is the charismatic and Pentecostal view.
3. a modified expression of the second view: that prophecy still occurs but is not inspired in the same way that Old Testament prophecy was. It is simply the utterance of spontaneous exhortations, teaching or praise. Wayne Grudem, an exponent of this view, defines such prophecy as 'telling something that God has spontaneously brought to mind'.[21]
4. that the word 'prophecy' refers today to preaching, especially extempore preaching.

With reference to the first view, it seems clear that some gifts must have ceased, namely the 'sign gifts'. When John the Baptist sent two of his disciples to ask Jesus whether or not he was the Messiah, Jesus replied, 'Go and tell John the things you have seen and heard: that the blind see, the lame walk, the lepers are cleansed, the deaf hear, the dead are raised, the poor have the gospel preached to them' (Luke 7:22). Now there is, by definition, only one true Messiah, *the* Messiah, Jesus Christ, our Lord. If the signs mentioned as proofs of his Messiahship could be performed by others they would lose their evidential value. Signs of the Messiah can be performed only by the Messiah, or, to a limited extent, those whom he specifically empowers (e.g. Luke 9:1–6). Similarly, the apostle Paul refers to signs and wonders and mighty deeds as indications of a true apostle. An apostle of Christ must have seen the Lord, been a witness of his resurrection, and have been called and commissioned by him (Acts 1:21–22; Luke 9:1–6; Acts 9:1–19; Gal. 1:1), and the proof that he was a genuine apostle was his ability to perform miracles. If others could perform them at will they would lose their authenticating value. God can perform miracles at any time as he wills, but it seems that he has not granted this ability to any person since the apostles.

There is further evidence that strongly indicates that prophecy in the sense of inspired revelation has ceased. First, in Daniel 9:24–27 we read that the angel Gabriel explained to Daniel that the 'seventy weeks' were to end with the destruction of Jerusalem, and also that in the same period 'vision and prophecy' would be sealed up. Athanasius, in his treatise *On the Incarnation*, interprets this passage in this way:

When did prophet and vision cease from Israel? Was it not when Christ came, the Holy one of holies? It is, in fact, a sign and notable proof of the coming of the Word that Jerusalem no longer stands, neither is prophet raised up nor vision revealed among them. And it is natural that it should be so, for when He that was signified had come, what need was there any longer of any to signify Him?[22]

Second, in Ephesians 2:20 the apostles and prophets are referred to as the 'foundation' of the church, with the Lord Jesus Christ being 'the chief cornerstone'. The foundation (singular) can be laid only once (see 1 Cor 3:10–11). It cannot be removed, and must not be altered or added to.

Third, we read in 1 Corinthians 13:8–10 that tongues and prophecy will cease when 'that which is perfect has come'. Some understand 'that which is perfect' to mean the completed canon of Scripture; others see it as the time when we shall see the Lord 'face to face'. There does seem, however, to be little point in saying that these things will end at the End!

Fourth, there may be significance in the apostle Peter's change of words from 'prophets' to 'teachers' in 2 Peter 2:1: 'But there were also false prophets among the people, even as there will be false teachers among you ...'

On the whole, therefore, the arguments for the cessation of inspired prophecy would seem to be weighty. Moreover, modern claims to predict the future are notorious for their fallibility.

If by 'prophecies' is meant uninspired utterances, off-the-cuff remarks and unprepared exhortations, there would seem to be no justification for gracing them with the label of 'prophecy'. On the other hand, as much of Old Testament prophecy consisted of preaching, there would seem to be some justification for the Puritan habit of referring to unprepared or unscheduled preaching as 'prophesying'.

Whether the term 'prophecy' is applied to present-day utterances or not, the cautionary word of verse 21 applies. When the apostle claimed respect for the Christian preacher, he did not claim infallibility. We are not to despise such preaching (v. 21), but test all that we hear and hold on to all that is good (v. 22).

How were the Thessalonians to test all things, and how do we do that today? By comparing what we hear with the written Word, just as the Bereans did in Acts 17:11. This was no innovation: 'To the law and to the testimony! If they do not speak according to this word, it is because there is no light in them' (Isa. 8:20). We are to search the Scriptures in order to make sure that what we hear is biblical. Then we are to hold on to what is good: we are to remember it, note it down, add it to our store of biblical knowledge but, above all, if it is a practical exhortation in line with God's Word, we are to put it into practice. How easy it is to be casual in our hearing of the exposition of God's Word! We must instead learn to treasure it.

We are also to look at the fruit of the teaching, the fruit produced by the teachers, and also consider their modes of life. Both these tests are implied in the words of Jesus in Matthew 7:15–23. There we are warned to beware of false prophets (v. 15) and we are told that 'by their fruits' we shall know them (vv. 16, 20). Even those who have prophesied, cast out demons and done wonders in the name of Christ (v. 22) are not necessarily genuine, for at the last day they will be rejected as those who have practised 'lawlessness' (v. 23). The Bible the early Christians used (the Old Testament) had already given similar warnings (Deut. 13; 18:20–22).

We are also to 'test the spirits' (1 John 4:1–3). We must not accept every new thing, especially any new bizarre thing, at face value. We need to ask God for the gift of discernment (1 Cor. 12:10).

STAY AWAY FROM EVERY SORT OF EVIL (V. 22)

Christians are to 'Abstain from every form of evil'. The word rendered 'form' ('appearance' in the KJV) has in some contexts the significance of a die or stamp used to mint coins. Like false currency which may look good but is worthless, teaching that does not have the ring of truth must, once tested, be rejected.

This verse, however, has further significance for us. We are to abstain from all forms of evil, even the very appearance of evil, in our daily living. Does something you are doing look doubtful? Is it likely to lead someone else astray? The story is told of a man who, one morning, examined his shirt collar to see if it was clean enough to wear again. His discerning wife remarked, 'If it's doubtful, it's dirty.'

We have an obligation both to our Lord and to other people to live pure lives. I once heard a Christian preacher, attempting to expound freedom from law and dependence on grace, erroneously say, 'If you feel you *ought* to do something, then it is wrong.' That is a complete misunderstanding of both law and grace, and a blatant contradiction of the New Testament which contains the word 'ought' nearly fifty times. We certainly '*ought*' to abstain from every form of evil. It is a command.

A dynamic conclusion! (vv. 23–28)

SANCTIFICATION AGAIN (V. 23)

Paul now prays that they will be sanctified by God in every part of their being so that when Christ returns they will be counted as blameless. These words are not to be taken as a technical description of the human being as threefold—spirit, soul and body—any more than the words of Jesus in Mark 12:30 are meant to describe the human nature as fourfold.

There is dynamite in these final words! Take the word 'sanctify'. Sanctification and holiness are basically the same word in both the Old and New Testaments. It may be helpful to think of sanctification as the process and holiness as the result. The basic meaning of the verb 'to sanctify' is 'to set apart' or 'to separate'. To be holy is to be separate *from* evil and set apart *to* God and his service.

The apostle has just commanded the Thessalonians to abstain from all forms of evil (v. 22). But man's unaided efforts are unlikely to be effective, so Paul prays that 'the God of peace Himself' will sanctify them 'completely', or 'through and through' (NIV). Sanctification is God's work, which he does through the Scriptures and by the Holy Spirit (see John 17:17).

Why does Paul here describe God as 'the God of peace'? Surely it is because peace with God is the only foundation upon which the work of sanctification can be carried out. The God of peace is the one who sends the Word, preaching peace by Jesus Christ (Acts 10:36). No one can ever be sanctified who is not reconciled to God. It is not possible to become holy until we are justified by faith and have peace with God through our Lord Jesus Christ (Rom. 5:1).

Notice how comprehensive Paul's prayer is, using the words 'completely', 'whole' and 'blameless'. Not a fragment of our being is to remain unsanctified, and not a whiff of compromise is to stain our character. This is the goal, though it will be completed only when we see Christ and are made like him (1 John 3:2–3).

This comprehensiveness is emphasized in the words 'spirit, soul, and body', a phrase which is intended to represent our total being. Some see the word 'spirit' as referring to the Godward aspect of our inner being, and 'soul' as referring to the animal side of our nature, the first relating to God and the second relating to the world. The trouble is that these two words are often used interchangeably, not only in hymns, Christian books and sermons, but also apparently in Scripture (compare John 12:27 with 13:21; Acts 2:27 with 1 Peter 3:18–19; Eccles. 12:7 with Isa. 10:18).[23] Each of them is used alone in contrast to the body to describe the whole person. Paul states that the unmarried Christian woman cares for the things of the Lord so that she may be holy in body and spirit (1 Cor. 7:34). Jesus warned the disciples that they should fear him who can destroy both soul and body in hell (Matt. 10:28). Such verses indicate that the words must be very similar in meaning. Add to that the words of Mary in the Magnificat, where she says, 'My soul magnifies the Lord, and my spirit has rejoiced in God my Savior' (Luke 1:46–47). This form of words, known as *parallelism*, is a characteristic of Hebrew poetry in which one line repeats the meaning of, contrasts with, or adds to, the previous line. However, when the two words are used together, as here in Thessalonians, it suggests that there is a slight difference in meaning, or at least of emphasis. In this case the meaning must be that *both* the aspect of a person's inner being that relates to God *and* the aspect that relates to ordinary life in the world are to be sanctified. In other words, we cannot be holy in our Christian activities and worldly in our everyday lives.

The word 'body' is much more straightforward. To be sanctified in body has both negative and positive aspects. We all know, or should know, whether our bodies are set apart from evil or not. Sexual immorality, pampering the body, excess in eating or drinking, laziness or dirtiness are incompatible with sanctification. On the positive side, Paul exhorts us in Romans 12:1–2 to 'present [our] bodies a living sacrifice, holy, acceptable to God, which is [our] reasonable service'.

We should not surrender our ears to gossip, lies, dirty stories or profanity, but rather to what is healthy, sound, edifying or necessary for our work. We should also guard what our eyes take in. To continue to hear or see evil things will make it difficult, if not impossible, to think on what is 'pure … lovely … of good report' (Phil. 4:8). The psalmist declared, 'I will set nothing wicked before my eyes' (Ps. 101:3), a verse we would do well to place on our television sets! Likewise, our mouths should not utter gossip, lies, profanity or other wrong words, but only what is helpful, true and edifying, in both our work and our leisure. There should be no great difference in moral quality between what we say in our daily lives and what we utter in the worship of God.

GOD, WHO IS EVER FAITHFUL, WORKS IN US (V. 24)

How does God work to sanctify us? He has provided all we need, all things that 'pertain to life and godliness' (2 Peter 1:3). His Holy Spirit will convict us of what is wrong and prompt us towards what is right. The Word of God, heard in preaching, read, studied, memorized, meditated upon and applied, will keep us clean (Ps. 119:9; John 15:3; 17:17; Eph. 5:26). And if we do sin, God has provided the means to be forgiven and cleansed through repentance and confession to him (1 John 1:7, 9; 2:2). He has also provided pastors, whose duty it is to '[c]onvince, rebuke, exhort, with all longsuffering and teaching' (2 Tim. 4:2; compare Heb. 13:17). God's faithfulness is the guarantee that he will do as he has said (see 1 Cor. 10:13).

ALL LEADERS NEED PRAYER! (V. 25)

Paul now requests prayer for himself. The mighty apostle asks these new Christians to pray for him, a request made several times in his epistles (2 Thes. 3:1; Rom. 15:30; Eph. 6:19; Col. 4:3; compare Heb. 13:18). No matter how young you are in the faith, never think that your prayers do not count, nor that your leaders, no matter how experienced, do not need them.

WARMLY GREET ONE ANOTHER (V. 26)

The 'holy kiss' was a greeting to acknowledge mutual membership of the body of Christ. In the Western world it has now largely been replaced by a warm handshake. Though the atmosphere of the family of God should never be icy, this greeting is intended to 'break the ice' and greet fellow-members of the Body of Christ.

THIS MUST BE READ TO ALL THE CHURCH (V. 27)

This verse contains surprisingly strong language. Why should Paul 'charge' them 'by the Lord' that his epistle be read to 'all' the brethren? It is possible that Paul thought the letter might be suppressed, or more likely that it might be circulated only among the leaders. On the other hand, it may be that the 'unruly' or disorderly elements might want to absent themselves from a reading of the apostle's letter. But nothing was to be kept back, and no one was to be missed out. The whole counsel of God was, and is, for the whole church.

THE CLOSING BENEDICTION (V. 28)

This underlines that the grace of God is always needed to fulfil God's commands: 'The grace of our Lord Jesus Christ be with you. Amen.'

Study questions

1. From the following Scriptures list some of the characteristics of the Day of the Lord: Acts 2:20; 1 Thessalonians 5:1–11; 2 Thessalonians 1:7–10; 2:2; 2 Peter 3:10; Revelation 16:14.

2. What should be our attitude towards Christian leaders, according to the following passages: Acts 17:11; 1 Thessalonians 5:12–13; Hebrews 13:7, 17; compare 2 John 9–11.

3. What criteria can we use to test teaching and/or experiences?

4. What is the difference (if any) between grieving the Holy Spirit (Eph. 4:30) and quenching the Spirit?

Notes

1 **F. F. Bruce,** *1 & 2 Thessalonians* (Word Biblical Commentary; Nashville: Thomas Nelson, 1982), p. 109.

2 **Charles A. Wanamaker,** *The Epistles to the Thessalonians* (NIGTC; Grand Rapids, MI: Eerdmans / Carlisle: Paternoster, 1990), p. 178; **Bruce,** *1 & 2 Thessalonians*, pp. 108f.; **Gene L. Green,** *The Letters to the Thessalonians* (Grand Rapids, MI: Eerdmans / Leicester: Apollos, 2002), p. 231.

3 **Green,** *Letters*, p. 232.

4 **Leon Morris,** *The First and Second Epistles to the Thessalonians* (NICNT; Grand Rapids, MI: Eerdmans, 1991), p. 151.

5 Ibid. p. 152.

6 Ibid.

7 **Bruce,** *1 & 2 Thessalonians*, p. 110.

8 **Green,** *Letters*, p. 238.

9 **Morris,** *First and Second Epistles*, p. 160.

10 **William T. Arnold,** 'Salvation', in **Walter A. Elwell, (ed.),** *Evangelical Dictionary of Biblical Theology* (Grand Rapids, MI: Baker / Carlisle: Paternoster, 1996), pp. 701f.

11 See, for example, **E. M. B. Green,** *The Meaning of Salvation* (London: Hodder & Stoughton, 1965).

12 'Bowing to the Lordship of Christ is the essence of salvation, and this attitude of submission is foundational to the whole life of the church. Wherever it exists the Lord has ground on which to work, even though understanding of his way be rudimentary; where it is absent there can be no real church' (**John Kennedy,** *The Torch of the Testimony* (Goleta, CA: Christian Books, 1965), p. 11).

13 **Morris,** *First and Second Epistles*, p. 167.

14 Ibid. p. 167.

15 **James Denney,** *The Epistles to the Thessalonians* (London: Hodder & Stoughton, 1892), p. 217.

16 Ibid. p. 220.

17 Ibid. p. 238.

18 **Jonathan Skinner,** *The Rise of Paganism: The Re-Emergence of an Old Ideology* (Darlington: Evangelical Press, 2006), pp. 134–135.

19 **William Hendriksen,** *1 & 2 Thessalonians* (London: Banner of Truth, 1972), p. 139.

20 **Morris,** *First and Second Epistles*, p. 177.

21 **Wayne Grudem,** *Systematic Theology* (Leicester: Inter Varsity Press / Grand Rapids, MI: Zondervan, 1994), p. 1049.

22 Cited in **David Chilton,** *The Days of Vengeance: An Exposition of the Book of Revelation* (Fort Worth: Dominion Press, 1987), p. 5.

23 '[T]he Bible does not use exact scientific language. It uses terms like *soul*, *spirit* and *heart* more or less interchangeably' (emphasis in original; **Anthony A. Hoekema,** *Created in God's Image* (Grand Rapids, MI: Eerdmans / Exeter: Paternoster, 1986), p. 293. Compare **Grudem,** *Systematic Theology*, pp. 473–474).

Part 2

The Second Epistle of Paul to the Thessalonians

Introduction

S econd Thessalonians was written a few months after the First Epistle in approximately AD 51. Paul wrote to respond to news he had received about the church, to comfort and encourage the believers, to deal with problems that were ongoing or had arisen since the first epistle had been sent, and to give further instruction on the Day of the Lord and the return of Christ.

Although the authenticity of this epistle has been challenged by critics rather more severely than that of the first epistle, there is no serious reason to doubt either its authenticity or its authorship.

Paul thanks God for the steady progress of the church and comforts them in their persecution. He corrects misunderstandings about the Day of the Lord, and gives instructions and commands about the behaviour of believers and situations in the church. He concludes with a blessing and final greetings. The three chapters conveniently divide as follows:

- thanksgiving for progress and comfort in suffering (ch. 1)
- explanation of the final things and correction of prophetic error (ch. 2)
- exhortation and commands concerning behaviour and attitudes to the wilfully disobedient (ch. 3)

Thanksgiving and encouragement (2 Thes. 1)

The greeting (vv. 1–2)

Paul was undoubtedly the author of this epistle, but Silas (Silvanus) and Timothy added their authority to it, as they were known to the Thessalonians and no doubt had fond memories of them. (For background information on Silas and Timothy, and on the church in Thessalonica, see the Introduction to Part 1 and Chapter 1 of this book.) Only in the Thessalonian epistles does Paul omit an appellation such as 'apostle' or 'bondservant' alongside his name. This church did not question his apostolic authority.

The apostle authenticates this letter in his own handwriting in 3:17, a necessary precaution as we shall see. By adding their names to the address, Silvanus and Timothy indicated that they joined Paul in the sentiments, encouragements and rebukes. No doubt they joined Paul also in praying about the letter and for the recipients.

This demonstrates that we do not actually have to preach the sermon ourselves in order to support it, back it up and pray for it. We do not have to write the letter to be behind it in its intentions and aims. We can join in the intention of a letter or a sermon by our agreement with its contents, our prayers for it, and our encouragements of the writer or preacher.

Preachers often need not merely our passive approval but our active encouragement. Moreover, the recipients of this letter needed to know that Silas and Timothy approved of it and agreed with it. A pastoral team not only needs to be united, but also to be seen to be united. If one member of a team is observed not to be fully supportive in a decision, teaching or discipline, the enemy of souls will be quick to find someone who senses the slight disunity and will seek to make capital out of it.

Quite probably Paul had discussed the letter's contents and its aim with Silas and Timothy as they prayed together for its effectiveness. Sermons, as well as apostolic letters, do not arise out of a vacuum but are the fruit of prayer, study, concern and love for the recipients. So preaching should be not only the result of the preacher's prayers, study and labour, but also the expression both of the pastoral team and ultimately of the whole church's concern and intention. The whole church does not prepare the sermon, but it should be behind the preacher and the sermon in its aims and intentions. Get behind your minister!

The address is identical to that in 1 Thessalonians except that Paul refers to 'our Father' instead of 'the Father'. The Lord Jesus Christ had taught his disciples to address God as 'our Father' (Matt. 6:9; Luke 11:2), and it became the regular designation in Paul's letters (1 Thes. 1:3; 3:11, 13; Rom. 1:7; 1 Cor. 1:3; 2 Cor. 1:2; Gal. 1:3–4; Eph. 1:2; Phil. 1:2; 4:20; Col. 1:2; 2 Thes. 2:16; Philem. 3). Now that he has got to know the Thessalonians better and has become assured of their progress (v. 3), he can comfortably refer to their joint spiritual parenthood. Salvation is much more than forgiveness of sins; it is incorporation into God's family throughout the world. Paul and the Thessalonian believers now have the same heavenly Father.

One characteristic theme of Paul's epistles is the phrase 'in Christ' and its equivalents ('in Him' or 'in the Lord Jesus Christ', etc.). Yet it is only in the Thessalonian epistles that he uses the phrase 'in God our Father' ('the' Father in 1 Thes.). The fact that Paul locates his addressees 'in God our Father and the Lord Jesus Christ' marks them out as regenerate and possessors of eternal life. 'The truth that Christians are in personal, spiritual, and eternal union with God is unique to Christianity; adherents of other religions do not speak of being in their god',[1] although some, such as Hindus, do aim at absorption into deity as their final goal.[2] The biblical truth of identification with Christ in this life, sometimes referred to as 'mystical union',[3] is one of the most glorious doctrines of the New Testament, especially as it implies union with God himself (John 14:23; 17:21, 23; Rom. 6:11; 8:1; 12:5; 16:7, 9–10; 1 Cor. 6:17; 15:22; 2 Cor. 5:17; Gal. 2:20; Eph. 1:1–3; 2:10; Phil. 1:1, 13–14; Col. 1:2; 3:3; 2 Peter 1:4).

The fact that Paul, without any explanation, links the Lord Jesus Christ with God our Father as the believer's spiritual location clearly affirms Christ's deity, as does his linking Father and Son as the source of grace and peace (v. 2), which has 'clear Christological implication'.4

PAUL'S DESIRE (V. 2)

Paul's greeting is not a mere formal or thoughtless introduction, for it expresses Paul's genuine desire for the Thessalonian believers and surely reflects the content of his prayers, too. He discards the common Greek greeting (*charein*) and instead combines the Hebrew greeting 'peace' (*shalom* in Hebrew, *eirēnē* in Greek) with the word 'grace' (*charis*). It is a deliberate change. 'This in itself is enough to note that Paul is thinking and not simply reacting as he writes his greeting.'5

Grace is the unmerited favour of God towards sinful men and women. It is that quality of God's attitude and action that brings us to salvation (Eph. 2:8–9). But it is more than that; the Thessalonians were already Christians. What more did Paul desire for them? He desired that they should be the continuing recipients of God's grace, 'grace for grace' (John 1:16). For grace is not only a *saving* attribute of God, but also a *keeping* and *equipping* attribute. It encompasses the whole saving work of God through Christ, 'not only the gift of salvation but also the continuous divine action by which he enables his people to do his will'.6 The term 'grace' is often used of 'the power with which the human being performs his or her gifted task'.7

Is the greeting a mere formality? What does it do in addition to being a warm expression of friendship? Neither grace nor peace can actually be imparted by a letter, though the contents may lead a person towards the source of grace and peace. They are God's gifts. The greeting therefore expresses the sincere desire of Paul and his company for the Thessalonian believers. He is saying, in effect, 'Our desire is that you will experience the ongoing grace of God and the resultant peace of God in your lives.' He would hardly profess this desire towards the recipients without also praying to God about this for them. Their progress was often the burden of his prayers for them (1:3, 11–12; 2:13, 16–17; 3:16).

How easy it is for us to allow trite and habitual greetings to trip off our lips. We so readily say, 'God bless you', perhaps without even thinking of its possible outcome, or of our responsibility to pray that desire into reality.

Thanksgiving and encouragement: God will repay (vv. 3–10)

UNCEASING THANKFULNESS (V. 3)

Paul felt moved to give thanks to God for the Thessalonian Christians because of the evident growth and progress of the church. 'Unceasing thanks are due from us to God.'[8] In the first epistle he simply gave thanks; now he is 'bound' to give thanks. It is not that he was reluctant to do so before, but that their remarkable progress called forth praise to God for them. He genuinely thanked God for their progress because it was an answer to his prayers for them (1 Thes. 3:12). Thanksgiving is often the weakest part of our prayers, especially thanking God for other people. We can remember to 'count our blessings' and thank God for what he has given to us personally, but how often do we genuinely spend time thanking God for various other people?

Paul uses the word 'ought' (*opheilō*), suggesting that to thank God for other people is a moral obligation. 'We owe it as a debt.'[9] Nor was this a 'one-off' thanksgiving, for he felt moved to do so 'always'. In this Paul and his companions were practising what they preached (1 Thes. 5:18). Their thankfulness was both the result of an inward conviction ('We are bound …') and an appropriate response to the outward evidence ('as it is fitting'). This, Paul indicated, was only right and proper.

So often today, Christians are impressed by spacious buildings and large congregations. The size and influence of the church and the popularity of the minister are what seem to count. But the elders of the church in Thessalonica are not even named and the church had no building. John MacArthur writes,

God never evaluates a church based on external features (cf. 1 Sam. 16:7). He is not impressed with innovative, clever repackaging of the gospel to make it more palatable for unbelievers. Nor are a church's elaborately staged worship services, political awareness, social prominence, or size reasons to boast before God. A church to be proud of is a place where the genuinely converted see their faith increase, their love grow, their hope endure despite persecution, and their focus remain singularly on God's kingdom.[10]

Why did Paul feel so obliged to thank God for them? Because of their remarkable spiritual growth. The intensive form of the verb 'to grow' (*huperauxanei*—to grow exceedingly) is found only here in the New Testament. What was this faith that was growing exceedingly? Was it simply trust in Christ? It would certainly have included that. Their faith in God was growing stronger day by day as, no doubt, they saw answers to prayer, studied the Scriptures and observed God at work in one another's lives. We saw in 1 Thessalonians that their faith was displayed in action but had suffered from 'certain deficiencies which required to be made good (1 Thes. 1:3; 3:10)'.[11] Now that faith was growing more and more. But growth in the faith of the Thessalonians would surely be more than growth in trust. The term 'the faith' is used in the New Testament to stand for the whole range of Christian doctrine and the life that should accompany it. It is used frequently in Paul's epistles and the Acts of the Apostles. For example, after Paul and Barnabas had, on the first missionary journey, preached the gospel in Derbe, they returned to Lystra, Iconium and Antioch, 'strengthening the souls of the disciples, exhorting them to continue in the faith …' (Acts 14:22).

Similarly, in Acts 16, on the second missionary journey, Paul and Silas ministered to the Christians in various cities and '[s]o the churches were strengthened in the faith …' (Acts 16:5; see also Rom. 1:5; 16:26; Eph. 4:13; Phil. 1:27; Col. 1:23; etc.). The faith, therefore, is more than simply trust in Christ for salvation. It includes that faith but also encompasses the apostolic doctrines, the truths of Scripture. More than that, 'the faith' stands for the whole of the Christian life: the practical outworking of those truths in the Christian life. Of course, even simple faith in Christ has doctrinal content, even though it may be very basic. The Thessalonians were not only learning to trust God more and more but were also undoubtedly growing in grace and in the knowledge of our Lord Jesus Christ (see 2 Peter 3:18).

However, this growth in the Thessalonians seems to have surpassed what might normally have been expected: it was growing 'exceedingly', in spite of persecution—perhaps, in some cases, because of persecution, for persecution tends to root out unreal Christians. Nor was this growth merely in head-knowledge of doctrine, and neither was it limited to growth in faith in Christ, for their love for one another was also increasing. Sadly, these aspects do not always progress together, step by step, in our lives.

In the first letter Paul had prayed that their love for one another might 'increase and abound' (1 Thes. 3:12; see also 4:9–10); now Paul thanks God that this prayer was answered. What was the evidence that their love for one another 'abounded'? After all, if love was only an emotion, an affection, it could not easily be seen. No doubt this love was revealed by the church members' attitudes to one another, their smiles, handshakes or embraces. However, it is more than likely that this love was also demonstrated in actions, deeds of service, practical caring for one another. The action of our Lord in washing the disciples' feet (John 13) has 'set the pace' for the whole church. Paul, in the epistle to the Galatians, urges, 'through love serve one another' (Gal. 5:13). It would seem, therefore, that Paul was referring, not to heightened emotion or even an excess of hugging and kissing, but rather to an increasing measure of practical service and care for one another. It was love in action.[12] Their growth included the practical outworking of love for one another. True Christian love (*agapē*) is the heart of genuine Christianity. The Ten Commandments are encapsulated in love for God and love for our neighbours (Matt. 22:34–40; Mark 12:28–33; compare 1 Cor. 13).

Ministers are sometimes disheartened by the fact that, while some church members are pressing on and growing in grace, others seem to be standing still or even regressing. What is so remarkable about the Thessalonian Christians is that the report Paul had received about the church indicated that all of them were growing in their love for one another; each one was growing in this fruit of the Holy Spirit.

The open secret

What was the secret of this remarkable growth in so young a church? If there is a secret, would not all true pastors like to know it? We dare not be dogmatic on this point, but we can suggest one or two factors that would no doubt have applied in this case.

We must mention in the first place the sovereign grace of God. The Almighty, for his own purposes, was pouring out his blessing upon the infant church. But the edifying influence of the Holy Spirit is rarely, if ever, totally separated from the work of God's servants. This is in no way to downplay the sovereign work of God, for he himself chooses to work through his servants. In Ephesians we are told that Christ himself gave 'some [to be] pastors and teachers, for the equipping of the saints for the work of ministry, for the edifying of the body of Christ ...' (Eph. 4:11–12). Here in Thessalonica the believers had received the apostles' doctrine direct from the apostle Paul himself, unsullied by man's contrary opinions and unclouded by the passage of time (compare Acts 2:42). The apostles had thoroughly taught the Thessalonians the truths of the gospel so that, young as the church was, they knew the basic doctrines thoroughly (1 Thes. 2:13; 5:1–2). Not that they had a perfect grasp of all doctrines and their implications—hence this epistle—but what they knew they had endeavoured to put into practice.

Sometimes churches, or individual Christians, are weak because they have not had a thorough grounding in basic doctrines. This needs to be an ongoing process because we can so easily forget what we have been taught and we need to be reminded until it becomes part of our personal knowledge. Furthermore, new converts, or even sometimes transfers from other churches, will need to be instructed in these truths. This teaching needs to be such that the church members make the truths their own: they need to hold the doctrinal and practical teaching, not only because the pastor teaches it, but also because they are convinced of its validity, its importance, its necessity and its application.

Alexander R. Hay raises the question why a church taught soundly by a godly pastor can, after a change of ministry, begin to hold doctrines contrary to what they have been taught. In a telling paragraph he argues that it is because the original doctrines have not become their own. They merely assented to what the former pastor taught, and when a new minister comes they begin to assent to what he teaches. Some, more discerning, leave, but the majority stay and accept the new direction. Hay writes, 'But why, after sound teaching so ably given, were they not strong enough and instructed enough to discern, refute and refuse the subtle, false doctrine so pleasingly presented? The answer is that the knowledge of the majority was never much more than head knowledge. For most of them it was really the pastor's knowledge and not their own.'[13]

With regard to the growth of the Thessalonians, the benefit they received from the apostolic teaching is not to be separated from the sovereign grace of God; rather it is a manifestation of God's grace that he provides shepherds who will teach the flock of God. 'I will give you shepherds according to My heart, who will feed you with knowledge and understanding' (Jer. 3:15; compare Eph. 4:11–12).

But there is another factor in the spiritual growth of churches. It is prayer. Oh dear! What a turn-off this is for some! But do not skip over this point. Part of the reason for our weakness as individuals and as churches is that we know we should pray—we know the value of it, we have read the promises—yet we rarely earnestly practise it. We do not put into practice what we know to be true in theory. That is why the 'Cinderella' of the church is the prayer meeting. Yet God has given us so many promises concerning prayer:

- 'Call to Me, and I will answer you, and show you great and mighty things, which you do not know' (Jer. 33:3)
- 'And whatever things you ask in prayer, believing, you will receive' (Matt. 21:22)
- 'Ask, and you will receive, that your joy may be full' (John 16:24)

Ministers are often fond of reading about, and citing, great men of God who spent much time in prayer, such as 'Praying Hyde', who saw great things happen in answer to prayer.[14] Mention could be made of such men as Andrew A. Bonar, Robert Murray McCheyne and William C. Burns, as well as countless others.[15] Evan Roberts was once asked for the secret of the 1904–1905 revival in Wales. He apparently replied, 'There is no secret; ask and you shall receive.' There is no doubt that prayer was a major factor in the work of the apostle Paul. Even in 2 Thessalonians 1 there is reference to his constant prayer (vv. 3 and 11).

In the first epistle Paul mentioned 'patience of hope' (1:3) along with their love and faith. Hope is omitted in 2 Thessalonians 1:3. Is that because of their confusion over whether the Second Coming had already occurred? Had they lost hope? That misunderstanding certainly needed to be corrected. However, hope is mentioned again at 2:16. The 'every one of you' (who were abounding in love) in verse 3 does not seem to match up with the 'some' at 3:11 who seemed to lack Christian faith and love and were walking 'in a disorderly manner'. F. F. Bruce suggests that 'these formed an uncharacteristic minority, whose waywardness, though regrettable, did not detract from the satisfaction with which the community as a whole was viewed'.[16]

LEGITIMATE BOASTING OR GENUINE APPRECIATION? (V. 4)

Paul told the Thessalonians that he boasted about them among the churches of God. In his first epistle to them he had indicated that the apostles did not need to say anything about them, as their lives testified to their conversion (1 Thes. 1:8). But now their progress was such that he could use it as an encouragement and perhaps a challenge to other Christians. When Paul writes that he boasts about the Thessalonian Christians, he is not saying something questionable. It does not conflict with the exhortation to 'glory in the LORD' (1 Cor. 1:31; 2 Cor. 10:17), as Paul is not boasting in what the Thessalonians have achieved, but in what God has wrought through them (compare Rom. 15:17–18; 2 Cor. 7:14; 9:2–4; 10:13–17; 12:5, 9; Gal. 6:14; 1 Tim. 1:12–16). Almost always in modern parlance the word 'boast' has a negative connotation, but it can also bear a positive nuance. The word translated 'boast' (*kauchaomai*) is used, with its cognate noun, in both a negative sense (e.g. Rom. 2:17, 23; 3:27) and a positive sense, as here. In a number of places the same word is translated 'to glory in' (e.g. 1 Cor. 1:31; 2 Cor. 10:17; etc.). In this verse Paul is using the word in a positive sense to indicate that he is telling others about their spiritual progress. The Thessalonians are his converts, and he is 'proud' of them.

We are sometimes reluctant to tell others how much we appreciate their spiritual growth. Obviously we want to avoid giving the devil an opportunity to tempt them with pride, but people do need encouragement, and sometimes they do not realize the good effect their lives are having. This may not be a bad thing on the whole, but they do also need positive feedback sometimes.

This was not mere flattery on Paul's part. Flattery is insincere and usually has a devious end in view. Jude speaks of those who were 'flattering people to gain advantage' (Jude 16). This was far from Paul's motive. His intention in boasting of the Thessalonians was no doubt to encourage and stimulate, even challenge, other Christians. Are we not all challenged and encouraged when we hear of outstanding blessing, or sacrificial service, in another part of the world? What Paul is describing in particular is the Thessalonians' patience and faith in the midst of persecution and tribulation (see Acts 17:5–8).

The word 'patience' (from *hupomenē*) is translated 'perseverance' in the NIV and 'endurance' elsewhere (Heb. 12:1; compare 2 Cor 1:6, where *hupomenē* is rendered 'enduring'). Its mention, perhaps, compensates for the omission of 'hope' alongside faith and love in verse 3. 'Patience' hardly expresses adequately the strength of this Greek word. Imagine you were sitting in a deck-chair on a sunlit beach enjoying an ice-cream and your friend asked you, 'How are you?' If you replied, 'Oh, I'm exercising patience', your friend might be amused, but he or she would hardly be impressed by your fortitude! Of course, your answer might be accurate if you were waiting for your husband or wife to return from somewhere else, or for the tide to come in so that you could go swimming. But those situations do not express the full meaning of *hupomenē*. William Barclay writes,

It is not the patience which can sit down and bow its head and let things descend upon it and passively endure until the storm is passed. It is the spirit which can bear things, not simply with resignation, but with blazing hope; it is not the spirit which sits statically enduring in one place, but the spirit which bears things because it knows that these things are leading to a goal of glory; it is not the patience which grimly waits for the end, but the patience which radiantly hopes for the dawn.[17]

Paul links patience with faith, as does James (James 1:3). Patience combined with faith is powerful, even in the midst of persecution and tribulations. Persecutions are brought about by the antagonism of other people; tribulations may include natural disasters and trials such as storms and shipwrecks, bereavement and failure of business enterprises. In all these circumstances the Thessalonians would 'endure' (*anechesthe*), or 'hold up'.

The fact that the Thessalonians were enduring persecutions and tribulations with patience and faith was newsworthy. The report of their victorious living would stimulate and encourage others who were probably facing the same trials.

THE PURPOSE OF SUFFERING (V. 5)

The purpose of suffering can sometimes be to test the character of the believer (1 Peter 1:7; 4:12; compare Deut. 8:2; Judg. 3:1–2). The word translated 'manifest evidence' (*endeigma*, sure token) is found only here in the New Testament, though the related word, *endeixis* (a pointing out, sign or demonstration), is found in Romans 3:25–26; 2 Corinthians 8:24; Philippians 1:28. It is cognate with the verb *endeiknumi* (to show or point out), and means an indication, token, proof or evidence. W. E. Vine writes that '*endeigma* indicates the token as acknowledged by those referred to', in other words, to the Thessalonians themselves;[18] it was a token to the Thessalonians.

This verse is rather puzzling at first glance. Why was their endurance under suffering a plain token or positive proof of God's righteous judgement? Was God judging them through these trials? Not necessarily, though God sometimes has to chasten those whom he loves (Heb. 12:3–11). But there is no hint of that disciplinary action here. What Paul is saying is that their behaviour while suffering rejection and dishonour at the hands of their neighbours was seen by God as a sign of honour, evidence of the genuineness of their faith, and proof that God had counted them worthy representatives of his kingdom (compare Acts 5:41; 14:22; 1 Thes. 2:12; Luke 20:35). Only true believers, filled with the Spirit of God, could behave consistently in such a way. Their suffering was not because they were more sinful than others (compare Luke 13:1–5); rather it was on behalf of the kingdom of God, which is equivalent to suffering for Christ's sake (compare Acts 5:41; 9:16; 14:22; Phil. 1:29; Rom. 8:17–18; 1 Peter 4:12–16).

This pastoral encouragement is often necessary today, for Christians are often puzzled as to why they suffer and unbelievers often do not appear to suffer. 'David (Ps. 73:1–14[19]) and Jeremiah (Jer. 12:1–4) were perplexed at the wicked prospering and the godly suffering',[20] and that is perfectly understandable. To adapt Matthew Henry on this verse, '[Christianity], if it is worth anything, is worth everything; and those [who] either have no religion at all, or none that is worth having, or know not how to value it ... cannot find it in their hearts to suffer for it.'[21] Their behaviour under such trials did not earn their salvation (Eph. 2:8–9; Titus 3:5); it proved the reality of it. We are justified by grace through faith in Christ (Rom. 5:1), but, as far as rewards are concerned, we shall be judged by works for Christ (Matt. 25:14–29; Luke 19:11–27; Rev. 20:4, 12; compare 1 Thes. 2:12; 1 Peter 1:6–7; 2 John 8). To quote Matthew Henry again, 'We cannot by all our sufferings, any more than by our services, merit heaven ...; but by our patience under our sufferings we are qualified for the joy that is promised to patient sufferers in the cause of God'[22] (see James 1:2; 1 Peter 1:6–7; Acts 5:41). Nor was this reaction mere Stoicism: they were joyful in their reception of the gospel (1 Thes. 1:6).

GOD WILL REPAY (V. 6)

While God's judgement is righteous in counting the Thessalonians worthy of the kingdom of God, it is also righteous and just in repaying with tribulation those who trouble the Christians: in relieving the persecuted and afflicting the persecutors. The verb 'to repay' (*antapodunai*) 'when predicated of God may denote either blessing or judgement'[23] (compare 1 Thes. 3:9; Luke 14:14; Rom. 12:19; Heb. 10:30).

The 'tribulation' (affliction, distress, suffering) is defined in verse 9 as the penalty of everlasting destruction. One aspect of this repayment we find hard to understand is that there will be varying degrees of punishment. We know that under the old covenant, punishment was to be according to deeds (e.g. Job 34:11; Ps. 62:12; Prov. 24:12; Isa. 59:18; Jer. 17:10; Ezek. 7:3), and that under the new covenant, believers will be rewarded according to their post-conversion behaviour, service and deeds (Matt. 10:41; 16:27; 25:34–40; Luke 6:22, 35; Rom. 2:10; 1 Cor. 3:8, 10–17; 2 Cor. 5:9–10; Col. 2:18–19; 3:23–25; 2 John 8). However, our Lord also taught that punishment will vary in severity according to people's sinfulness or depths of depravity (Luke 10:13–16; 12:47–48; compare Heb. 10:26–31).

God's judgement is sure and perfectly balanced, as indicated by the verb 'repay' (*antapodidomi*, to give back, recompense; see also Deut. 32:35; Luke 13:2–5; Rom. 1:18–32). He will afflict those who afflict us (the words translated 'tribulation' and 'trouble' are from the same root; see similar constructions in Gen. 12:3; Zech. 2:8; Matt. 18:6–10). Those who persecute will be punished. This will not necessarily be in time, but it will inevitably follow the return of Christ. Paul's argument is perfectly congruent with the rest of Scripture (e.g. Gen. 18:25b; Ps. 1:4–6; 9:17; Prov. 1:24–31; 16:5; Matt. 10:28; Rom. 2:3; Col. 3:25; Heb. 12:25). Punishment of the wicked must be just, as God is perfect. 'God is not capricious but rather judges justly.'[24] All nations have laws which forbid and punish wrongdoing according to their standards, and if this is right for man, it is surely right for God the Creator to punish those who sin against him. The wicked are not always punished in this life as they deserve, so future retribution is in accordance with man's sense of justice as well as with the teaching of Scripture.

PAYMENT DAY (V. 7)

'When is this retribution going to be exercised?' is a question that would naturally arise in the minds of the persecuted believers. Paul replies by linking judgement with the future return of Christ. '[T]he emphasis on the vengeance of God is calculated to encourage the brothers and sisters in the face of great adversity, supplying them with an eschatological perspective that will enable them to evaluate their present situation rightly ... [O]ur modern glib rejection of the notion of divine intervention and judgement stands corrected by these words.'[25]

In his letters, Paul often uses the word *parousia* ('presence' or 'coming') to refer to Christ's return. In this verse, however, he employs the term *apocalupsei* (*apokalupsis*—'revelation' or 'unveiling'), which suggests a dramatic and surprising aspect of these events (compare 1 Thes. 2:19; 3:13; 4:15; 5:23; 2 Thes. 2:1 with 1 Cor. 1:7; 1 Peter 1:7, 13; 4:13). This is significant because Christ is hidden at present (1 Peter 1:8), and the last sight the world had of him was as a victim dying on a cross. The early Christians were sometimes accused of atheism[26] because their God could not be seen, but on the great day of Christ's return all will see him (Matt. 24:30; Rev. 1:7). The next view of him will be as the glorified and triumphant Lord and Judge. Even in the days of his flesh the Lord's true nature was hidden from the world. As Charles Wesley expressed it, Christ was 'veiled in flesh'.[27] Christ will be 'revealed from heaven', which speaks of both his origin and his authority.

When Jesus ascended into heaven, two angels told the disciples, 'This same Jesus, who was taken up from you into heaven, will so come in like manner as you saw Him go into heaven' (Acts 1:11). But his 'revelation', while also personal and visible, will be dramatically different, for he will return 'with His mighty angels' (2 Thes. 1:7). He ascended alone; he will return with his angelic retinue. The phrase 'mighty angels' is literally 'angels of his power'. Sometimes angels appeared, in both Old and New Testaments, as more or less ordinary men, perhaps to avoid alarming those to whom they appeared. Occasionally, however, their wholly other nature was manifest, to the terror of those who saw them (see, for example, Dan. 10–11[28]). Some of these appearances are generally regarded as 'theophanies', pre-incarnation manifestations of the second Person of the Trinity.

Paul does not change, still less contradict, what he wrote about the end times in his first epistle, as some critics claim; rather he explains, expands and fills out the earlier teaching. Just as the wicked will be punished, so the believers will be given 'rest'. The translators quite rightly supply the word 'give' which is not in the original. This is important because, while the wicked deserve the punishment, believers do not deserve this 'rest' on their own merits. It is a gift of God's grace to those who have trusted in Christ for salvation. The word translated 'rest' (*anesin*) is a noun meaning ease, rest, peace or tranquillity. It indicates the lifting of pressure caused by persecution, but in the context it also implies participation in God's own kingdom and glory (1 Thes. 2:12). This privilege will be shared with the apostles ('with us'; compare 1 Cor. 4:9–13). As far as the persecutors and the persecuted are concerned, the Day of Judgement will bring about an 'ethically appropriate'[29] reversal of roles (compare Luke 16:25).

Present rest

Is rest only to be received at the end of time, then? Certainly there is to be a glorious rest in heaven. The Puritan Richard Baxter wrote a beautiful book about heaven called *The Saint's Everlasting Rest*. That will be a glorious, perfect and complete rest. But there is also a rest to be received in this life. Hebrews 3–4 speaks of this present rest using the analogy of entering Canaan. Hymns (and some preachers!) sometimes speak of entering heaven as entering Canaan, which, though it is a beautiful thought, is not an accurate analogy. Canaan is not really a type of heaven because there were unbelievers, sin, warfare and enemies in Canaan.

Moreover, Canaan had to be gained through warfare and expelling enemies.

The great John Owen, in his magisterial seven-volume commentary on the Epistle to the Hebrews, explains persuasively that chapters 3 and 4 of that epistle do not refer to heaven but to the gospel rest into which we enter now. He acknowledges that there is a rest to be received in heaven, but the rest spoken about in Hebrews is peculiar to the gospel and gospel times, in that it is compared and contrasted with the rest offered under Moses. The writer is presenting an antithesis, contrasting two peoples: those in the wilderness and the Hebrews he is addressing. The 'rest' the Israelites in the wilderness failed to enter was the settled state of God's solemn worship in the land of Canaan. The antithesis of that is not heaven, but the settled state of church worship we can now enjoy in Christ. The whole design of the author is not to contrast heaven, immortality and glory with the law or what the Israelites had in Canaan, for no one ever doubted that heaven is above both Canaan and even our present state.

For Owen, then, this present 'rest' mentioned in Hebrews is peace with God (Rom. 5:1), freedom from a servile bondage in ritual worship, deliverance from the yoke and bondage of Mosaical institutions, freedom and liberty of spirit, and rest in God's Son, who is our peace. The words in Hebrews 4:3 that are in the present tense indicate a present entrance. Moreover, the author is exhorting sincere believers to persevere, not primarily so that in the end they may enter heaven, but in order to enter the present rest in Christ.[30] Yes, there is a present rest, even in the midst of conflict, as Paul and Silas demonstrated as they praised God even in prison (Acts 16:25).

Future rest

But here in 2 Thessalonians Paul is speaking of the future complete rest which the persecuted believers will enjoy when the Lord Jesus Christ returns, and which will contrast sharply with the punishment the wicked will endure. This is the rest of which Richard Baxter wrote. There will then be a relaxation from the tension and a rest from warfare which is not possible in this present world. When our Lord was arrested in the Garden of Gethsemane he could have called on twelve legions of angels[31] to come to his assistance (Matt. 26:53), but he refrained from doing so in order to fulfil the purpose for which he had come and to follow the path laid down for him by the Father. But when he returns there will be no need for such restraint. The angels who will accompany him then (1 Thes. 3:13; Matt. 16:27; 24:30–31; 25:31; Mark 8:38; Zech. 14:5) are described here as 'mighty', or, more literally, 'angels of his power' (*angelōn dunameōs autou*). Angels are certainly powerful (2 Peter 2:11), but here they are executives of Christ's judicial power (compare Gen. 19:1, 11; 2 Sam. 24:16; 2 Kings 19:35; 2 Chr. 32:21; Ps. 35:5; Matt. 13:41–42; Acts 12:23; Jude 14–15; Rev. 15:1).

TAKING VENGEANCE (V. 8)

This vengeance must not be confused with man's revenge. It is not retaliation, still less an outburst of anger. It is the execution of deserved judgement (compare Isa. 66:4, 15; 1 Peter 2:14; Luke 18:3, 5, 7; 21:22; Rom. 12:19; Heb. 10:30). In Daniel 7:13–14, the Ancient of Days gives authority to 'One like the Son of Man'. This is paralleled by John 5:27, where we read that the Father has given the Son authority to execute judgement 'because He is the Son of Man' (compare 1 Thes. 4:6; Mark 8:38; Acts 10:42; Isa. 66:15–16). The return of Jesus Christ, referred to in 2 Thessalonians 1:7 as his 'revelation' (*apokalupsis*), will be an awesome and terrifying event: awesome for all, and terrifying for unbelievers, for he will return in 'flaming fire',[32] exercising full 'vengeance' (*ekdikēsin*: retribution, full punishment, justice, vengeance) on those who 'do not know God' and who 'do not obey' the gospel of our Lord Jesus Christ (see Judg. 2:10; 1 Sam. 2:12; Ps. 9:17;

79:6; Jer. 2:8; 9:3, 6; Hosea 4:1, 6; 5:4; John 8:54–55; 17:3; Gal. 4:8; 1 Thes. 4:5; Titus 1:16; compare Exod. 5:2).

This is not an innocent or inadvertent ignorance but 'that inexcusable refusal to know God',[33] a deliberate suppression of the truth which prevents people from knowing God (see Rom. 1:18–21; compare 2:14–15). The fact that this ignorance is linked with disobedience is important. Those who do not know God and those who do not obey the gospel are the same people. They are not two classes; this is a synonymous parallelism expressing two aspects of the same sinful rebellion (see Jer. 10:25; Ps. 79:6; Acts 6:7; Rom. 1:5, 18–32; 2:8; 6:17; 10:16; 15:18; 16:26; Heb. 5:9; 1 Peter 1:2, 14, 22; 4:17). To wilfully refuse to believe and know God is tantamount to disobeying the gospel (see Isa. 53:1; Rom. 2:8; 10:16). Salvation is a free gift to be received, but the gospel is a command to be obeyed (Acts 17:30; 26:20; compare Heb. 10:26–31). God's retribution is not selfish, sinful or vengeful, as man's usually is. It is a manifestation of his justice (Deut. 32:35; Ps. 1:4–6; Isa. 66:15–16; Ezek. 33:17–20; Matt. 3:12; 25:41, 46; Luke 20:15–18; 21:22; Rom. 3:5; compare 12:19; Heb. 10:30; 2 Tim. 4:14; Rev. 6:10).

Flaming fire

Fire is often associated with manifestations of God in Scripture. In Genesis, when God made a covenant with Abraham, 'a smoking oven and a burning torch ... passed between [the] pieces' of Abraham's offering (Gen. 15:17). We must not imagine a literal stove floating between the pieces of the sacrificed animals; this was the nearest the writer could get to describing the manifestation of God's presence. When the Angel of the Lord addressed Moses, a bush burned with fire yet was not consumed (Exod. 3:2). When the Ten Commandments were given, Mount Sinai was covered in smoke because 'the LORD descended upon it in fire' (Exod. 19:18). Fire touched Isaiah's lips to purge away his felt uncleanness (Isa. 6:6). Ezekiel's vision of God involved 'a great cloud with raging fire engulfing itself' (Ezek. 1:1–4, 13, 27). John the Baptist prophesied that Jesus would baptize with the Holy Spirit and fire (Matt. 3:11; Luke 3:9, 16), and fire licked the heads of the disciples on the Day of Pentecost (Acts 2:3). Hebrews 12:29 states that 'our God is a consuming fire'. The fire that will accompany Christ's Second Advent (Dan. 7:9–10; Mal. 4:1) symbolizes not only Christ's deity and glory, but also his 'consuming vengeance against his foes'.[34]

There are numerous references to fire in the Book of Revelation, but for our purposes the most significant are, perhaps, those that refer to the glorified Lord as having 'eyes like a flame of fire' (Rev. 1:14; 2:18; 19:12). There are many similar verses in the Bible.[35] It would be thoroughly biblical to say that fire is frequently linked with manifestations of the divine presence.

Not knowing God

Not to 'know God' is not to have eternal life, for eternal life consists in knowing God and Jesus Christ (John 17:3), a knowledge in which we are intended to grow and progress (2 Peter 3:18; Phil. 3:12–14). In apostolic preaching, obedience to the faith was a prominent element (Acts 6:7; Rom. 1:5; 15:18; 16:26; compare 1 Peter 1:2). Head-knowledge, mere belief in the facts, is not enough, as James makes clear in his epistle (James 2:19). While it is gloriously true that we are saved by grace through faith and not by works, God intends that good works should follow our conversion (Eph. 2:8–10; compare 1 John 1:6; 2:3–6; 3:10, 14; 5:2–3).

PUNISHMENT FOR EVER? (V. 9)

The final state of those who have rejected the knowledge of God and rebelled against his gospel is described in such horrifying terms in the New Testament that, were it not that our Lord Jesus Christ himself supplied many of these descriptions, we might be inclined to ignore them, as indeed some Christians have done (Matt. 3:12; 13:42, 50; 25:46; compare Jude 13; Rev. 21:8). There is no suggestion of a second opportunity to escape this judgement and be saved, for the 'verdict, as its execution, will be final'.[36] Those who do not know God and have not obeyed the gospel will pay the penalty of everlasting destruction, which contrasts with God's gift to believers: eternal life (John 3:16; Rom. 2:7; 5:21; 6:22–23; Gal. 6:8). These words 'everlasting' and 'destruction' require examination.

Everlasting destruction

First let us take the word 'everlasting' or 'eternal' (*aiōnion*). Some argue that the word really means 'age-long' and that therefore an end to the punishment is envisaged; others argue that words mean different things in different contexts. That last point is, of course, true enough. But in Matthew 25:46 both these objections are answered, for we read that those condemned at the Judgement will go away into eternal punishment, but the righteous will go into eternal life, exactly the same Greek term being used for 'everlasting' punishment and 'eternal' life. Moreover, the overwhelming weight of New Testament evidence is for the word 'eternal' (*aiōnios*) to be interpreted as 'without end'. For example, this adjective is used of God (Rom. 16:26), the Holy Spirit (Heb. 9:14), heaven (Luke 16:9), salvation (Heb. 5:9), redemption (Heb. 9:12), the new covenant (Heb. 13:20), God's kingdom (2 Peter 1:11) and the gospel (Rev. 14:6). The most reasonable conclusion is that the things so described will last for ever.

It is sometimes asked if it is fair or just to punish someone eternally who has sinned in time. Is everlasting punishment a just retribution for even seventy or more years of sin? Part of the problem with this objection is that human beings barely recognize the true nature of sin. We understand crime, which is an offence against the state or another person or persons; we understand vice, which is an offence against ourselves; but we do not understand the seriousness of sin, which is an offence against God (Ps. 51:4). We can convict a person of crime or vice, but only the Holy Spirit can really convict a person of sin (John 16:8–11). Another point is that people do not cease to sin when they die. Their rebellion against God and their rejection of Christ continues. As they have chosen in this life, so they will continue to choose for eternity (Rev. 14:11; 22:11).

In his book *Biblical Teaching on the Doctrines of Heaven and Hell*, Edward Donnelly points out that human beings are incompetent to decide how God should deal with sin. Our standards are all distorted and warped. To illustrate his point he writes,

Imagine a group of young professionals enjoying a meal in any big-city restaurant. Not an eyebrow will be raised if someone mentions that they have recently had an abortion. A reference by another to their same-sex 'partner' will elicit no disapproval. But if one of the party were to light a cigarette in a no-smoking section of the restaurant? Shock, horror, unanimous disgust! Is exhaling tobacco smoke more reprehensible than sexual perversion or killing an unborn child? Are such people competent to make moral judgements, to decide how God should deal with sin? They cannot even distinguish between wickedness and bad manners.[37]

Moreover, the length of time it takes to sin bears no relationship to its seriousness. Murder may be committed in a moment; malicious gossip may continue for years.

With regard to the everlasting nature of hell, Donnelly writes,

We must remember, too, that those who are in hell continue to sin, incurring more guilt to all eternity. The divine sentence is, 'He who is unjust, let him be unjust still; he who is filthy, let him be filthy still' (Rev. 22:11). As John L. Dagg puts it, 'A sinner cannot become innocent by being confirmed in sin ... The future condition of the wicked is chiefly terrible, because they are abandoned by God to the full exercise and influence of their unholy passions, and the consequent accumulation of guilt for ever and ever.' In other words, those in hell become ever more guilty and accumulate ever more sin, which deserves ever increasing punishment. After countless ages, they have more to answer for than when they were first condemned.[38]

While this eternal punishment will consist, in part, of banishment from the benign 'presence' (literally, 'face', 2 Thes. 1:9) of the Lord (see Matt. 25:41; Rev. 6:16; compare Isa. 2:10; 1 Peter 3:12) and 'from the glory of His power', the Greek text suggests that the condemning presence of the Lord and his glorious power are the source of the eternal destruction (compare Num. 16:46; Ps. 34:16; 96:13; Isa. 2:10, 19, 21; Jer. 4:26; Ezek. 38:20; Rev. 6:16; 20:11). God will be present in hell since he is omnipresent (Ps. 139:7–8), but it will be a wrathful and condemning presence. Those in heaven will know a glorious, welcoming, though awesome presence (Rev. 22:3–5). Imagine a mother hugging a sobbing child who has just been knocked down by a careless cyclist. She directs her anger towards the cyclist while at the same time hugging and caressing the child. If a mere human can be both angry and loving at the same time to different people, it is not difficult to imagine how an omnipresent God can be both angry and loving at the same time.[39]

In this life, even unbelievers benefit from God's general providence. Rulers are provided to restrain evil (Rom. 13:1–7), Christians exercise a preserving influence as salt and light (Matt. 5:13–14), rain falls on the just and the unjust (Matt. 5:45), and angels are constantly active (Ps. 103:20–21; Heb. 1:14). It must be inconceivably terrible to be in a place from which all restraints and good influences are removed, not being in heaven and seeing the 'glory of His power', but rather enduring God's displeasure. 'Cast out from the presence of the Lord is the sting of eternal death; the law of evil left to its unrestricted working, without one counteracting influence of the presence of God, the source of all light and holiness (Isa. 66:24; Mark 9:44).'[40]

Jesus spoke more about hell than about heaven, so we must face the reality of this awful destiny for the unsaved. Having said that, a number of Scriptures teach that punishment will be graded according to guilt and enormity of sin. We do not know how this will be done but Jesus taught that it is so (Matt. 10:14–15; 11:20–24; Mark 12:38–40; Luke 10:10–15; 12:42–48; compare Rom. 2:5–7).

Everlasting *destruction*

The word translated 'destruction' (*olethron*) also calls for comment. It does not mean cessation of being, but ruin or destruction, especially in the sense that the object is no longer suitable for its original purpose. The British landscape is littered with ruins of old barns, churches and monasteries which are destroyed but still exist. In 1 Thessalonians 5:3 this 'destruction' is compared to labour pains, which do not result in the cessation of the mother's being (though in a few cases they do lead to death). In 1 Corinthians 5:5 the word is used 'of the effect upon the physical condition of an erring believer for the purpose of his spiritual profit' and in 1 Timothy 6:9 'of the consequences of the indulgence of the flesh, referring to physical ruin and possibly of the whole being'.[41]

Since this word is qualified by the word 'eternal' or 'everlasting', it cannot refer to annihilation. If something is annihilated it ceases to exist, so the adjective 'everlasting' would be meaningless.[42] Because of their trials the Thessalonians needed this reassurance of future judgement and recompense, and this doctrine must be taught today to encourage persecuted believers.

WHEN HE COMES IN THAT DAY (V. 10)

The Judgement will take place when Jesus returns (compare Ps. 96:13) to be glorified 'in His saints'. Who are these holy ones ('saints') in whom Christ will be glorified? The holy ones in 1 Thessalonians 3:13 are the angels who will accompany the Lord on his return, but here it is believers who are in view. Although the reference could be to the 'mighty angels' of verse 7, the parallelism of the next clause confirms that they are 'all those who believe'.

Believers are regularly called 'saints' in the New Testament (Acts 9:13; Rom. 1:7; 15:25, 31; 1 Cor. 1:2; 16:1; 2 Cor. 1:1; 9:1; Phil. 1:1; Col. 1:2, 4; compare 1 Thes. 4:7). There is a Day yet to come when the Lord Jesus will return to be glorified and admired by the saints. God should be glorified here and now in this life by believers (Matt. 5:16; John 15:8; Rom. 15:6, 9; 1 Cor. 6:20; 10:31; Phil. 1:11; 1 Peter 4:11), so this is something beyond that. However, all our present efforts are limited and unworthy of Christ's true glory, being partly veiled by our inherent sinfulness. But when Christ returns he will be glorified in a new way in his saints as they mirror his glory, for believers will be transformed and glorified 'in a moment, in the twinkling of an eye' (1 Cor. 15:51–52; John 17:10, 22; compare Isa. 49:3). The amazing thing is that we shall be glorified with him (Rom. 8:17; Col. 3:4), though it is as well to bear in mind that in this life glorification is related to suffering (Rom. 8:18; 2 Cor. 4:17; Col. 3:4–5; 1 Peter 1:6–7). The Lord Jesus Christ is already glorified in heaven (Rev. 1:13–16; 5:9–14), but here on earth he is ignored, despised and vilified by many unbelievers, and even believers do not yet see him (1 Peter 1:8). But on that Day he will be admired among all believers, of whom those still on earth will see their Lord for the first time.

Not only so, but our most fervent praise in this present life is muted by trials, sorrows and unbelief. But on that Day these hindrances will all be swept away and our praise and worship will be pure and complete. That will be a day of retribution and ruin for those who opposed Christ or refused to believe in him, but it will be a day of rest and glorification for true believers, for they will share in his glory (Phil. 3:21; 1 John 3:2; Rom. 8:18–19). As we then see our fellow-believers transformed, we shall marvel at Christ's work in them. Christ will be marvelled at because his amazing grace has so transformed them into his likeness (1 John 3:2).

This glorious experience will include the Thessalonian believers because they 'believed' the gospel of Christ and the 'testimony' of the apostles, who were his witnesses (2 Thes. 1:10; compare 2:14; 1 Thes. 1:5; 1 Cor. 1:6).

Prayer and glory (vv. 11–12)

'With this end in view'[43] the apostles constantly pray that these believers may be counted 'worthy' (by God) of the call to holiness here and glory hereafter (1 Thes. 2:12; 4:7; 5:24; Eph. 4:1; compare Phil. 3:14). Paul, for whom prayer is a way of life, now assures them that he 'always' prays for those who were saved through his ministry (compare 2:16–17; 3:1–5, 16), and he reveals why he prays for them so much. Prayer for the flock is one of the most important continual tasks of a faithful pastor. It was the background to all Paul's teaching, preaching, evangelizing, writing, discipling, travelling and even suffering (Rom. 1:9–10; 2 Cor. 13:7, 9; Eph. 1:15–17; 3:14–21; Phil. 1:4, 9–11; Col. 1:3, 9–11; 1 Thes. 1:2; 3:10–13; 5:23; 2 Tim. 1:3; Philem. 4, 6).

Teaching is normally restricted to certain times and places; prayer can be offered at any time and in any place. Teaching, preaching and discipling are somewhat circumscribed by the pastor's strength and the hearers' patience! Prayer, however, is relatively unlimited as God never wearies and his ear is always open to our cries (Deut. 4:7; Ps. 145:18–19; Heb. 4:16; 7:25). Paul prays that their lives will be consistent with their profession. Since they are publicly identified as Christians, he prays that their behaviour will match their reputation (compare 1 Thes. 2:12; 4:1; Eph. 4:1; Col. 1:10).

Perhaps we shall never know just how much we owe to those who pray for us. Blessed are those who have Christian friends who regularly pray for them! But we all have One who regularly makes intercession for us (Rom. 8:26; Heb. 7:25). We Christians will pray for one another when we are ill or have a pressing need, but do we remember to pray for one another that we may live up to our Christian calling? This may sound presumptuous or proud, but it need not be so. We need all the help we can get, and the New Testament is full of references to meeting one another's needs. We are to serve one another (Gal. 5:13; 1 Peter 4:10) in the courtesies of life (John 13:14); bear one another's burdens (Gal. 6:2); receive one another (Rom. 15:7); and provide hospitality for one another (1 Peter 4:9). Our ministries to one another may include admonishing (Rom. 15:14), exhorting (Heb. 3:13; 10:25; 1 Thes. 5:11) or teaching one another (Col. 3:16), but they certainly include praying for one another (James 5:16).[44]

A question that sometimes arises is, if God knows everything (is omniscient) and is sovereign, why do we need to pray?[45] The fact is that God, in his sovereignty, has decreed to work through his people's prayers. This is sometimes described as God's part and man's part: our part is to pray and God's part is to answer. Of course, we are not *only* to pray, for God will not do for us what we can do for ourselves. This was Peter's experience in Acts 12:5–10. There are many examples of this in Scripture. God elects to salvation (Eph. 1:4; Rom. 8:28) and grants repentance and faith (Acts 11:18; Eph. 2:8–9), but man has to repent and believe (Acts 2:38; 16:31; 17:30). Though sanctification is a work of God's Spirit in applying the Scriptures, man's obedience is involved. When Daniel saw from Jeremiah's prophecy that the Babylonian captivity would last seventy years, he nevertheless prayed earnestly with fasting that the promised deliverance would come (Dan. 9:2–19). The Scriptures themselves are inspired by God, yet they are also human documents with varying styles and vocabulary according to the skill of the writers (2 Tim. 3:16; 2 Peter 1:21).

Paul again acknowledges their common faith when he prays that 'our God' will count them worthy of their calling (v. 11). This is the effectual call that brings people to salvation (John 6:37, 44; 17:6, 11–12; Acts 13:48).[46] Sadly, as we shall see, some in the Thessalonian church were not walking 'worthy' (3:6, 11). The phrase 'count ... worthy' could also be translated 'make … worthy'. Although Paul is praying that God will count or make them worthy, nevertheless he also exhorts them to live worthy lives. Prayer and exhortation go together (Rom. 13:13; 1 Cor. 7:17; Col. 1:9–10; Eph. 4:1; 5:2, 8; 1 Thes. 2:11–12).

The remainder of verse 11 is translated by the NIV as 'and that by his power he may fulfil every good purpose of yours and every act prompted by your faith'. Is the desire for goodness (*eudokian agathōsunēs*) theirs or God's? It should go without saying that it is God's good pleasure that we should live holy lives (Eph. 1:4; Phil. 2:13; Col. 1:22; 1 Peter 1:16). But God does beget in believers a desire for goodness, and so it is almost certainly that desire which is in Paul's mind, because the 'work of faith' is the Thessalonians' (1 Thes. 1:3). Even so, not only the desire but also its outworking are wrought in believers by God (1 Thes. 5:23–24; Gal. 5:22–23). Therefore, since 'good pleasure' (*eudokia*) is mostly used of God (Eph. 1:5, 9; Phil. 2:13), it perhaps should be translated 'fully perfect in you all goodness according to his gracious purpose',[47] which would, of course, include begetting that desire in them. '[W]ork of faith' is faith manifested by work (James 1:4). Of course, faith's work is really God's work in and carried out by man (Phil. 2:13). This work is 'with power', that is, manifested powerfully (Col. 1:11, 29).

GLORIFYING THE LORD (V. 12)

Our whole lives should be lived to the glory of God (1 Cor. 10:31), and that includes bringing glory to the 'name' (reputation) of our Lord Jesus Christ. If we do not live up to our profession, the name of the Lord Jesus Christ is dishonoured; but if by his grace we seek to 'walk just as He walked' (1 John 2:6), he will be glorified. The believer's graces, worked in us by the Holy Spirit (Gal. 5:22–23), redound to Christ's glory, and his glory, as Head, reflects glory on the members (John 21:19; Gal. 1:24; 1 Peter 4:14; compare Isa. 28:5 with Isa. 62:3). The phrase 'the grace of our God and the Lord Jesus Christ' has only one article, implying the inseparable oneness of God and the Lord Jesus Christ.

Why does Paul pray this? In order that the Lord Jesus Christ may be glorified in the Thessalonians. And why should we pray like this? In order that Christ may be glorified in the lives of our friends. The glory of the Lord should always be our aim (Matt. 5:16; 1 Cor. 6:20; 10:31; 1 Peter 4:11), for this is also the Holy Spirit's aim (John 16:14). The astonishing thing is that Paul prays that the Thessalonian believers may also be glorified in Christ! We wretched, helpless sinners are glad enough to be forgiven, cleansed from our sins and promised a place in heaven, but to be glorified also? This is almost unbelievably amazing. Yet it is true.

We suffer with Christ in order that we may be glorified with him (Rom. 8:17). This is so certain that it is spoken of in the past tense in Romans 8:30: 'these He also glorified'. Part of this glory will be a glorious body like his (Phil. 3:21; 1 Cor. 15:43–53; 1 John 3:2; compare 2 Cor. 5:1–5), designed and adapted for the new heavens and the new earth, a body that will last for ever. This new body will be essential as our present bodies could not exist in God's presence. No man can see God and live (Exod. 33:20). Our God is a consuming fire (Heb. 12:29). But the resurrection bodies we shall be given, glorious bodies, will be able to exist in the presence of God and bear the intense light of that 'uncreated beam'.[48]

This does not imply that we shall be glorified for anything we are or have done in ourselves. It is all 'according to the grace of our God and the Lord Jesus Christ'. In a sense, the glorifying of the saints will reflect glory to the Lord. Just as a beautiful painting glorifies the artist, a magnificent building glorifies the architect and a lovely, fragrant garden glorifies the gardener, so the glorified saints will reflect the glory of the Lord and his wonderful plan of salvation. He will be glorified in his saints (v. 10).

Well might we sing with A. T. Pierson,

Chapter 6

All these once were sinners, defiled in His sight,

Now arrayed in pure garments in praise they unite:

Unto Him who hath loved us and washed us from sin,

Unto Him be the glory for ever! Amen.[49]

Study questions

1. Examine the countries in the '10/40 window'[50] and find out how persecuted Christians are coping.

2. Find out from suitable agencies, such as Barnabas Fund, how you could help the persecuted believers practically in these countries.

3. Why is it that, so often, persecuted believers grow spiritually and stand firm in the faith, while those under more tolerant regimes tend to stagnate?

4. Have you experienced suffering or persecution for Jesus's sake? What was your response? What should our reaction be if and when such things come upon us?

Notes

1 **John MacArthur, Jr.,** *1 & 2 Thessalonians* (The MacArthur New Testament Commentary; Chicago: Moody Press, 2002), p. 224.

2 'In Hinduism, nirvana is the extinguishing of worldly desires and attachments, so that the union with God or the Absolute is possible' (**John Bowker, (ed.),** *The Oxford Dictionary of World Religions* (BCA edn.; London: Oxford University Press, 1997), p. 703).

3 **Sinclair B. Ferguson** and **David F. Wright, (eds.),** *New Dictionary of Theology* (Leicester: Inter-Varsity Press, 1988), pp. 697ff.

4 **Gene L. Green,** *The Letters to the Thessalonians* (Grand Rapids, MI: Eerdmans / Leicester: Apollos, 2002), p. 278.

5 **Andrew H. Trotter, Jr.,** 'Grace', in **Walter A. Elwell, (ed.),** *Evangelical Dictionary of Biblical Theology* (Grand Rapids, MI: Baker / Carlisle: Paternoster, 1996), p. 314.

6 **Green,** *Letters*, p. 86.

7 **Elwell,** *Dictionary of Biblical Theology*, p. 315.

8 **Richard Francis Weymouth,** *Weymouth's New Testament in Modern Speech* (London: James Clarke & Co., [n.d.]).

9 *Jamieson, Fausset and Brown Commentary* (PC Study Bible; Seattle, WA: Biblesoft, 2006). Henceforth referred to as JFB.

10 **MacArthur,** *1 & 2 Thessalonians*, p. 230.

11 **F. F. Bruce,** *1 & 2 Thessalonians* (Word Biblical Commentary; Nashville: Thomas Nelson, 1982), p. 144.

12 In a fine sixteen-page essay on *agapē* and *agapan* **William Barclay** writes, 'Love is practical (Heb. 6:10; 1 John 3:18). It is not merely a kindly feeling, and it does not limit itself to pious good wishes; it is love which issues in action' (*New Testament Words* (London: SCM, 1964), p. 28).

13 **Alexander Rattray Hay,** *The New Testament Order for Church and Ministry* (Barnston: New Testament Missionary Union, 1947), pp. 290f.

14 **Captain E. G. Carré, (ed.),** *The Life of John 'Praying' Hyde* (South Plainfield, NJ: Bridge Publishing, [n.d.]).

15 Mention is made of these and others in **D. M. M'Intyre,** *The Hidden Life of Prayer* (Stirling: Stirling Tract Enterprise/Marshall, Morgan & Scott, [n.d.]).

16 **Bruce,** *1 & 2 Thessalonians*, p. 145.

17 **Barclay,** *New Testament Words*, p. 144.

18 **W. E. Vine,** 'Token', in *Expository Dictionary of New Testament Words*, vol. iv (London: Oliphants, 1973), p. 141.

19 Psalm 73 is actually ascribed to Asaph, though JFB speaks of David being perplexed.

20 JFB.

21 **Matthew Henry** on 2 Thes. 1:5 in *Commentary on 2 Thessalonians*, in *Commentary on the Whole Bible* (PC Study Bible; Seattle, WA: Biblesoft, 2006).

22 Ibid.

23 **Bruce,** *1 & 2 Thessalonians*, p. 149.

24 **Green,** *Letters*, p. 286.

25 Ibid. p. 287.

26 A frequent charge. See **J. Stevenson, (ed.),** *A New Eusebius: Documents Illustrative of the History of the Church to AD 337* (London: SPCK, 1960), pp. 8, 19, 21, 62, 71.

27 **Charles Wesley,** 'Hark! The Herald Angels Sing', 1739.

28 See also Gen. 16:7–13; 18:1–2; 19:1, 15; 21:17; 22:15; 24:7, 40; 28:12; 31:11; 32:1; Exod. 3:2; Num. 22:22–27, 31–35; Josh. 5:13–15; Judg. 2:1–4; 6:11–24; 13:2–25; 2 Sam. 24:16–17; 1 Kings 19:5, 7; 2 Kings 1:3, 15; 19:35; Zech. 1:9–14; 2:3; 3:1–6; 4:1, 4–5; 5:5, 10; 6:4–5; Matt. 1:20–25; 2:13, 19; 4:11; 28:1–8; Mark 16:5–8; Luke 1:11–20, 26–38; 22:43; 24:4–7; John 20:12–13; Acts 5:19; 8:26; 10:3, 7; 12:7–10; 27:23.

29 Bruce, *1 & 2 Thessalonians*, p. 150.

30 John Owen, *An Exposition of the Epistle to the Hebrews*, vol. iv (Grand Rapids, MI: Baker, 1980), pp. 215ff. and 256ff.

31 This is a massively powerful army. Consider what one angel did in 2 Kings 19:35–37, when he killed 185,000 Assyrians. What could twelve legions do?

32 The phrase 'in flaming fire' is identical to the phrase in the LXX (*en puri phlogos* or *en phlogi puros*) at Exod. 3:2, which may be why Justin argues that it was Christ before his incarnation who appeared to Moses (**Bruce,** *1 & 2 Thessalonians*, p. 150).

33 Bruce, *1 & 2 Thessalonians*, p. 151.

34 JFB.

35 See, for example, Exod. 13:21–22; 14:24; 24:17; Lev. 9:23–24; 10:2; Num. 9:15–16; 11:1–3; 14:14; 16:35; 26:10; Deut. 1:33; 4:11–12, 15, 24, 33, 36; 5:4–5, 22–26; 9:3, 10, 15; 10:4; 18:15–16; 32:22; 2 Sam. 22:9, 13; 1 Kings 18:24, 38; 2 Kings 1:10, 12; 2:11; 6:17; 2 Chr. 7:1, 3; Neh. 9:12, 19; Ps. 11:6; 18:8, 12–13; 21:9; 50:3; 68:2; Isa. 66:15–16.

36 Green, *Letters*, p. 292.

37 Edward Donnelly, *Biblical Teaching on the Doctrines of Heaven and Hell* (Edinburgh: Banner of Truth, 2001), p. 25.

38 Ibid. pp. 27f.

39 For a fuller explanation see **Donnelly,** *Doctrines of Heaven and Hell*, pp. 40ff.

40 JFB.

41 'Destroy, Destruction', in **Vine,** *Expository Dictionary*, vol. i, p. 304.

42 See also 'Destroy, Destruction', in **Elwell,** *Dictionary of Biblical Theology*, pp. 168ff.

43 Bruce, *1 & 2 Thessalonians*, p. 155.

44 Other references to 'one another' include loving one another (John 13:34–35; 15:12–13, 17; 1 Thes. 3:12; 4:9–10; 1 Peter 1:22; 1 John 3:11, 23; 4:7, 11–12; 2 John 5); being kind to one another (Eph. 4:32); preferring one another (Rom. 12:10); tolerating or being patient with one another (Eph. 4:2; Col. 3:13); and being of the same mind (Rom. 12:16; 15:5). Our relations with one another include remaining at peace with one another (Mark 9:50); remembering that we are members of one another (Rom. 12:5; Eph. 4:25); submitting to one another (Eph. 5:21; 1 Peter 5:5); confessing our faults to one another (James 5:16); and having fellowship with one another (1 John 1:7). Our courtesy towards one another should include greeting one another (Rom. 16:16; 1 Cor. 16:20; 1 Peter 5:14; 2 Cor. 13:12); caring for one another (1 Cor. 12:25); considering one another (Heb. 10:24); waiting for one another (1 Cor. 11:33); and edifying one another (1 Thes. 5:11; compare Rom. 14:19). The other side of the coin is that we should not judge one another wrongly (Rom. 14:13); we must not lie to one another (Col. 3:9), speak evil of one another (James 4:11) or grumble against one another (James 5:9).

45 See **Douglas Kelly,** *If God Already Knows Why Pray?* (Fearn: Christian Focus, 2007).

46 See also Rom. 1:6–7; 8:28, 30; 9:24; 11:29; 1 Cor. 1:2, 9, 24, 26; 7:17–18; Gal. 1:6, 15; 5:8; Eph. 1:18; 4:1, 4; Col. 3:15; 1 Thes. 2:12; 4:7; 5:24; 1 Tim. 6:12; 2 Tim. 1:9; Heb. 3:1; 9:15; 1 Peter 1:15; 2:9, 21; 3:9; 5:10.

47 JFB.

48 From **Thomas Binney,** 'Eternal Light! Eternal Light!', 1826.

49 **Arthur Tappan Pierson,** 'With Harps and with Vials', 1874.

50 The 10/40 window is an area of the world that contains the largest population of non-Christians in the world. The area extends from 10 degrees to 40 degrees north of the equator, and stretches from North Africa to China. (Visit: 1040window.org/; and see '10/40 Window' at: en.wikipedia.org/.)

The great apostasy and the revelation of the Lord from heaven (2 Thes. 2)

Some of the Thessalonian Christians were greatly disturbed by false information they had received to the effect that the Day of the Lord had already come, that is, that Christ had already returned or was about to do so. The apostle reminds them of what he had previously taught, namely, that Christ will not return until two things have happened: a great falling away of professing Christians, and the appearance of a powerful antichrist, the 'man of sin'. Christ will then return in glory and destroy the man of sin. Paul then assures the Thessalonian believers of his prayers and counsels them to stand fast.

Don't be alarmed (vv. 1–2)

Paul now introduces an exhortation by making a respectful and brotherly request to the Thessalonians (see 1 Thes. 4:1; 5:12; compare Phil. 4:3; 2 John 5). The request seems to sound a note of urgency and includes a reminder of the teaching already received as well as an exhortation to take heed to what follows. It concerns the return of Christ and the Thessalonians' attitude towards this event. The apostle had previously written about the suddenness of Christ's return (1 Thes. 5:1–11) and the necessity of being prepared for it. Now it seems that some might have misunderstood the teaching on suddenness to mean immediacy (1 Thes. 5:2–6).

However, this misunderstanding was not only about the Second Advent of Christ, but also about 'our gathering together to Him'.[1] The use of a single definite article links the two events together[2] so that they 'are aspects of the same eschatological consummation and cannot be separated temporally or theologically, as some have suggested'.[3] Paul had already informed them that at the return of Christ neither the living nor the dead would have an advantage, for the resurrected saints and the still-alive saints will be 'caught up together … to meet the Lord in the air' (1 Thes. 4:15–18).

Although this teaching was intended to comfort them, some had begun to panic lest they had somehow missed the great event. The problem was that some extraneous communication had been given which may have suggested that Christ had already returned, or at least that the Day of the Lord had already begun to dawn, and some of the Thessalonian Christians thought they had somehow missed out on it. They thought there had been a 'secret rapture' and that they had been left behind. The apostle now seeks to refute this wrong teaching and provide correct instruction, for no true believer will be left behind.

So Paul urges them not to be suddenly, or hastily, shaken or continually disturbed by whatever they had heard or read that suggested they had been excluded from the great events surrounding our Lord's return (v. 2). The verbs Paul uses suggest that, while the false communication had been received and the shaking had occurred at one particular point in time, their troubled state was ongoing.[4] This reminds us that, while false doctrine may be received in a moment, its effects may be felt for a long time. The Thessalonians are counselled to 'retain their mental equilibrium'.[5] The Lord Jesus Christ himself warned about the possibility of Christians being disturbed about eschatological events (Matt. 24:6; Mark 13:7; Luke 21:8–19).

In these days of promiscuous publishing, especially on the Internet, Christians are more likely to read or hear contrary teaching than ever before. The multiplicity of media is a mixed blessing. Radio, television and the Internet can all be put to good and profitable use, but they can all be channels of error, too. Some Christians seem to believe anything they see in print, and this danger applies just as much to the Internet, if not more so. Pastors need constantly to guard the flock (Acts 20:28) and to instruct them on how to be discerning, founding them on the Scriptures and warning them against false teaching. Not every web site, or radio or television message (or, for that matter, every sermon preached) can be trusted, although faithful pastors will seek to guard their own pulpits. Every religious message that is heard 'needs to be examined through the lens of apostolic teaching as contained in Scripture'.[6] Here, however, a note of caution needs to be sounded. It is possible to become so extreme in smelling out errors that every slight deviation or opinion that varies from the self-appointed 'devious-doctrine detector' is jumped upon.

When I was a student at Bible college, a fellow-student, who was going abroad, disposed of a box of books. As I and other students knelt by the box to share them out I asked one if he would like a certain book by a well-known evangelical preacher. 'No, thank you,' he replied quite firmly. 'Why not?' I asked, anxious to learn. 'Because in the parable of the sower he interprets the seed sown as persons,' he replied. So because of one perceived error the whole of that godly man's teaching was rejected.

On one occasion when I was preaching, I mentioned a number of biographies that would benefit those who read them. Afterwards a man accosted me and charged me with leading people astray because I mentioned in my list the name of one particular godly and famous evangelical preacher, who, this man alleged, had gone astray in his latter years (a charge I knew to be false). This man subsequently sent me more than fifty pages copied from magazines and the Internet criticizing this preacher. So while we must be careful not to be led astray by false doctrine, we must also avoid the Pharisaical habit of condemning every opinion that deviates from our own.

SHAKEN BY FALSE TEACHING (V. 2)

The Thessalonians must have been badly shaken by this supposed revelation because the same word translated 'shaken' (*saleuthēnai*) is used of the shaking of the foundations of the prison when the earthquake occurred in Acts 16:26 (see also Matt. 11:7; 24:29; Luke 6:38; Acts 4:31; Heb. 12:26). This word is qualified by 'soon' (or 'quickly'; *tacheōs*). The NIV renders the phrase 'easily unsettled'. Notice that they were not to be shaken 'in mind' (*noos*) or understanding. They were not to change their opinions so quickly, switching from the teaching they had previously received from the apostles.[7]

There is a dangerous anti-scriptural trend to contrast the head and the heart. Generally speaking, when people use that contrast they are differentiating between knowing a mere fact (head-knowledge) and having a deep conviction (heart-knowledge). However, that distinction is unscriptural because when the Bible uses the word 'heart', more often than not it means the mind.[8] The danger of this false distinction is that some Christians come to believe that feelings and emotions are more important than knowledge. Gordon H. Clark writes, 'In our day the anti-scriptural contrast between the head and the heart has vitiated the personal Christianity of thousands of believers ... this widespread denigration of the intellect and therefore of the truth, has resulted in minimizing all deception on the ground that knowledge is worthless, while feeling, emotion, ecstasy is the essence of sanctification.'[9]

To be unsettled or shaken quickly or easily indicates a measure of immaturity (see 2 Cor. 11:3). They were, after all, fairly new Christians, even though they had progressed so rapidly. Pastors need to ground their young believers securely in the faith as there is so much that could unsettle them in these days. Leading men and women to Christ, or seeing them converted through sermons, is not enough. They need to grow in grace and the knowledge of the Lord Jesus Christ (2 Peter 3:18).

Conversion is the beginning, not the end, of the Christian life. Too many spiritually newborn babies are abandoned at birth!

It is clear that the apostle did not know for certain what the source of this false teaching was, so he covers various possibilities by mentioning 'spirit', a shorthand term for prophecy (e.g. 1 Cor. 12:10; 1 John 4:1–3), 'word' or 'letter, as if from us'. The first would most probably refer to an utterance claiming to be from the Lord, a supposed prophecy. The second would be an address or sermon, or perhaps even a comment on one in a discussion. The third seems to be a forged letter, pretending to be from the apostle himself. Some might have based their misunderstanding upon an 'inspired word' or 'prophecy', while others might have claimed that this is what they understood Paul to have said, either in his preaching or perhaps through a mishearing or misunderstanding when Paul's first letter was read out in the assembly. Forged letters were not uncommon in the first few centuries of the Christian church. Perhaps this is why the apostle tells the Thessalonians that he always signs his own letters himself (3:17).

It is, however, possible that someone had misinterpreted what the apostle had taught either by word of mouth or in his first epistle. F. F. Bruce suggests that 'another possibility is that the Thessalonians had recently been exposed to teaching which moved some of them to accept a realized, or even over-realized eschatology, not unlike that with which Paul takes issue in 1 Cor. 4:8 …'[10] (see 2 Tim. 2:18). Someone could have deliberately set out to misinterpret the apostle's teaching and so deceive the Thessalonian Christians. However it came about, they were being deceived, led astray or deluded into false doctrine (v. 3, *exapataō*—to be deceived thoroughly[11]). Whichever was the medium, the false message was that the Day of the Lord had already come.

Some have suggested that the error assumed that the Day was imminent. But the verb used (*enestēken*) normally means 'is present', not 'is imminent'.[12] A different Greek expression is used by Paul to mean 'at hand' (Phil. 4:5). This teaching had stirred up insecurity concerning the Thessalonians' own part in the coming glory (see vv. 13–17), just as this topic had previously raised concerns about the fate of their departed loved ones (1 Thes. 4:13–18). Paul urges them not to be disturbed. Christians need to be like the Bereans, who searched the Scriptures daily to check what was being taught them (Acts 17:11). The Bereans, it seems, were more careful than the Thessalonians in checking messages by the Scriptures.

Why needn't the Thessalonians have been alarmed? Because that Day would not arrive before something else had occurred (compare Mark 13:7). The return of Christ, Paul teaches, will not occur until certain other things have happened first, including the appearance of 'the man of sin' (v. 3), or 'man of lawlessness' (NIV).

At various times in history Christians have been wrongly informed that the Lord was to return at a certain time, and, in some cases, they have sold everything or gone up to a mountain to wait for him. The Bible does tell us to be ready to meet the Lord at any time, but it does not tell us when he will return. At the time of writing my wife and I have our house on the market in preparation for a move nearer our family. The house has to be ready for inspection by a prospective buyer. But that does not mean we are constantly looking out of the window or waiting by the front door in case someone should come. There is a difference between readiness and expectancy. We must be ready to meet the Lord at any time because, though he may not personally return today, he may take us home to be with him at any time.

Don't be deceived (vv. 3–4)

Leon Morris remarks that this is an 'extraordinarily difficult passage',[13] not least because there is no parallel passage with which to compare it. But what is clear is that Paul cuts the ground from under the feet of the deceivers by explaining that there is no way the Day of the Lord could have arrived because certain outstanding and unmissable events must occur first.

The words 'Let no one deceive you' suggest that a deliberate attempt had been made to lead the Thessalonians astray, either by misinterpreting the apostle's teaching or by introducing false teaching. Christians must not allow themselves to be deceived by any means or in any way, for there are many ways by which the enemy will seek to deceive us. Although Paul is dealing with the particular deception that the Thessalonians had fallen into, he issues a general warning about deception. The New Testament is replete with such warnings.[14]

The Day of the Lord will not come before two things have happened. In the original Greek there is a grammatical ellipsis in verse 3, for Paul does not actually say what it is that must be preceded by these two things. Obviously the Day of the Lord is meant, so the various translations supply the words (as shown in the NKJV by the italics in 'that Day will not come'). The word 'first' does not indicate the order of these two events, but rather states that the two together must precede the Day of the Lord.

There will be a 'falling away', or 'apostasy' (*apostasia*) before Christ's return. Falling away is, sadly, all too common an occurrence. The Lord Jesus Christ warned that this would happen (e.g. Matt. 24:10–12; compare 1 Tim. 4:1). This does not mean that genuine Christians will ultimately fall away and be lost (see John 10:28), even though some may grow cold or backslide for a time (Rev. 2:4; 3:3, 15), but it does mean that many in the professing church will abandon the faith (Matt. 24:10–13; 1 Peter 4:17). John Calvin, preaching on 'The Sure Foundation' in 2 Timothy 2:19, spoke of those who profess to be Christians but prove they are not elect by falling away, remarking, '... it is no small matter to have the souls perish who were bought by the blood of Christ.'[15]

Paul is referring to what is obviously a major event in which political revolt and religious apostasy are combined.[16] The word *apostasia* is preceded by the definite article: *the* falling away.[17]

The other event is that 'the man of sin' or 'lawlessness' will be revealed.[18] Such a figure was foreshadowed in the persecutions of Antiochus Epiphanes (ruled 175–164 BC; see Dan. 7–8;[19] 11:36–45; Mark 13:14–27). 'Lawlessness' is used in the New Testament as a synonym for 'sin' or 'iniquity' (Rom. 4:7; 2 Cor. 6:14; Titus 2:14; Heb. 1:9; 10:17; 1 John 3:4). The falling away will have a leader. 'He is not called "lawless" because he has never heard of God's law, but because he openly defies it!'[20]

The man of lawlessness is not Satan, as he is distinguished from Satan in verse 9. Neither, according to Hendriksen, should he be identified with the beast out of the sea of Revelation 13 and 17. In the Book of Revelation the four beasts of Daniel's prophecy (Dan. 7) are combined into one composite beast, and since the four beasts in Daniel represent kingdoms, the composite beast cannot refer to one person. Hendriksen holds that the beast out of the sea 'must refer to anti-Christian government whenever and wherever it manifests itself'.[21] Nor is the man of lawlessness a personification of a political system or social tendency. The phrases 'exalts himself', 'sits as God' (2 Thes. 2:4) and will be 'slain' (v. 8, RV, ASV and NASB) indicate that an individual is referred to.[22]

Although the word 'Antichrist' is found only in John's epistles, many interpreters identify the man of sin with the Antichrist, because just as the man of sin will be revealed at the end of time, when the returning Lord will destroy him (2:8), so also, according to John's epistles, the Antichrist will come in 'the last hour' (1 John 2:18; compare 4:3; 2 John 7).[23] Antichrist can mean both one who opposes Christ and also one who purports to replace Christ.[24] But as John makes clear, although there will be one individual in which such opposition is focused, there are many antichrists throughout history; the man of lawlessness will be the epitome of all that preceding antichrists have stood for.[25]

The phrase 'son of perdition' (v. 3) means one destined for destruction, who is therefore doomed. The expression is applied to Judas Iscariot in

John 17:12. The term 'destruction' (*apōleias*) means ruin or loss, not of being but of well-being. It may refer to things, signifying their waste (Matt. 26:8; Mark 14:4), or to people, signifying their spiritual and eternal perdition (John 17:12; 1 Tim. 6:9; 2 Peter 3:16).[26] Here the latter usage is in mind (see v. 8), and the term is frequently used in the New Testament of the destruction of those who oppose God and his purposes (Matt. 7:13; Rom. 9:22; Phil. 1:28; 3:19; Heb. 10:39; 2 Peter 3:7; Rev. 17:8, 11).

So the return of Christ will not occur until these two events—the great apostasy and the appearance of the man of sin—have come to pass.

WHO IS THIS PERSON? (V. 4)

The son of perdition wishes to be worshipped as God. It is a fact of history that several Roman emperors wished to be worshipped as God, though none actually sat in the Jewish temple and proclaimed himself to be God. Some early Christians thought this 'son of perdition' was Nero, because of the intensity of the persecution he carried out. But Marcus Aurelius and Diocletian, among others, also persecuted Christians, and, by all accounts, more severely than Nero. The individual at the end of time cannot be a Roman emperor, unless there is to be a resurrected Roman empire.[27]

The identity of the 'temple' in verse 4 has been the subject of much debate. It has been suggested that there is an allusion to the profaning of the temple in Jerusalem by Antiochus Epiphanes in 169 BC, an event that Daniel described as the 'abomination of desolation' (Dan. 9:27; 11:31; 12:11) and which Jesus referred to as prefiguring what would take place before his return (Matt. 24:15; Mark 13:14). However, although such allusions would have been well known to Paul, it is unlikely that the Thessalonians would have had these references in mind. In any case, how could this being sit in the temple of God when the Jerusalem temple, still standing when Paul wrote, would no longer exist?

This thought, together with Ezekiel 40 onwards, has given rise to the idea that the Jewish temple will be rebuilt. But that does not necessarily follow. In the first place, the passages in Ezekiel are almost certainly symbolic. In the second place, the *church* is now the temple of God in which God dwells (1 Cor. 3:16–17; 6:19; Eph. 2:19–22; compare Rev. 3:12).

The idea of a future temple with a Levitical priesthood and animal sacrifices contradicts the New Testament (e.g. Heb. 8:1–10:17), while many details of the proposed temple described in Ezekiel, such as specifications, certain dimensions and the materials to be used, are lacking. The proposed division of the land (Ezek. 47:13–48:35) among the twelve tribes is highly idealized, and a trickle of water becoming a mighty river within a few thousand metres would seem to be impossible (Ezek. 47:1–12). Consequently, Duane A. Garrett writes, '[Ezekiel's] vision is a prophet-priest's portrayal of the glories of the kingdom of God. The calamity of the exile has been reversed. Worship is orderly and beautiful. Leadership is subservient to God. There is a place for every one of God's people, and there is neither want nor need. Most importantly of all, the Lord is there (48:35).'[28]

It is easy to see, therefore, that this prediction in 2 Thessalonians could be fulfilled by some powerful figure taking authority in the church, opposing what the Bible teaches about God and claiming deity. However, Bruce thinks this meaning is unlikely as there was no united church organization at the time when Paul wrote, so such an idea would not occur to the readers. He suggests that the Jerusalem temple is in view, but understood in a metaphorical sense, equivalent to the son of perdition taking his seat on the throne of God; in other words, usurping both the divinity and the authority of God.[29]

In any case, this person sets himself up above 'all that is called God', so all religions are included, not just the Christian church (compare Acts 17:23; 1 Cor. 8:5; Dan. 11:36–37). This would include such religions as the emperor cult. In AD 27 Emperor Octavian received the title 'Augustus' and his divination was celebrated throughout the empire. A temple devoted to him was built in Thessalonica, so the Thessalonians would have recognized such allusions. It is total authority over all religions that is predicted of the man of lawlessness.

Remember what you have been taught (vv. 5–6)

The Thessalonians were not to be deceived into thinking that the return of Christ had already occurred. The apostle gently chides them by asking, 'Do you not remember … I told you these things?' Paul thus reminds them of what he had continually taught them while with them. This was not new information. The Thessalonians had already received enough teaching to enable them to evaluate and reject the false doctrine. The apostle repeatedly reminds them of what he had taught (1 Thes. 2:9; 3:4; 4:1–2; 5:1–2; 2 Thes. 3:10). If only we knew what he had said! What must have been clear to them in this reminder, since they had heard his teaching, is obscure to us. However, the Lord has given us all we need to know about the return of Christ. It seems they may have forgotten or misapplied some of Paul's teaching, or perhaps simply failed to apply what they knew. This is still a human problem today.

How many Christians cannot remember what was preached the previous Sunday? Just as serious a problem today, if not more serious than forgetting what has been preached, is the failure to apply it to our lives. This is probably the greatest failure in the church today, especially in the West: the failure to apply the Word of God to our daily living. If the teaching is true, as confirmed by a study of the Word of God, and is relevant to our lives today, how can Christians be helped to remember and apply what has been taught? One way is to take notes of the sermon—a valuable discipline. Another way is to get a recording of the message and listen to it again; but it takes as long to hear the recording as it did to listen to the sermon in the first place. This technology was obviously not available to the Thessalonians. But even having the notes in our heads or on paper, or even in digital form, does not deal with the problem. Carefully-considered, prayerful obedience is what is required (Luke 6:46; Matt. 7:24–27; John 15:14).

There are, however, three simple techniques that can help our memories; these were available to the Thessalonians and are equally available to us:

- Listen carefully—intently—with the intention of remembering (Luke 8:18). This may be helped by taking brief notes.
- Meditate on the message heard (Josh. 1:8; Ps. 1:2). This technique seems to be much neglected today. It means thinking about the message, turning it over in our minds, and seeking to apply it to our lives and situations. Thomas Watson wrote, 'A Christian without meditation is like a soldier without arms, or a workman without tools. Without meditation the truths of God will not stay with us; the heart is hard, and the memory slippery, and without meditation all is lost.'[30]
- Talk about it to others (Mal. 3:16). This may be in a formal or informal discussion, or even just repeating the gist or main thoughts of the sermon to others.

One authority has said that half the new material taken in is forgotten after the first half-hour; two-thirds after nine hours; three-quarters after six days; and four-fifths after a month. But that has to be qualified by the way we take things in and what we do with what we hear.

For example, broadly speaking, the average person who pays attention to a sermon or lecture will remember only 10 per cent of what he or she hears, but up to 70 per cent of what he or she says, discusses or repeats. Perhaps after every good sermon, or after our personal Bible reading, we ought to ask ourselves, 'What am I going to do about this?' We should at least ask ourselves, 'Is there something in this sermon or passage I need to do?'

'YOU KNOW' (V. 6)

The Thessalonian Christians had obviously been taught about these things by Paul, so again they knew what he was referring to. We, however, do not. Even St Augustine admitted that he was unable to discover what Paul meant.[31] What or who was restraining this power or person of lawlessness? Some have suggested that this restraining power is the Holy Spirit. But there is no biblical evidence that the Spirit will be taken away, especially in the light of Jesus's promise that he will abide with believers for ever (John 14:16). However, others, mainly those holding a dispensationalist view of eschatology, believe this refers to the rapture, so when all believers are snatched away, the Holy Spirit will go with them.[32] John MacArthur, himself a dispensationalist, rejects this interpretation, stating that it is 'impossible' that the Holy Spirit should be removed from the world at that time, as he is omnipresent.[33]

Many scholars, following Tertullian (c. AD 160–c. AD 220), suggest that the power restraining the man of lawlessness was the Roman empire, with its imposed law and order. F. F. Bruce remarks that '… a certain reticence can be detected in the references made to [this restraining power] in the letters; this can best be explained if more explicit language was liable to cause trouble should the letter fall into the wrong hands.'[34]

Fresh in the memories of both the Thessalonians and the apostles would have been the riots fomented under the pretext that the apostles were 'acting contrary to the decrees of Caesar, saying there is another king—Jesus' (Acts 17:5–8). Though the Roman empire has long since gone, the principle of law and order, in varying degrees and in different ways, remains. The best interpretation would seem to be 'the power of well-ordered human rule'. If this interpretation is correct, it seems that Paul is saying that, as long as law and order prevail, the man of lawlessness will be unable to be revealed with his 'program of unprecedented unrighteousness, blasphemy and persecution'.[35]

God is sovereign and he sets up rulers and authorities so that total anarchy and the complete victory of evil cannot occur (Rom. 13:1; compare Dan. 4:34–35; Titus 3:1; 1 Peter 2:13). If the man of sin had been allowed to come forth in the days when Paul was writing, humanly speaking, the church might have been overwhelmed at birth. This restraining power seems to be impersonal, perhaps a principle ('what is restraining', v. 6) and yet personal ('He who now restrains', v. 7).

We should note, however, that some scholars, finding difficulty with the idea of a restraining power or person, interpret the participle normally translated 'restraining' (*to katechōn*, neuter, v. 6) or 'restrains' (*ho katechōn*, masculine, v. 7) in quite a different way. They see this term as being in some way aligned with 'the man of sin' and so interpret this word as meaning 'seized' or 'possessed' rather than 'restrains'. They thus see this admittedly difficult passage as referring to someone who is 'possessed', or to the power of demonic possession which is already at work in the world.

According to this view, before Christ comes, this demonically possessed person, or power of demon possession, will give way to the man of lawlessness. Instead of interpreting verse 7 as a restraining power being taken out of the way, they understand it in an active sense, as the possessed one stepping aside for the revelation of the man of lawlessness.[36]

Another approach understands the two participles (*to katechōn*, v. 6, and *ho katechōn*, v. 7) to mean 'possessing', 'ruling over', 'holding sway' or 'prevailing'. That which holds sway is 'the mystery of lawlessness'. This power, personified as 'he', prevails until he is out of the way, when the man of lawlessness will be revealed. The general idea is that a power of lawlessness or iniquity now prevails which, before Christ returns, will give way to the personification of rebellion and lawlessness in the man of sin.[37]

The mystery of iniquity (vv. 7–12)

The word translated 'mystery' in the New Testament means something that is hidden or secret, rather than something which is unintelligible. With regard to the expression 'the mystery of lawlessness' (v. 7), Leon Morris wisely comments, 'We can never, by our own reasoning, plumb the depths of iniquity, the reason for its existence, or the manner of its working.'[38] This hidden corruption was already at work, even within the church.

The way Paul deals with problems in his other epistles, especially in 1 Corinthians and Colossians, illustrates that fact. Pastors need to warn their flocks about false doctrines and practices. I know of one church in recent years, where, after a godly pastor left, disaster struck in the form of false doctrine. One of the leaders remarked, 'Our pastor taught us carefully what was right, but never warned us about what was wrong.'

Some years ago, when a booklet was published by a fellowship of churches exposing the dangers of the 'Toronto Blessing', a minister stood up in that fellowship's National Council and objected, saying that they should not publish negative publications but only positive ones. If that attitude had been taken by the apostles, much of the New Testament would never have been written!

In a sermon on 2 Timothy 2:16–18, John Calvin wrote,

When he nameth Hymeneus and Philetus, he showeth that we must not spare them, who, like scabby sheep, may infect the flock, but we must rather tell everyone, what kind of men they are, that they may beware of them. Are we not traitors to our neighbours when we see them in danger of being turned from God, and do not inform them of it? A wicked man that goeth about to establish perverse doctrine, and cause offences in the church, what is he but an impostor? If I dissemble when I see him, is it not as though I should see my neighbour in danger, and would not bid him beware?

If the life of the body ought to be so precious to us that we would do all in our power to preserve it, of how much more importance is the life of the soul!

Those who endeavour to turn everything upside down, will come and sow their false doctrine among the people, in order to draw them into a contempt of God. These ... are they that have erred, and endeavoured to overthrow the faith of the church: and yet we suffer them. Men will frequently say, must we be at defiance with them? Must we cast them off, that they may fall into despair? This is said by those who think we ought to use gentleness; but what mercy is it to spare one man, and in the mean time to cast away a thousand souls, rather than warn them? ...

Satan cometh with his poison and plagues, that he may destroy all. We see the flock of God troubled and tormented with ravenous wolves, that devour and destroy whatsoever they can. Must we be moved with mercy towards a wolf; and in the mean time let the poor sheep and lambs of which our Lord hath such a special care, let them, I say, perish? When we see any wicked man troubling the church, either by offences or false doctrine, we must prevent him as much as lieth in our power: we must warn the simple, that they be not misled and carried away; this, I say, is our duty.39

We must resist corruption and false teaching. But there is a restraining power beyond what pastors and teachers can accomplish. The implication of this passage is that one day this restraining power or person will be removed and evil will be allowed full rein.

As we have seen, the Holy Spirit himself cannot be removed. However, if the one who restrains is understood to be the Holy Spirit, it could mean that the Holy Spirit's influence, in terms of his restraining power, will be withdrawn from influencing authorities. More likely is the suggestion mentioned above (under v. 6) that the Roman empire's principle of law and order is referred to, in which case this could extend to the general principle of law in society.40 Evil, as an impersonal force, ever threatens to boil over in society, and will continue to do so; hence the need for the rule of law (Rom. 13:1–7).

THE LAWLESS ONE DESTROYED (V. 8)

'[T]hen' contrasts with the 'now' of verse 6. The man of lawlessness will be 'revealed'. Three times Paul uses this verb to describe the man's appearance, emphasizing that this is no ordinary person coming on the scene, but one associated with the supernatural. This unleashed manifestation of lawlessness will find its focus in one person, the man of lawlessness.

The apostle John, in his first epistle, refers to 'the Antichrist', but points out that there are many 'antichrists' (1 John 2:18; 4:3). In some sense the man of lawlessness may be identified with the Antichrist. There is the ongoing historical aspect ('lawlessness', v. 7, and 'many antichrists', 1 John 2:18) with the final personification of lawlessness and opposition to Christ. The apparent triumph of evil will, however, be short lived. Christ will decisively defeat the man of lawlessness.

When this personification of evil is revealed, the Lord will overthrow and destroy him. There will be a twofold destruction, or two instruments of destruction. The 'breath of His mouth' may refer to the Holy Spirit (Gen. 2:7; John 20:22), or the Holy Scriptures which are 'God-breathed' (2 Tim. 3:16), but more likely refers to Christ's own personal power. Christ's breath will 'consume' the man of lawlessness (*analiskō—expend, consume, destroy*). This matches the picture in Revelation in which Christ goes out on a white horse to make war, with 'a sharp sword' coming out of his mouth (Rev. 1:16; 19:15, 21; compare Eph. 6:17; Isa. 11:4). The Word of God, which is the 'sword of the Spirit' (Eph. 6:17), is the weapon God uses throughout history to make war with evil. This is the instrument we must use today to defeat evil and to accomplish God's will in our lives and in the church.

The other power which will destroy the man of lawlessness is the appearing (*epiphaneia*) of Christ, translated here as 'the brightness of [Christ's] coming'. In other words, this is not so much an instrument as the presence of the Lord himself. The word *epiphaneia* means basically 'appearing' and was used of a Roman emperor visiting a city, though with implications of splendour or even divinity (see also 1 Tim. 6:14;

2 Tim. 1:10; 4:1, 8; Titus 2:13).[41] But it is very appropriate to include the idea of brightness, as the Lord, when he appears will be glorious (1:7–10; compare Rev. 1:12–17). Moreover, the word has been translated as 'dawning'.[42] The mere appearance of the Lord in all his glory is enough to put an end to the man of sin.

The word used here for 'destroy' (*katargeō*—to abolish, destroy, make void, utterly defeat; compare Rom. 3:31; 4:14; 1 Cor. 1:28; Gal. 3:17; Eph. 2:15; 2 Tim. 1:10) is stronger than *analiskō* (consume), in that it implies that Christ will bring the enemy to nothing; he will completely dispose of him. Paul repeatedly uses this verb in connection with the final judgement (1 Cor. 2:6; 6:13; 15:24, 26; 2 Tim. 1:10).

A foretaste—a mere glimmer—of this brightness was witnessed by three privileged apostles on the Mount of Transfiguration, when Christ's glory momentarily broke through the veil of his flesh (Matt. 17:2; Mark 9:3; compare 2 Peter 1:17–18). Already in this letter the apostle has referred to Christ being revealed from heaven 'in flaming fire' (1:8). There are hints throughout Scripture of the manifestation of God being linked with fire (e.g. Gen. 15:17; Exod. 3:2–3; 19:18; Ezek. 1:4; Heb. 12:29). When John saw the glorified Son of Man in his vision on Patmos, Christ's eyes were like a 'flame of fire' and his face was 'like the sun shining in its strength' (Rev. 1:14, 16). When God's glory is revealed, evil must flee, dissolve or be destroyed.

THE LAWLESS ONE DEFINED (V. 9)

Paul does not underestimate the man of sin. He will be destroyed, not because he is weak, but because the Saviour is infinitely stronger. Immature Christians sometimes make derogatory remarks or jokes about Satan, or foolishly challenge evil spirits, but we are safe only because we are in Christ, not because the enemy is weak. A thoughtful reading of Jude 8–9 should correct this error.

The 'coming' of the lawless one will be in accordance with the powerful activity of Satan, his master.[43] There will be a mighty display of power, supernatural events and wonders. But all this display will be based upon falsehood, which originates in unrighteousness. The word 'coming' is *parousia*, or presence, which, according to Bruce, 'probably suggests a parody of Christ's parousia'.[44] This seems to be confirmed by the fact that the apostle Peter uses the same three words—'power' (or 'miracles'), 'signs' and 'wonders'—of the works of Jesus in Acts 2:22 (compare Acts 2:43; Gal. 3:5; Heb. 2:4).

The words 'lawless one' do not appear in the original Greek. Since this may confuse readers, translators have quite rightly inserted the words to make it clear whose 'coming' is being referred to. We see also that the lawless one, or man of sin, is distinguished from Satan, though Satan works through him. Indeed, he works powerfully in signs and wonders (compare Matt. 24:24). Note, however, that they are 'lying' wonders; it is not that they are not real, but that they do not express the truth. As Os Guinness writes, 'Reality is not to be mistaken for legitimacy.'[45] Some real supernatural events, signs and wonders are Satanic in origin.

It is most important that Christians realize that manifestations of power—such as people falling down, or supernatural signs and other things that cause people to be amazed—do not necessarily indicate the presence or working of God. The Lord Jesus Christ made that abundantly clear in Matthew's Gospel: 'Many will say to Me in that day, "Lord, Lord, have we not prophesied in Your name, cast out demons in Your name, and done many wonders in Your name?" And then I will declare to them, "I never knew you; depart from Me, you who practice lawlessness!"' (Matt. 7:22–23).

UNRIGHTEOUS DECEPTION (V. 10)

This man of sin will make himself known 'with every art that cunning can invent and unrighteousness suggest, in order to delude and deceive'.[46] This appearance of the man of lawlessness will deceive those who are perishing (compare 1 Cor. 1:18; 2 Cor. 2:15; 4:3). Those taken in by this unrighteous deception (literally, 'deceit of unrighteousness') will eventually perish, because they did not accept the love of the truth. Refusal to believe the truth lays a person open to all kinds of errors. 'To embrace error, however powerfully and plausibly it may be presented, is dangerous business. In our age, when truth is increasingly viewed as relative and personal, thoughts about the power and consequence of embracing error move to the periphery.'[47]

True Christians may be temporarily deceived, but the elect of God can never finally perish (John 10:27–28). What is it that keeps people from being deceived and so lost? It is receiving the 'love of the truth'. It is not merely knowing the truth; the devils know the truth and tremble (James 2:19). Rather it is loving the truth, embracing it, considering it the most important thing to know. A person's eternal destiny is 'bound up with his or her relation to the truth'.[48] Receiving the love of the truth is the way to be saved. Jesus said, 'I am the way, the truth, and the life. No one comes to the Father except through me' (John 14:6). Receiving the love of the truth is equivalent to receiving Christ, who is the truth (John 1:12–13).

A STRONG DELUSION (V. 11)

Those who do not receive the love of the truth but have 'pleasure in unrighteousness' (v. 12) will therefore be given by God a 'strong delusion' to occupy their minds (*energeia*—strong, working, active). They will become deluded or confused, unable to distinguish truth from error. When people deliberately choose unrighteousness or unbelief, God, after giving them time to repent, confirms them in their unbelief. Pharaoh is an example. When faced by the miracles performed by Moses and Aaron, he at first hardened his heart himself. After he did this several times, the Lord confirmed his stubbornness and hardened his heart for him. This was a judicial hardening (see Exod. 7:13–14, 22; 8:15, 32; 9:7, 12, 35; 10:20, 27; 11:10). When King Ahab of Israel hated God's true prophets, the Lord permitted him to be deceived by a lying spirit in the mouths of the false prophets (2 Chr. 18:1–22). When people pursue impurity, God gives them up to it (Rom. 1:24, 26, 28; compare 11:8).

We should bear in mind, however, that God is not 'the deliberate author of this infatuation',[49] but rather it is the 'god of this age' who has blinded their minds (2 Cor. 4:4). The same principle is found in Revelation 22:11: 'He who is unjust, let him be unjust still; he who is filthy, let him be filthy still ...' Once people are in this state, they will believe anything. A current example is the atheistic evolutionist who, seeing the incredible beauty and design in nature, stubbornly insists that it came about by chance. Some evolutionists have even suggested that beings from another planet brought life to the earth![50] They will not believe the truth so are ensnared by a lie.

This verse expresses an important truth concerning moral law. There is no moral law independently of God. Nor is there, as some imagine, a contest between Satan and God, with God being slightly stronger. The fact is, Satan is a created being with limited powers; God is the almighty Creator.

Leon Morris puts it succinctly: 'God is using the very evil that people (and even Satan) do for the working out of his purpose. They think that they are acting in defiance of him, but in the end they find that those very acts in which they expressed their defiance were the vehicle of their punishment.'[51]

UNBELIEF RESULTS IN CONDEMNATION (V. 12)

Because they will not believe the truth, which involves rejecting unrighteousness, they will be condemned (*krinō*). At the final judgement all the deluded ones will be condemned.

'The Greek word—*krinō*—means to judge, determine, decide; and then to condemn: Rom. 2:27; 14:22; James 4:11; John 7:51; Luke 19:22; Acts 13:27. It may be applied to the judgement of the last day (John 5:22;

8:50; Acts 17:31; Rom. 3:6; 2 Tim. 4:1), but not necessarily.'[52] In this context it implies condemnation, but the emphasis is upon the justice of God's act.

Unbelief is usually a matter of morality, because truth and falsehood have 'moral implications'.[53] People who take pleasure in unrighteousness love their sins and will not give them up (Rom. 1:32; 2:8). There is a double contrast here between truth and unrighteousness (*adikia*—wickedness) and between not believing and delighting in. Taking pleasure in unrighteousness of necessity means disbelieving the truth (Rom. 1:18). To believe the truth requires repentance.

Stand fast in the truth (vv. 13–15)

CHOSEN BY GOD (V. 13)

Paul now resumes the theme of thanksgiving expressed in the introduction (1:3). Now that the Thessalonians' uncertainty has been dealt with and the matter of the man of sin cleared up, he confesses to a duty, a strong desire, to thank God for the Thessalonians, who are beloved by God. He does not congratulate himself on the effect of his preaching, but rather acknowledges the true source of salvation: God himself.

The fact that Paul 'always' gives thanks for them not only reveals Paul's constant thankfulness but suggests the Thessalonians' consistency. Ministers are sometimes constantly concerned about particular church members, whether because of their erratic walk or their lukewarm faith (see Rev. 3:15–16). How encouraging it is to have church members who are constant, and for whom we can always give heartfelt thanks!

The first word 'But ...' expresses a contrast between those he has just mentioned and the Thessalonians. The damnation of the lost is contrasted with the salvation of Paul's converts. They have been chosen (*haireomai*—to take or choose for the purpose of showing special favour[54]) by God 'from the beginning'. This must mean that they were chosen from before creation (Eph. 1:4–5; Rom. 8:29–30). An alternative reading of 'from the beginning' (*ap' archēs*) is 'firstfruits' (*aparchēn*), for which the textual evidence is slightly stronger.[55] In this case they would be the first converts in Thessalonica.

How is this election worked out in time? Through 'sanctification by the Spirit and belief in the truth', which are the Godward and manward aspects of salvation (*en hagiasmos*—sanctification, holiness, consecration, with *en* used in an instrumental sense). God works by his Spirit and grants the gifts of repentance and faith which those chosen then exercise (Eph. 2:8–9; Acts 5:31; 11:18; 2 Tim. 2:25). Sanctification and belief in the truth are not the causes of election but the means God uses to save people. We are saved, not *because of* sanctification and faith, but *through* sanctification and faith. Paul has already taught the Thessalonians that sanctification is both God's will (1 Thes. 4:3, 7) and God's work (1 Thes. 5:23), but they are not to be passive (1 Thes. 4:3–8). Sanctification is an ongoing work of the Holy Spirit in time (1 Cor. 6:11) and it will be completed when Christ returns and is 'glorified in his saints' (1:10; compare Rom. 15:16; 1 Cor. 15:51–54; 1 Thes. 5:23; 1 Peter 1:2; 1 John 3:2–3).

CALLED BY THE GOSPEL (V. 14)

God issues the call to salvation through the gospel (1 Thes. 2:12; 4:7; 5:24; compare Gal. 1:6–7). Paul gives a brief summary of the facts of the good news in 1 Corinthians 15:1–8. Preaching the gospel is the means God normally employs to call sinners to salvation, though sometimes the call comes directly, as in the ministry of Jesus and the conversion of Saul of Tarsus (Acts 9). Whichever way the call comes, it is God who calls, not man (Rom. 8:30; 1 Cor. 1:9; Gal. 1:6, 15; 5:8; 2 Tim. 1:8–9; 1 Peter 1:15; 2:9; 5:10; 2 Peter 1:3).

This call does not rely upon the eloquence of the preacher but on the power of God (1 Cor. 2:1–5). Salvation is not a mere alternative way of life, or an opinion some may hold; it is a transforming experience in which the believer is brought from guilt to pardon (Acts 10:36, 43; 13:38–39; Rom. 5:1; 8:1), from slavery to freedom (Gal. 3:13, 22–26; 4:1–7), from blindness to sight (Luke 4:18; John 8:12; 9:25; 12:46; Acts 26:18; 2 Cor. 4:4–6), from alienation to a share in divine citizenship (Eph. 2:11–13, 19; Phil. 3:20) and from death to life (Eph. 2:1, 5; Col. 2:13; compare Rom. 6:4–5). Its wonder and beauty are encapsulated in the phrase 'the glory of our Lord Jesus Christ'. We are called to glory (Rom. 5:2; 8:17–18, 30; Col. 1:27; 1 Thes. 2:12; 1 Peter 5:10; compare John 17:22, 24).

However, a note of caution needs to be sounded here. Not all Christians have a dramatic or dynamic conversion, especially those converted in their youth. Many Christians do not realize what wonderful things have happened to them, still less what is laid up for them, until they are taught about them. This is precisely what Scripture is doing in the verses cited above. Christians need to be taught about these blessings and thus enter into the enjoyment, appreciation and experience of them.

THEREFORE STAND FAST (V. 15)

'[S]tand fast' comes from the Greek *stēkete* (present imperative: 'go on standing'; compare Rom. 14:4; 1 Cor. 16:13; Phil. 1:27; 4:1). Paul encourages his readers to stand firm as though his life depended on it (1 Thes. 3:8). In view of their amazing destiny, all Christians must be encouraged to stand fast. At times in this life, everything may seem to be against us, but the prospect of eternal glory with Christ is an enormous encouragement to remain steadfast in our beliefs and practices in the face of opposition, discouragement or persecution.

One way of doing this is to hold firmly to the traditions taught by the apostles in word and writing—'our epistle': not to teaching coming from another source (1 Cor. 11:2; compare Gal. 1:14; Col. 2:8). In fact, in this context, Paul's main concern is that they 'stand fast' in the teaching they have received (compare Acts 2:42; Eph. 4:14). The apostles were the channel of communication from Christ, and the Holy Spirit led them into all truth so that they could 'teach others also' (2 Tim. 2:2). Paul passed on what he had received (Gal. 1:11–12; compare John 15:26–27; 16:13–14; 1 Cor. 11:2, 23; 2 Tim. 1:13; 2:2; Heb. 2:3).

There are good traditions and there are bad traditions. The good traditions are those passed down from Christ and his apostles (1 Cor. 11:2, 23; compare Rom. 6:17; Jude 3). The bad traditions are those man-made ones which contradict or distort the truth (Matt. 15:2–3; Mark 7:3, 5, 8–9, 13; Col. 2:8). Such dangerous traditions are still being produced.

A prayer for his readers (vv. 16–17)

These two verses are equivalent to a prayer that the Lord Jesus Christ and God the Father will comfort and strengthen the Thessalonian believers. Although both the Lord Jesus Christ and God the Father are grammatical subjects in the sentence, the verbs 'comfort' and 'establish' are in the singular, which again stresses their unity. Here the Lord Jesus Christ precedes God the Father, whereas in 1 Thessalonians 3:11 God the Father is named first. The Father and the Son are 'so completely united in action that either may be named before the other without making any difference to the sense'.[56]

The Thessalonians will not be able to stand fast and cling to the authentic traditions unless God in Christ encourages and strengthens their hearts. The linking of Christ's name with that of God the Father underlines his deity. The 'consolation' that God has already given them is not temporary, nor ephemeral, but 'everlasting'. It is based upon the love of God for them (Rom. 8:37; Gal. 2:20; John 3:16; 1 John 4:9). God has also given them 'good hope by grace' (compare Rom. 15:4, 13).

The prayer is that God will 'comfort' (compare 2 Cor. 1:3–4), that is, strengthen, their hearts (the whole inner man), and 'establish' them in 'every good word and work'. Words and deeds must go together. Deeds authenticate the words; words explain the deeds (see Matt. 5:16; Luke 24:19; Acts 7:22).

Christians are always in need of encouragement. Our speech and service, words and work should not only be good but also ongoing. They should not be merely a flash in the pan, an occasional word of witness or a good deed, but an established pattern of godly living. The New Testament contains a strong emphasis upon 'good works' (see Rom. 2:7; 2 Cor. 9:8; Eph. 2:10; Phil. 1:6; Col. 1:10; 1 Tim. 2:10; 6:18; 2 Tim. 2:21; 3:17; Titus 1:16; 3:1). Sometimes preachers are so zealous to preach and safeguard the liberating truth that we are saved by grace through faith without works, that they may be in danger of giving the impression that good living is not very important. Ephesians 2:10 should not be separated from Ephesians 2:8–9.

Study questions

1. Look for mention of the return of Christ in Paul's other letters and compile a list of the details.
2. Examine our Lord's teaching on the end times. What is the significance of Matthew 24:34?
3. Apparently, when John Wesley[57] was asked what he would do if he knew that his life were to end the next day (we may apply this to either his death or the return of Christ), he replied that he would carry on as he had planned. What does that suggest about his faith and his lifestyle?
4. Since no one knows when Christ will return, what are the really essential lessons we should learn from this chapter?

Notes

1 **Leon Morris** remarks that the cognate verb is used of the gathering of the elect (Matt. 24:31; Mark 13:27), and that the only other occurrence of the noun is in Heb. 10:25, where it refers to the gathering of the believers for worship. But even in that verse the Day of the

Lord is mentioned. (**Leon Morris,** *The First and Second Epistles to the Thessalonians* (NICNT; Grand Rapids, MI: Eerdmans, 1991), p. 213.)

2 Ibid.

3 **Gene L. Green,** *The Letters to the Thessalonians* (Grand Rapids, MI: Eerdmans / Leicester: Apollos, 2002), p. 301.

4 Paul uses an aorist infinitive for the verb translated 'shaken' (aorist passive infinitive, *saleuō*— to be shaken, agitated), and a present infinitive for 'troubled' (present passive infinitive, *throeō*—to be disturbed, troubled, frightened). This suggests that the shaking occurred at one point in time, while the 'being troubled' is an ongoing state.

5 **Morris,** *First and Second Epistles.*

6 **Green,** *Letters*, p. 305.

7 Ibid. p. 303.

8 See Appendix 1 on the meaning of 'heart' in Scripture.

9 **Gordon H. Clark,** *First and Second Thessalonians* (Jefferson, MD: Trinity Foundation, 1986), p. 87.

10 **F. F. Bruce,** *1 & 2 Thessalonians* (Word Biblical Commentary; Nashville: Thomas Nelson, 1982), p.165.

11 This word is used only by Paul—in Rom. 7:11; 16:18; 1 Cor. 3:18; 2 Cor. 11:3; 1 Tim. 2:14— though the verb without the strengthening prefix, *ex*, is found in James 1:26.

12 Both **Bruce** (*1 & 2 Thessalonians*, p. 165) and **Morris** (*First and Second Epistles*, p. 216) explain that the word must mean 'is present'.

13 **Morris,** *First and Second Epistles*, p. 217.

14 See Appendix 2 on deception in the New Testament.

15 Reprinted in **John Calvin,** *The Mystery of Godliness and Other Sermons* (Morgan, PA: Soli Deo Gloria, 1999), p. 83.

16 **Bruce,** *1 & 2 Thessalonians*, p. 166.

17 'The word *apostasia* is derived from the verb *aphistēmi* which when used intransitively means "to fall away" or "to become apostate". As used in 2 Thessalonians 2:3 *apostasia* is preceded by a definite article: *the* apostasy or *the* rebellion … [W]hat is predicted here is a final, climactic apostasy just before the end time. This apostasy will be an intensification and culmination of a rebellion which has already begun' (**A. A. Hoekema,** *The Bible and the Future* (Exeter: Paternoster, 1979), pp. 153f.).

18 Most modern versions prefer 'lawlessness', as early manuscript evidence, such as Aleph and B, have it, whereas the majority text has 'sin'. However, **Gordon Clark** points out that the verse has 'sin' when cited by the early writers Irenaeus, Tertullian, Hippolytus, Origen, Eusebius, Ambrosiaster, Ephraem, Cyril of Jerusalem, Ambrose, Chrysostom, Pelagius, Jerome,

Theodora, Augustine, Theodoret and John of Damascus. It is of little importance, for John states that 'sin is lawlessness' (1 John 3:4). (**Clark,** *First and Second Thessalonians*, p. 86.)

19 For a discussion of the 'horns' of Daniel 7–8 see **Edward J. Young,** *Daniel* (Edinburgh: Banner of Truth, 1979 repr.).

20 **William Hendriksen,** *1 & 2 Thessalonians* (London: Banner of Truth, 1972), p. 170.

21 Ibid. p. 171.

22 The textual evidence varies between *anaireō*, 'to take away, destroy or kill', and *analiskō*, 'to consume'. **W. E. Vine** states that 'the best texts' have *aneireō*, 'to slay' (*Expository Dictionary of New Testament Words*, vol. iv (London: Oliphants, 1973), p. 40). This verb is used in Matt. 2:16; Luke 22:2; and Acts 2:23 with the sense 'to kill violently'. This makes sense, as in vv. 3 and 4 he is clearly seen to be a person.

23 **Bruce** has a useful ten-page excursus on Antichrist, *1 & 2 Thessalonians*, pp. 179ff.

24 Wycliffe, Luther and the Westminster Confession (XXV, 6) identify the Antichrist with the pope, because of the papacy's claim that the pope represents Christ. Few would be so specific today, if only because the Antichrist comes at the end of time.

25 **Hendriksen**, *1 & 2 Thessalonians*, p. 172.

26 **Vine,** *Expository Dictionary*, vol. i, pp. 302–304.

27 After the death of the Roman emperor Nero (AD 37–68), there was a widespread belief that he would return; this is known as the 'Nero redivivus' myth. Some have identified the beast of Rev. 13:1–18 with Nero. This has led some commentators to identify Nero with the man of sin. However, it is worth bearing in mind that Nero had not yet become emperor when the Thessalonian epistles were written. See **F. L. Cross, (ed.),** *The Oxford Dictionary of the Christian Church* (London: Oxford University Press, 1958), p. 945; **Hendriksen,** *1 & 2 Thessalonians*, pp. 170ff.; **J. Stuart Russell,** *The Parousia* (1887; Grand Rapids, MI: Baker, 1983), pp. 457ff.

28 **Walter A. Elwell, (ed.),** *Evangelical Dictionary of Biblical Theology* (Grand Rapids, MI: Baker / Carlisle: Paternoster, 1996), p. 233.

29 **Bruce,** *1 & 2 Thessalonians*, p. 169.

30 Cited in **Joel R. Beeke,** *Puritan Reformed Spirituality* (Darlington: Evangelical Press, 2006), p. 79.

31 'I frankly confess I do not know what he [Paul] means' (*The City of God*, XX, p. 19, cited in **Geoffrey W. Bromiley, (gen. ed.),** *The International Standard Bible Encyclopedia*, vol. iii (Grand Rapids, MI: Eerdmans, 1988), p. 92).

32 See **Elwell,** *Dictionary of Biblical Theology*, p. 909.

33 **John MacArthur, Jr.,** *1 & 2 Thessalonians* (The MacArthur New Testament Commentary; Chicago: Moody Press, 2002), p. 279.

34 Bruce, *1 & 2 Thessalonians*, p. 176.

35 Hendriksen, *1 & 2 Thessalonians*, p. 181.

36 This view is explained in detail in **Green,** *Letters*, pp. 314–317.

37 For a full discussion of this viewpoint see **Charles A. Wanamaker,** *The Epistles to the Thessalonians* (NIGTC; Grand Rapids, MI: Eerdmans / Carlisle: Paternoster, 1990), pp. 249–257.

38 Morris, *First and Second Epistles*, p. 229.

39 John Calvin, *The Mystery of Godliness and Other Sermons* (Morgan, PA: Soli Deo Gloria, 1999), pp. 59ff.

40 Bruce, *1 & 2 Thessalonians*, pp. 178ff.

41 Morris (*First and Second Epistles*, p. 231), cites the Bauer/Arndt-Gingrich Greek Lexicon, which defines epiphany as a technical term for 'a visible manifestation of a hidden divinity, either in the form of a personal appearance, or by some deed of power by which its presence is made known'.

42 Bruce, *1 & 2 Thessalonians*, p. 172.

43 Hendriksen, *1 & 2 Thessalonians*, p. 184.

44 Bruce, *1 & 2 Thessalonians*, p. 173.

45 Os Guinness, *The Dust of Death* (London: IVP, 1973), p. 311.

46 From **Adam Clarke,** *Commentary on 2 Thessalonians*, chap. 2 (PC Study Bible; Seattle, WA: Biblesoft, 2006).

47 Green, *Letters*, p. 322.

48 Ibid. p. 323.

49 Bruce, *1 & 2 Thessalonians*, p. 174.

50 This was actually suggested by **Richard Dawkins** when interviewed by Ben Stein (DVD *Expelled*, NPN Videos, 2010).

51 Morris, *First and Second Epistles*, p. 235.

52 From **Barnes'** *Notes on 2 Thessalonians*, chap. 2 (PC Study Bible; Seattle, WA: Biblesoft, 2006).

53 Bruce, *1 & 2 Thessalonians*, p. 175.

54 Bruce (ibid. p. 190) remarks that this is the only place in the New Testament where the simple word *hairesmai* is used of God's choosing his people. But the sense here is similar to that of *eklegesthai* used elsewhere, e.g. Eph. 1:4.

55 Bruce (ibid.) points out that the textual evidence for 'firstfruits' (*aparchēn*) is stronger than that for 'from the beginning' (*ap' archēs*), though in what sense the Thessalonians were 'firstfruits' is not clear. They were obviously not the firstfruits of Macedonia, as the Philippian church was established before theirs (see Rom. 16:5; 1 Cor. 16:15). Bruce concludes with the intriguing remark that the church as a whole is the firstfruits of mankind to God. Then Bruce makes this thought-provoking comment: 'It is a travesty of God's electing grace to suppose that, because he chose some for salvation, all the others are thereby consigned to perdition. On the contrary, if some are chosen for special blessing, it is in order that others may be blessed through them and with them. This is a constant feature in the pattern of divine election throughout the Bible story, from Abraham onward. Those who are chosen constitute the firstfruits, bearing the promise of a rich harvest to come' (p. 191). See also **Green, Letters**, p. 326.

56 Bruce, *1 & 2 Thessalonians*, p. 195.

57 This saying has also been attributed to others, such as D. L. Moody and C. H. Spurgeon. The point is valid even if the provenance is uncertain.

Final requests and exhortations (2 Thes. 3)

God's servants need prayer (vv. 1–2)

PRAY FOR US (V. 1)

'Finally' (*to loipon*—'for the rest') is used either to signal the approaching end of the letter or the transition to another section, as in Philippians 3:1. Paul now exhorts the Thessalonians to pray for the apostolic team in order that the word of the Lord may 'run', that is, have free course, and 'be glorified' (compare Ps. 147:15). Both verbs are in the present subjunctive, suggesting 'continue to run' and 'continue to be glorified'. This is an allusion to the Olympic Games, where an athlete runs without hindrance and receives honour as the winner of the race. Paul used this analogy several times (Rom. 9:16; 1 Cor. 9:24–27; Gal. 2:2; 5:7; Phil. 2:16; compare Heb. 12:1–2). The point is that prayer was needed so that the Word of God would spread rapidly, meet with no obstruction and be honoured, not just as the word of man but, as it was in fact, the Word of God (compare 1 Thes. 2:13).

But how best is the Word of the Lord 'glorified'? Surely it is when it transforms lives and glorifies God. James Denney writes,

A message from God that did nothing would not be glorified: it would be discredited and shamed. It is the glory of the gospel to lay hold of men, to transfigure them, to lift them out of evil into the company and the likeness of Christ. For anything else it does, it may not fill a great space in the world's eye; but when it actually brings the power of God to save those who receive it, it is clothed in glory.[1]

The apostle knew the value and importance of prayer and often asked his correspondents to pray for him (e.g. Rom. 15:30–32; 2 Cor. 1:11; Eph. 6:19; Phil. 1:19; Col. 4:3–4; 1 Thes. 5:25). In this he was not so much concerned about his own personal safety (he seemed to care little about that) as for the freedom to proclaim the gospel (see Acts 14:14–20; 19:30–31; 21:4, 9–13; 2 Cor. 4:7–12; 11:22–23; Phil. 1:19–30; 3:7–14; Col. 1:24–29). Paul was writing from Corinth and may have had in mind the opposition he had received there, which called forth a vision from the Lord to encourage him (Acts 18:5–6, 12–13, 9–10). He admits in his first letter to the Corinthians that he had gone there in 'weakness, in fear, and in much trembling' (1 Cor. 2:3).

How often do we preachers approach a new situation in that frame of mind? Are we not more often filled with self-confidence? When did you last tremble before preaching or witnessing? A rapid expansion of the gospel had occurred among the Thessalonians (1 Thes. 1:8; compare Acts 17:4) but it did not happen everywhere (Acts 14:5–6, 19–20). Why did this happen in Thessalonica? Ultimately, it was the sovereign will of God, but within God's sovereign pleasure we might point to the fact that the preaching in Thessalonica was notable for the power that accompanied it (1 Thes. 1:5). God in his wisdom and providence has made the success of the gospel dependent, to a certain extent, on the prayers of believers. Why he should do this we do not know, but this is what the Bible teaches (1 Chr. 16:11, 35; 2 Chr. 7:14; Ps. 18:3; 50:15; 56:9; 91:15; Jer. 33:3; Matt. 7:7–8; Mark 9:28–29; Luke 11:13; 18:1; Eph. 6:18–19; Phil. 4:6; 1 Thes. 5:17; Heb. 4:16; etc.).

This should encourage us all to engage in fervent prayer for the success of the gospel. The church is weak when prayer is lacking. This is why Paul asked for prayer. Paul's imperative 'pray' is in the emphatic position in the sentence, which suggests how important he regarded this request. Moreover, it is a present imperative, emphasizing the need to go on praying. But why did he ask for prayer for themselves? Why not just ask that prayer be made that the gospel might have free course and be honoured? The answer in part is surely that the condition of the messengers greatly influences the success of the message.

Writing to Timothy, the apostle points this out, saying, '… in a great house there are not only vessels of gold and silver, but also of wood and clay, some for honor and some for dishonor. Therefore if anyone cleanses himself from the latter, he will be a vessel for honor, sanctified and useful for the Master, prepared for every good work' (2 Tim. 2:20–21). God's messengers need the physical and mental strength, the wisdom and the knowledge for the task, but, above all, the power of the Holy Spirit, who is given in answer to prayer (Luke 11:13). They must be spiritually fit for the work. It is challenging and moving to realize that the mighty apostle Paul asked these new Christians to pray for him and his colleagues. But the significance and power of prayer does not reside in the age or maturity of those who pray, whatever their experience, but in the God to whom they pray.

E. M. Bounds, in his justifiably famous book *Power Through Prayer*, wrote that the church is looking for better methods, while God is looking for better men. He also wrote that it takes twenty years to make a sermon because it takes twenty years to make a preacher.[2] The saintly Robert Murray McCheyne remarked that his people's greatest need was his own holiness. On the same theme, Professor James S. Stewart, in his book *Heralds of God*, quoted a certain bishop Quayle as asking and answering this question: 'Preaching is the art of making a sermon and delivering it? Why, no, that is not preaching. Preaching is the art of making a preacher and delivering that. It is no trouble to preach, but a vast trouble to construct a preacher.'[3]

Mary E. Maxwell expressed this truth in her hymn 'How I Praise Thee, Precious Saviour':

Just a channel full of blessing,
To the thirsty hearts around;
To tell out Thy full salvation,
All Thy loving message sound.

Channels only, blessed Master,
But with all Thy wondrous power
Flowing through us, Thou canst use us
Ev'ry day and ev'ry hour.

UNREASONABLE OPPOSITION (V. 2)

Another reason why the apostles needed prayer was so that they might be 'delivered from unreasonable and wicked men'. The Greek word translated 'unreasonable' (*atopōn*) means out of place, then absurd, unusual, strange; then improper, unreasonable and even wicked. It occurs only four times in the New Testament and is translated differently each time: 'wrong' (Luke 23:41; 'amiss' in the KJV), 'fault' (Acts 25:5), 'harm' (Acts 28:6), and 'unreasonable' here, the only place where it is applied to people rather than things. The literal meaning of 'out of place' could also present the idea of 'baffling'. How can it be that something that transforms people's lives, produces love, service, kindness and honesty, and gives people eternal hope, should be opposed? It is certainly 'unreasonable' to reject it out of hand. Given the facts of the reality of God, his holy nature and man's sinfulness, the gospel is altogether reasonable. Those who oppose it are unreasonable. More than that, they are sinful, since 'all have sinned and fall short' of God's glory (Rom. 3:23), but some are more obviously opposed to the gospel than others.

The late John Marshall, who regularly preached in the open air in Hemel Hempstead, was once aggressively heckled by a woman. After a brief interchange John remarked, 'You know, I believe that if Jesus Christ were alive today you would crucify him.' 'I would, I would,' shouted the woman.[4]

Although the NIV renders the word *atopōn* as 'wicked' (ESV, 'evil'), it does not necessarily mean that here. Not all who speak 'out of place' are wicked, at least overtly. They may be well-meaning but misguided people who place undue emphasis upon a certain aspect of truth or practice.

They may simply be gripped by a misunderstanding or even a certain doctrinal error. Such people can often cause ministers pain or heartache.

Adam Clarke, in his commentary on 2 Thessalonians, says that the word 'signifies ... disorderly, unmanageable; persons out of their place—under no discipline, regardless of law and restraint, and ever acting agreeably to the disorderly and unreasonable impulses of their own minds.'5

Some are unreasonable, while others are quite clearly evil (*poneros*, 'wicked'). This is a concept that the modern world is hardly willing to accept. According to the humanistic outlook, people may be unfortunate, mistaken, fallen into bad company, come from dysfunctional backgrounds and so on, but they are rarely acknowledged to be actually evil, for sin is not recognized by society today.

'[F]or not all have faith.' This statement has been variously understood by commentators. On the surface it states the obvious: that not all are believers, though some have 'faith' in lucky charms or idols. The word 'faith' has the definite article, so literally it means 'the faith', the true faith, the gospel. This has led some to interpret the statement as meaning that not all embrace the Christian faith, or are prepared to do so. Another variant is that not all people have the disposition which would cause them to receive the testimony of the apostles. However, the same word is applied to the Lord in the next verse and there it obviously means 'faithful', so there is a play on words here. There are few people we can safely trust, but the Lord is faithful.

Security in Christ (vv. 3–5)

HOW TO BE ESTABLISHED (V. 3)

Paul now turns his attention to the Thessalonians in order to assure them that they are secure because 'the Lord is faithful'. Usually he writes of the faithfulness of God (1 Cor. 1:9; 10:13; 2 Cor. 1:18; compare Heb. 10:23;

1 Peter 4:19; 1 John 1:9), but in this context it is quite in keeping to speak of the faithfulness of 'the Lord' Jesus Christ. He will establish them (*stērizō*, to establish or confirm; compare Luke 22:32; Rom. 1:11; 16:25; 1 Peter 5:10).

New Christians need to be established in the faith. This is accomplished by prayer, teaching and example. To be established is to be built upon a firm foundation (Matt. 7:24–29; 1 Cor. 3:10–12). The three thousand who were converted on the Day of Pentecost 'continued steadfastly in the apostles' doctrine and fellowship, in the breaking of bread, and in prayers' (Acts 2:42).

To establish new converts today demands a definite programme, a specific agenda. A discipling arrangement could be set up, either for an individual or for a group.[6] The aims should be clear-cut and specific, with definite goals in mind. If we aim at nothing we are bound to hit it! For example, if a church needs an elder or elders, especially if there have been none before, it is not enough just to look around for the likeliest man. Teaching on eldership should be given. The whole of the pastoral epistles could be expounded, not just chapter 3 of the First Epistle to Timothy. The congregation will then begin to look for and recognize eldership qualities within the membership, and any whom the Lord is calling will begin to adjust their lives accordingly.

Paul also assures his readers that the Lord will guard them (*phulassō*— to watch or guard) from the evil one (*tou ponērou*—the evil). This could mean either evil in general or the evil one in particular, as in the Lord's prayer; most commentators prefer 'evil one'. God normally guards his people through pastors and elders who will pray for them (John 17:15) and will be on the alert to watch for predators (Jer. 3:15; Acts 20:28–31; 2 Tim. 4:1–5).

The devil goes around 'like a roaring lion, seeking whom he may devour' (1 Peter 5:8). Christians, therefore, are safe so long as they remain close to the Lord and do not trespass on the devil's territory. Jesus said, '[T]he ruler of this world [i.e. Satan] is coming, and he has nothing in Me' (John 14:30). In other words, the devil had no point of access, no 'landing strip' or leverage point in Jesus which would have enabled him to gain entrance into our Lord's life. But if Christians engage in activities that are forbidden in God's Word or, at best, are very dubious, they allow the enemy to begin to influence their thinking and ultimately their behaviour. For example, if Christians read pornographic literature, which is mental adultery, not only are they sinning in that act, but also they are making themselves vulnerable to further temptation. Likewise, if Christians, in direct disobedience to God's Word, attend spiritistic séances or play with Ouija boards, they are straying onto the devil's territory and laying themselves open to serious trouble.

Of course, it is not only the most obvious sins that lay us open to the devil's attacks. Sometimes, when speaking to a small group, such as at a ladies' meeting, I will ask, 'Are any of you involved in witchcraft?' After waiting for a moment or two for various expressions to register, such as puzzlement or surprise, I then turn to 1 Samuel 15:22–23a and read,

Has the LORD as great delight in burnt offerings and sacrifices,
As in obeying the voice of the LORD?
Behold, to obey is better than sacrifice,
And to heed than the fat of rams.
For rebellion is as the sin of witchcraft,
And stubbornness is as iniquity and idolatry.

Notice the three words depicting serious sins—'witchcraft', 'iniquity' and 'idolatry'—and how rebellion and stubbornness are counted as parallel to them. Why did God's prophet say that rebellion is as the sin of witchcraft? Surely because it is as bad as witchcraft in God's eyes. But could it be also that it is as good as witchcraft *in the devil's eyes*? In other words, rebellion against God will enable the enemy to get into an individual's life, or into the life of a church, just as easily as if witchcraft were practised. The same goes for stubbornness against God's commands.

Being guarded by God implies remaining under his control and being obedient to his Word.

WE ARE PERSUADED (V. 4)

In the Greek, the phrase translated 'we have confidence' uses the perfect tense, suggesting an ongoing confidence regarding the Thessalonians' future obedience. Although they had 'boasted' about the Thessalonians, the apostles had confidence not in people but in the Lord, because he is faithful. We can be disappointed by people if we put our trust in them. Sometimes we do have to rely on others to get jobs done or fulfil responsibilities, but our confidence must always ultimately be in the Lord. Paul's confidence that they would obey was a generalization, because there were individuals among them in whom he could hardly be confident (1 Thes. 3:6; 5:14; 2 Thes. 1:3; 3:11).

As an apostle, appointed by the Lord, Paul could command the church. Ministers and elders do not have apostolic authority today, but they do have a certain authority. Strictly speaking, the only authority a pastor has is the spiritual authority inherent in the message he preaches. Having said that, there is a measure of authority that goes along with the office of minister. This will vary from denomination to denomination, and from church to church. It is also linked to some degree with the personality of the minister. But whatever the church or denomination, there will be times when the minister may have to '[c]onvince, rebuke, exhort' (2 Tim. 4:2).

One thing, however, is clear, and that is that a minister should never be a dictator. Autocracy is quite out of place in the pastoral office. On the other hand, democracy is not a biblical concept either. The meeting in Acts 15 was not comparable to a modern church meeting; it was a meeting of apostles and elders of the 'mother church' together with representatives of one other church to decide the grounds upon which Gentiles might come into the church. The churches in the New Testament appear to have been autonomous (see Rev. 1–3).

As far as local-church government is concerned, the ideal is a plurality of spiritually minded leaders in a local church. Happy is the man who has one or more godly leaders alongside him to share in the rule and guidance of the church. But even if there are elders who actively lead, or 'rule', the church (1 Tim. 3:4–5; 5:17; Heb. 13:7, 17, 24; compare 1 Peter 5:3), they would be wise to seek to carry the church with them in major decisions. To spring major changes on a church without prior warning or consultation is not good practice and can lead to serious trouble. The elders do not need to abdicate their leadership; there are ways of preparing a church for change which do not involve surrendering the right to decide issues. It is helpful if the church constitution spells out the elders' role and the manner in which issues are to be decided.

LOVE AND STEADFASTNESS (V. 5)

Hearts need to be directed 'into the love of God' and 'the patience' or steadfastness of Christ. 'The love of God is the grand motive and principle of obedience; this must occupy your hearts: the heart is irregular in all its workings; God alone, by his Spirit, can direct it into his love, and keep it right (*kateuthunai*—to direct), give a proper direction to all its passions, and keep them in order, regularity and purity.'[7]

Paul's wish for these Christians is tantamount to a prayer that 'the Lord' will direct their hearts—the whole inner person, mind, will and emotions—into the love of God and steadfastness of Christ (compare 1 Chr. 29:18). Since the Holy Spirit is the 'executive member of the Godhead' and it is he who produces the fruit of holy character in us (Gal. 5:22–23), it is possible to take the word 'Lord' in this verse to refer to him. If the phrase 'the Lord' does indeed refer to the Holy Spirit (as in 2 Cor.

3:17–18), this verse would be Trinitarian; however, the most natural interpretation is 'the Lord Jesus Christ'.

The phrase 'love of God' may mean either God's love for them, which is Paul's normal usage (Rom. 5:5, 8; 8:39; 2 Cor. 13:14; Eph. 2:4) and overwhelmingly the main emphasis in the New Testament (John 3:16, etc.), or their love for God. Since our love for God is generated by his love for us, perhaps both should be included (see 1 John 4:10).[8] Love of (for) God will show itself in faithful attendance at the means of grace, holy living and obedience to the Word of God. This love of God is not only a divine attribute and a favourable attitude towards other believer, 'but also a divine, dynamic force within them, a principle of life in their innermost being'.[9] Love for God will also be linked with love for others (Mark 12:29–31; 1 John 3:11).

Just as God's love for us produces love for God in us, so the 'patience' or steadfastness of Christ would give rise to a similar quality in the Thessalonians. What is the 'patience of Christ'? It is patience during all their sufferings and persecutions such as Christ manifested under his. He bore meekly the 'contradiction of sinners against himself' (Heb. 12:3, (KJV); and when he was reviled, he did not revile in return (1 Peter 2:23).

Steadfastness or patience (*hupomenē*) is not, however, mere passivity; it is a patient enduring, 'a bearing-up under'. It is God-given restraint in the face of opposition or trials. When Paul employs the term it is nearly always in connection with opposition or hostility towards Christ and his followers, such as tribulation (Rom. 5:3–4), reproach (Rom. 15:3–4), suffering (2 Cor. 1:6; 2 Tim. 3:10), affliction (2 Cor. 6:4) and warfare (1 Tim. 6:11–12). Though endurance (*hupomenē*) and longsuffering (*makrothumia*; often translated as 'patience': Heb. 6:15; James 5:8; compare 1 Thes. 5:14) are very similar, they should be distinguished, for *hupomenē* is related to circumstances, while *makrothumia* is exercised towards people.[10]

The heart is the whole inner person, mainly the mind, but including the will and emotions. Having 'the love of God and ... patience of Christ' means more than mere mental assent to these aspects of character; they are to be wholehearted inclinations. Into these matters we need the Lord to 'direct' us. How are we directed into such aspects of character? Surely it is by the application of the Word of God through preaching, teaching, reading, meditation and prayer, as enlivened by the Holy Spirit.

Separation from disorderly behaviour (vv. 6–7)

SEPARATION IS A NECESSITY (V. 6)

This passage is very similar in content to what Paul writes in 1 Thessalonians 4, except that the tone is now more severe. There were those in the church who had 'obstinately disregarded'[11] Paul's instructions while he was with them (see 3:10) as well as his exhortations in his first letter (1 Thes. 4:11–12; 5:14). Now he had to take up the matter again, but entreaty is replaced by command. The Thessalonian church members are commanded to keep away from (*stellesthai*—to stand aloof, keep away from, or to avoid; used only here and in 2 Cor. 8:20) those who are walking in a disorderly fashion. He puts their submission to the test by a particular command (*parangellō*—to command, order or charge).

Paul had already tactfully anticipated their obedience and prepared the way for this solemn charge by using this verb in verse 4. He emphasizes that he really means it by repeating the verb in verses 10 and 12. The verb was used of the Lord Jesus Christ (Matt. 10:5; Luke 8:29; 9:21; Acts 1:4; 10:42), and Paul used it when instructing the churches in moral behaviour (1 Cor. 7:10; 11:17; 1 Tim. 6:13–14). He now commands the whole church with regard to their attitude to those who are behaving in an unruly manner.

Direct biblical commands, such as the Ten Commandments (Exod. 20:1–17), are not options or suggestions. Paul commands the

Thessalonians to steer clear of those who behave in a disorderly (*ataktos*—undisciplined or unruly) manner and who are not living according to the 'tradition', that is, the oral teaching that Paul has given them (v. 10; compare 1 Thes. 4:11–12; 5:14). In spite of the teaching given while Paul was with them, and the subsequent instruction in his previous letter to them, some members of the church had simply continued to live as they had before.

Green suggests that this behaviour should be understood against the background of the practice of patronage which was 'pervasive in the ancient world' and in which clients depended on their patron for food, money and representation. The patrons benefited from the honour accrued by having so many clients.[12] It is not clear, however, that this explanation fits the circumstances. These people were 'undisciplined' and were refusing to work, thus bringing dishonour on the church.

Paul now exercises his apostolic authority, which is essentially the authority of Christ delegated to him, by issuing a command. This is a very strong command as it is issued 'in the name of our Lord Jesus Christ'—not just Paul's Lord, but their Lord also.

Before considering this command in detail, it would be as well to ask why Paul considered it necessary for the Thessalonians to separate themselves from such people. After all, they were 'brothers'. It is a sad fact of church history, even recent church history, that this command has been applied in a very strict and extreme manner over relatively trivial matters, causing much grief and suffering, even among families.[13] So why in certain circumstances is it necessary for Christians to steer clear of 'brothers' who are behaving in an unruly manner and not according to biblical teaching? There are several reasons:

- To associate with such people must be displeasing to God (see Num. 16:26; Matt. 18:17; Rom. 16:17; 1 Cor. 5:11).
- Other Christians might be influenced and drawn into their unruly behaviour.

- Such behaviour is a bad example to the world and mars the witness of the church, so that unbelievers will despise the church.
- If people are not living according to apostolic teaching, not only are they departing from the faith but also they are likely to deliberately lead others astray.

But how should this action be taken, and on what basis should separation take place? Our Lord, in Matthew 18:15–20, outlines a procedure that should be followed in the case of personal offences. In the Thessalonians' case the situation had not reached the final stage described in Matthew 18, as the offender was still regarded as a brother. From time to time in his epistles, Paul gives instructions on how to deal with various errors (see Rom. 14:1–15:7; 16:17–18; 1 Cor. 1:10–14; 3:1–4; 5:1–6:11; Gal. 6:1–5; Phil. 2:1–4; 4:2–3; 1 Tim. 1:3–6; 5:1–2; 6:3–5; 2 Tim. 2:24–26; 4:2–4; Titus 1:10–14; 3:9–10). Clearly, in the light of these Scriptures, such disciplinary actions should be taken carefully, gently, patiently, and with much prayer, teaching and exhortation—but also firmly and without compromise of either behaviour or doctrine.

If possible, and if appropriate, the disciplined person should be followed up and offered pastoral help. To 'walk' in this kind of context (2 Thes. 3:6) means to live or behave, so walking disorderly (*ataktōs*) means behaving lazily or in an unruly or undisciplined manner. In the context it applies to those who were refusing to work. Today it could apply to those who are dishonestly living on state benefits, or who are 'working the system'. Such behaviour is not only unworthy but brings dishonour on the name of Christ and upon his church.

PAUL'S EXAMPLE (V. 7)

The apostle now refers to the standard set by the apostolic team. They were not at all unruly or ill-disciplined in their behaviour or lifestyle. It is perfectly proper for Christians to follow the good example of older or more experienced Christians. Paul exhorted the Corinthians to follow him, but added the safeguard 'as I imitate Christ' (1 Cor. 11:1; compare 1 Thes. 1:6; 1 Cor. 4:16; Phil. 4:9). Good Christian biographies and missionary accounts can be of great value to young Christians. Also, the lives and examples of older Christians in the church can be an inspiration to others. Sadly, they can also hinder if those older Christians do not live up to their profession.

The effect of our lives on others is perhaps not preached upon or discussed as often as it should be (see Matt. 5:16). The example set by ministers, elders and other church officers is of supreme importance (1 Tim. 3:7; 4:12; 2 Tim. 3:10). An ounce of example is worth a ton of teaching, and if the former contradicts the latter, the teaching is in vain. No one is perfect except our Lord Jesus Christ, who was and is holy in his deity and perfect in his humanity. We are all sinners and liable to fall. A true Christian will know that immediate repentance and cleansing are necessary (1 John 1:5–10). Nevertheless, some sins are more obvious, public and harmful to the church than others. A Christian may become convicted of pride or unclean thoughts, and may repent, confess the sin to God and be forgiven and cleansed without harming anyone else. But if he or she is openly arrogant and boastful, or commits adultery, the Christian is bringing shame on his or her profession.

Some sins, in my view, debar men from office. For example, if a church treasurer embezzles church funds and is then found out, he may repay the money, repent and be forgiven, but he should not normally be restored to dealing with money for two reasons: first, because he may be tempted again; second, because he will have forfeited the trust of the church. If a youth worker or Sunday school teacher is found to be sexually abusing children, he or she may repent, be forgiven and be restored to Christian fellowship, but should not be restored to dealing with children again, for the same reasons. If a minister has an affair, he may break off the illicit relationship, truly repent, be forgiven and be restored to Christian fellowship, but he should not be restored to the pastoral ministry. Not only has he disgraced his profession, grieved God and harmed other lives, but he will also have forfeited the trust of his church members.[14]

Support of Christian workers (vv. 8–9)

BURDEN OR OBLIGATION? (V. 8)

In the first epistle, Paul stated that he and his team supported themselves in order to avoid any charge of mercenary motives in preaching the gospel (1 Thes. 2:5, 9); here he declares that their labour was also an example to the idle. He states that they did not want to be a burden (*epibareō*—to be a burden, to weigh down) to the Thessalonians. The Philippians did not regard it as a burden to contribute to the support of the apostles (Phil. 4:15–16), sending to him more than once while he was in this very city of Thessalonica (for the hospitality Paul enjoyed while in Philippi see Acts 16:15, 34, 40). Many Thessalonians would no doubt have regarded it as a privilege to contribute to the support of those who brought them the message of salvation, but as Paul observed idlers among them who would have made his practice a pretext to justify themselves, he set aside his rights. His reason for doing the same thing at Corinth was to point out how different were his aims from those of the false teachers who sought to profit from their preaching (2 Cor. 11:9, 12–13). As it happened, it was at the very time and place of writing these epistles that he is expressly said to have worked at tent-making with Aquila (Acts 18:3).

It is perfectly scriptural for Christian workers engaging in full-time ministry to be supported by the churches. Both our Lord and Paul himself made this clear (Matt. 10:10; Luke 10:7–8; 1 Cor. 9:3–18; 1 Tim. 5:17–18). However, the apostles waived this right in Thessalonica in order to set an example to the idle people in the church. They did not expect free meals or living expenses, although Paul did, on other occasions and from other churches, accept financial support (Phil. 4:16; 2 Cor. 11:8–9; compare Gal. 6:6). But he wrote firmly against those who would turn ministry into money-making (Acts 20:33–35; 2 Cor. 2:17; 1 Tim. 3:3, 8; 6:9–10; Titus 1:7; compare Heb. 13:5; 1 Peter 5:2; 2 Peter 2:3). The apostolic team provided their own food by working hard.

The word translated 'labor' (*kopos*) means laborious toil, difficulty or manual labour. This is emphasized by the word translated 'toil' (*mochthos*) which means hard labour, strenuous toil or hardship. In other words, the work the apostles engaged in to provide their own food was no mere token employment; it was genuine hard labour. They obviously worked long hours, for Paul uses the phrase 'night and day'. In certain missionary situations God's servants have to be employed in secular occupations in order to gain access to particular countries, even if the missionary societies provide for them in other ways. Even in the West some Christian workers support themselves with either full- or part-time employment in secular jobs, such as education or medicine. In this case the apostle wanted some, at least, of the Thessalonians to follow (literally 'imitate') their example of working hard.

WHY THEY WORKED (V. 9)

Paul explains why they engaged in such strenuous labour. He first points out that as God's servants they had a right to financial support, a point he makes elsewhere (1 Cor. 9:4–9). But they were endeavouring to set an 'example' (1 Thes. 1:5–7; 2:14; compare 1 Cor. 4:12) to those who would not work. Bruce writes,

It would have been more difficult for the church to discipline its members who lived … at the expense of their fellows, if they could have pleaded that this was what the missionaries did. But if those who were entitled to be supported by others chose rather to support themselves, how much more should those who had no such entitlement earn their own living![15]

This seems to be a constant concern of Paul's, or at least a matter of considerable sensitivity, as he had already referred to this in the first epistle (1 Thes. 2:5, 9; 4:11), though in that case it seems his motive was to avoid any appearance of mercenary motives.

Warnings against idleness (vv. 10–12)

NO WORK, NO FOOD (V. 10)

Those who were unwilling to work should not eat (compare 1 Thes. 4:11; Eph. 4:28). Paul is not concerned here with those *unable* to work, but with those *unwilling* to work. These were obviously not the poor and needy, the disabled or seriously sick. The Bible teaches constantly the necessity of caring for the poor, and both the individual and the church are exhorted to care for them (Matt. 6:2–3; Gal. 2:10; 1 Tim. 5:4; Heb. 13:16).[16] The Thessalonians needed to be taught that it was not right to 'sponge' off other people, particularly to eat bread at another's expense. This is one of the dangers of the welfare state; it can make people dependent and encourage laziness. 'It is a sin to minister to necessities that are merely artificial.'[17] Paul had already taught them about this when he was with them.

The verb 'commanded' (*parēngellomen*) is in the imperfect tense, suggesting that they issued this command more than once. It is sometimes overlooked that the fourth commandment is not just about taking one day in seven as a day of rest, but also about working for the other six days (Exod. 20:8–11; compare Gen. 3:17–19; Ps. 128:2; Prov. 10:4–5; 12:11; 19:15; Eph. 4:28; 1 Thes. 4:11–12). Paul wanted them to follow (*mimeomai*—'imitate', from which our word 'mimic' derives) the apostles' example by working hard. Sometimes mere teaching is not enough. People need to see a living example of what is to be done. Ministers, elders and other Christian workers cannot expect church members to obey teaching that they themselves are not practising. One way of helping people is to train them by working alongside them.

THE PROBLEM STATED (V. 11)

Paul has heard, presumably from Timothy, that there are some 'who walk among' (*peripatountas en*) the Thessalonians, either as church members or those associated with them, who have not heeded his previous exhortations (1 Thes. 4:11–12; 5:14) and are still not working at all. They are idle. They are not busy but are busybodies. There is a play on words here, as the word translated 'busybodies' is literally 'working around' (*mēden ergazomenous alla periergazomenous*, literally, 'nothing working but working-around'). This second participle (*periergazomenous*) is found only here in the New Testament (though the noun form is found in Acts 19:19[18] and 1 Tim. 5:13) and means 'to meddle in that which is not one's concern' (compare 1 Peter 4:15, where another noun is used). They were not working but they were working around: they were busybodies (compare 1 Tim. 5:13). It is one thing to be always busy; it is a different matter to be busy about the right things.

A STERN COMMAND (V. 12)

This is a very strong exhortation from Paul. He commands (*parangellō*) and exhorts (*parakaleō*) 'through our Lord Jesus Christ'. These two verbs have appeared before in these letters ('command' in 1 Thes. 4:11; 2 Thes. 3:4, 6, 10; 'exhort' in 1 Thes. 4:1, 10; 5:14). Combining the two emphasizes the authority of Paul and the urgency of the command, while adding the words 'through our Lord Jesus Christ' puts the authority beyond doubt. In other words, this is no mere opinion or preference of Paul's: it has Dominical authority behind it.

Notice that these people are commanded to work 'in quietness' and for their own food. Busybodies often do make a fuss and commotion, even when they are not working. In many communities one can find at least one person who talks too much, and such people need to be encouraged to hold back and let others speak. Busybodies who talk too much and who are always complaining or expressing their opinions can be a trouble in a church and may need tactful counselling. A mild form of this is the eager person who always answers questions in a discussion group, so robbing others of a chance to contribute. There are various ways of dealing with this. One way is to ask, 'Now can someone who has not spoken yet answer this question?' Another way, if sitting in a circle (the best seating arrangement for a discussion), is to ask the group to speak in turn, beginning with the person next to the offender and then moving around the circle away from the guilty party! If all else fails, a quiet word in private, explaining the need for others to be able to contribute, may be needed. The situation among the Thessalonians was much more serious, of course, which is why Paul takes such a strong line.

Encouragement and explanation (vv. 13–15)

A WORD OF ENCOURAGEMENT (V. 13)

After such a strong word Paul now mollifies his readers with a word of encouragement. They are not to 'grow weary' (or become discouraged or lose heart, *ekkakeō*) in doing good. It is a human weakness that we can grow tired of constantly working hard at our Christian lives, especially if we have received a strong exhortation or rebuke. Christians always need encouragement. It is a wise pastor who follows, and also prefaces, if possible, hard words with words of appreciation and encouragement. It is also sound psychology!

HOW TO RESPOND TO THE WILFULLY DISOBEDIENT (V. 14)

As important as rebuke and exhortation are, how the church deals with the wilfully disobedient is also very important. A wrong approach here can undo all the good done by teaching. It is fatal to gloss over the disobedience and go on as though nothing has happened. Such neglect leaves the boil unlanced, the sore unhealed and the teaching unconfirmed. This point has already been touched upon, but here Paul gives some specific guidance.

First, the offender must be noted, that is, marked and observed. This implies that the church knows about the problem. In our Lord's teaching in Matthew 18, the final stage in dealing with the unrepentant one is 'tell it to the church', whatever the 'it' is (v. 17). The church is to be informed.

The second instruction is that the church members are not to 'keep company' (mix or associate with) the offender (*me sunanamignusthai*). This verb is found only here and in 1 Corinthians 5:9, where both the offence and the punishment are more serious. What is the purpose of this treatment? '[T]hat he may be ashamed.' He has got to feel the cold wind of lack of fellowship. This can be very tricky and, as has been mentioned, certain Christian groups have been extreme in their application of such teaching as this. In such cases they have insisted on applying verse 14 but without taking into account verse 15. However, it is not only the effect upon the sinning brother or sister that has to be borne in mind. If Christians are living lazy and disorderly lives, they are giving a bad impression of the local church and of Christianity in general.

A NECESSARY MODIFICATION (V. 15)

Paul hastens to add that such a person must not be treated as an 'enemy' but rather warned or admonished as a 'brother'. Such a person is still a Christian, though a wayward one. James Denney points out that, in addition to separation and admonition, this exhortation adds love as an essential element in the process of discipline. He writes,

Withdraw from him, and let him feel he is alone; admonish him, and let him be convinced he is gravely wrong; but in your admonition remember that he is not an enemy, but a brother. Judgment is a function which the natural man is prone to assume, and which he exercises without misgiving. He is so sure of himself, that instead of admonishing, he denounces; what he is bent upon is not reclamation, but the annihilation, of the guilty. Such a spirit is out of place in the Church; it is a direct defiance of the spirit which created the Christian community, and which that community is designed to foster. Let the sin be never so flagrant, the sinner is a brother; he is one for whom Christ died. To the Lord who bought him he is inexpressibly valuable; and woe to the reprover of sin who forgets this.[19]

In Galatians 6:1 Paul issues a necessary caution that those who seek to correct others should consider themselves lest they 'also be tempted'. This caution has at least two applications. First, there should be a spirit of humility lest, while seeking to correct others in one error, the one seeking to help may be erring in another direction.

Second, a person seeking to counsel another might be drawn into that particular error. For example, I know of a case where a woman seeking (wrongly) to counsel a man concerning sexual deviations was herself drawn into those same deviations. Apart from the error of a woman attempting to counsel a man, in most cases of disciplinary counselling at least two counsellors should be involved in order to safeguard against emotional involvement or false accusation. The discipline Paul is advocating here is obviously not the same as excommunication, as, for example, in 1 Corinthians 5. The fact that the offender is to be admonished as a brother means that the channels of communication are to remain open.

The word translated 'admonish' (*noutheteō*) means to admonish, rebuke, exhort or instruct.[20] Circumstances alter cases, and how this instruction is to be carried out depends upon the circumstances, the people involved, the opportunities available and, supremely, the willingness of the subject(s) to listen (see Gal. 6:1). It has been said that there are two types of churches: those where problems are dealt with, and those where they are ignored. This can be applied not only to matters of church discipline, but also to the content and aims of preaching. Church leaders should not wait until there is a problem requiring church discipline before they act. The example of the apostle is clear in this matter. When he saw or heard of a behavioural problem he dealt with it in a letter or in his teaching. To ignore such problems can be as bad as, or worse than, being overstrict.

I know of a case in which some young men once behaved rather badly and inappropriately while helping on an evangelistic mission. This was serious enough for the matter to be reported back to the pastor of the church they came from. However, he simply remarked, 'Boys will be boys', and ignored the matter. He was not being a faithful shepherd.

Dealing with behavioural problems in the church through preaching has to be done sensitively and tactfully. It is quite out of order to preach at an individual from the pulpit, and few ministers would stoop so low. This is not what is in mind; rather it is the need for teaching over a period to deal with a general trend. To fire off a red-hot sermon on gossip or adultery in the middle of an exposition of Psalm 23 is perhaps not the best way to deal with such problems! But teaching on behaviour, dress, the use of the tongue, and so on, can be woven into teaching over a period.

For example, how should we deal with the common problem of declining attendance at the main prayer meeting? Surely this problem should be dealt with by teaching on the value and importance of prayer, and by expounding the promises and commands, giving plenty of examples and illustrations of the benefits and blessings of prayer. In addition, individual encouragement or counselling may be appropriate, including explanations of how to take part in a prayer meeting.

The closing benediction (vv. 16–18)

A FINAL APPROPRIATE BLESSING (V. 16)

Paul pronounces or desires the blessing of peace. This may include peace with God, peace in their own minds and consciences, peace among themselves, and peace with all people. He desires peace 'in every way':

that is, they should use every effort to promote it (Rom. 12:18; Matt. 5:9; Heb. 12:14).

Though peace in our hearts or in the church is sometimes difficult to maintain, it is always desirable. Any peace worth having must ultimately be given by the Lord of peace. It is not in us either to give it or maintain it.

The title 'Lord of peace' is given here to Christ just as it is given to the Father elsewhere (Rom. 15:33; 16:20; 2 Cor. 13:11). Literally, he gives 'the peace'; the peace which is his alone to give, and which is both inward and outward.

Spiritual and moral problems in a church are often likely to disturb the peace of the fellowship. For example, there is a danger of people taking sides. One of the hardest things in a church is to agree with the discipline of a family member or a close friend. Yet our allegiance to Christ should be stronger than our human attachments. Paul's preceding instructions could also be likely to generate dispeace, so Paul reminds his readers that God is a God of peace, and he expresses the desire that God will grant them peace in the midst of conflict. In the first letter, his prayer was to the 'God of peace' (1 Thes. 5:23); here it is to the 'Lord of peace', that is, the Lord Jesus Christ (compare Num. 6:26; John 14:27). Notice how all-encompassing this blessing is: Paul emphasizes this wish by praying that it will be for all the church, 'always' and 'in every way' (compare Luke 24:36; Rom. 15:13; and note the use of 'always' in Acts 2:25; 10:2;). This peace, of course, is not merely the absence of strife but the overarching sense of God's presence even in the midst of storms. The prayer 'The Lord be with you all' is in full accord with Christ's promise in Matthew 28:20.

THE AUTHENTICATING SIGNATURE (V. 17)
Because of the possibility of forgery (see 2:2) Paul signs the letter with his own hand as a proof that the epistle is genuine. This also reminds us that Paul dictated his letters to a secretary and then added his own personal

greeting and signature. He always took a very close personal interest in his converts. Skilful letter-writing is a great art. Much good can be done through personal correspondence. The rise of the Internet and emails may have changed this skill, if not harmed it, but letter-writing should not be overlooked as a pastoral tool. After the Revd Charles Simeon of Cambridge died in 1836, several hundred copies of letters he had written were discovered in a sideboard. He not only wrote letters but also copied each of them, and all by hand, of course. Many other men of God have had a profound effect by their letters, which, since they are a source of social history, are also extremely valuable for research.[21]

BLESSING THROUGH CHRIST (V. 18)

With these words Paul is saying, 'The (undeserved) favour, blessing and influence of our Lord Jesus Christ be with you all (be your constant companion). May you ever feel his presence, and enjoy his benediction!' The closing benediction is in this instance not Trinitarian but simply in the name of 'our Lord Jesus Christ'. This does not suggest that the blessing is in any way inferior or defective, for all our spiritual blessings come to us through Christ, including the grace of God (Eph. 1:3–7).

Conclusion

In this, one of Paul's shortest letters, the great apostle has focused on encouragement, exhortation and, especially, eschatology. On the doctrine of the last things he provides details not found anywhere else in the New Testament. He warns against false teaching and unruly behaviour, especially idleness, and instructs how to deal with offenders. His heart sings with encouragement and thanksgiving, even while it smarts from the suffering of his friends. He offers care when it is needed and commands as required. Even just within these three chapters there is plenty of instruction for every church member and for all Christian leaders.

Chapter 8

Study questions

1. Examine Paul's teaching in his other epistles about the Christian's attitude to those in error, and explain any apparent differences.
2. Find out what procedures your church has in place for cases of church discipline.
3. How seriously do you take the practical exhortations of the New Testament?
4. Prayer has many aspects. How balanced is your prayer life with regard to the elements of praise, thanksgiving, petition and intercession?
5. How should we go about seeking to help others who appear to be going astray doctrinally? morally? in commitment and attendance at the means of grace?

Notes

1 **James Denney,** *The Epistles to the Thessalonians* (London: Hodder & Stoughton, 1892), p. 362.
2 **E. M. Bounds,** *The Complete Works of E. M. Bounds on Prayer* (Grand Rapids, MI: Baker, 1990), pp. 447–448.
3 **James S. Stewart,** *Preaching* (The Warrack Lectures; first published in September 1946 under the title *Heralds of God*), (London: English Universities Press, by arrangement with Hodder & Stoughton, 1955), p. 165.
4 I was with a group of ministers to whom John Marshall recounted this incident.
5 **Adam Clarke,** *Commentary on 2 Thessalonians*, chap. 2 (PC Study Bible; Seattle, WA: Biblesoft, 2006).
6 The subjects dealt with while discipling an individual or a group will vary according to need, but may include the meaning of repentance and its ongoing necessity; the meaning of faith; assurance of forgiveness; the security of the believer in Christ; the importance of the Bible for the Christian; the necessity of prayer; how to have a devotional time; the importance of belonging to a church; the necessity of commitment and regular attendance; the importance and practice of worship; victory over sin and temptation; obedience to God and respect for authority; separation from sin; how to listen to the Word preached; how to read the Bible; Bible study methods, and how study differs from reading; Scripture memorization; meditation in the Word; applying Scripture to life; the sovereignty of God; the deity of Christ; the cross,

atonement, substitution; the Lordship of Christ; love—for God and others; the Holy Spirit; the importance of sound doctrine; the importance of godly living; witnessing—why and how; personal testimony—content and how to give it; the danger of pride; humility; the holiness of God; the will of God; giving/tithing; the support of missions; discernment; worldliness; heresies and cults; election; reading other books; the use of time; self-discipline.

7 **Clarke,** *Commentary.*

8 **Leon Morris** cites Lightfoot to the effect that the two senses are 'combined and interwoven' (**Leon Morris,** *The First and Second Epistles to the Thessalonians* (NICNT; Grand Rapids, MI: Eerdmans, 1991), p. 251).

9 **William Hendriksen,** *1 & 2 Thessalonians* (London: Banner of Truth, 1972), p. 197.

10 Ibid. p. 198.

11 **John MacArthur, Jr.,** *1 & 2 Thessalonians* (The MacArthur New Testament Commentary; Chicago: Moody Press, 2002), p. 304.

12 **Gene L. Green,** *The Letters to the Thessalonians* (Grand Rapids, MI: Eerdmans / Leicester: Apollos, 2002), p. 342.

13 Readers may be able to supply their own examples, but how this spirit invaded a whole 'denomination' is described in **F. Roy Coad,** *A History of the Brethren Movement* (Exeter: Paternoster, 1968), ch. 13.

14 This matter is carefully and sensitively dealt with in **John H. Armstrong,** *The Stain That Stays: The Church's Response to the Sexual Misconduct of its Leaders* (Fearn: Christian Focus, 2000).

15 **F. F. Bruce,** *1 & 2 Thessalonians* (Word Biblical Commentary; Nashville: Thomas Nelson, 1982), p. 206.

16 See also James 2:15–16; 1 John 3:17; compare Exod. 23:11; Lev. 19:9–10; 25:25–28, 39–43; Ps. 41:1–3; Prov. 28:27; 31:9; Isa. 58:6–7; Dan. 4:27; Matt. 19:21; Luke 18:22; 19:8; Acts 20:35; Rom. 12:13.

17 **Clarke,** *Commentary.*

18 In Acts 19:19 the noun *perierga*, which means literally 'superfluous works', is used in the technical sense to mean 'magic'. See **F. F. Bruce,** *The Acts of the Apostles: The Greek Text with Introduction and Commentary* (2nd edn.; London: Tyndale, 1952), p. 359.

19 **Denney,** *Epistles*, pp. 384f.

20 **Jay E. Adams** has built a whole system of counselling based upon this word; he calls it 'Nouthetic Counselling'. Adams was unhappy with the importing of secular psychotherapeutic ideas into Christian counselling. For a helpful survey of this tendency and the problems it brings see **Dr E. S. Williams,** *The Dark Side of Christian Counselling* (London: Wakeman Trust/Belmont House Publishing, 2009).

Chapter 8

21 See **H. C. G. Moule,** *Charles Simeon* (London: Inter-Varsity Fellowship, 1948). Many volumes of letters by Christian ministers have been published, such as *Letters of John Newton* (London: Banner of Truth, 1960); *D. Martyn Lloyd-Jones: Letters 1919–1981* (Edinburgh: Banner of Truth, 1984). These, and other volumes like them, can be most instructive and edifying.

The meaning of 'heart' in Scripture

Before we consider the way the word 'heart' is used in Scripture, it may be helpful to see how the Bible presents the state of the heart and what God does for it.

The state of the heart

The heart is full of iniquity (Gen. 6:5; Prov. 11:20; Eccles. 8:11); it is a fountain of evil (Mark 7:21–23); it is darkened or blind (Rom. 1:21; Eph. 4:17–18), hard (Mark 6:52; Rom. 2:5) and deceitful (Jer. 17:9).

What God does for the heart

He knows it (Jer. 17:10; Mark 2:7–9); he cleanses it (Ps. 51:10; Isa. 1:18; Acts 15:8–9); he renews it (Ezek. 36:25–27); he dwells in it (Eph. 3:17); he fills it with love and peace (Rom. 5:5; Col. 3:15).

Even from those Scriptures it should be obvious that by 'heart' it is not the wonderful organ that pumps blood around our body that is meant. When a person has a heart-transplant operation, he or she does not become another person! Nor do those Scriptures fit well with the idea of emotion alone.

What is meant by the word 'heart'

In Genesis 8:21 God speaks of the 'imagination of man's heart'. But imagination is one of the functions of the mind. The word 'heart' is also used to represent the will, as when the Lord says to Moses, 'Pharaoh's heart is hard' in Exodus 7:14 (compare 1 Sam. 7:3; Luke 21:14). Our will is exercised by our minds. After Peter's powerful sermon on the Day of

Pentecost we read that the hearers were 'cut to the heart'; in other words, their consciences were pricked, again a function of the mind. We read of storing Scripture in our hearts (Ps. 119:11), that is, memorizing it, a function of the mind (compare 1 Sam. 21:12). Although sometimes the word 'heart' refers to the emotions (e.g. Ps. 4:7; Isa. 35:4; Luke 24:32), emotions are felt in the mind, which in turn affects the body. It is clear, therefore, that the word 'heart' in Scripture means primarily the mind (see Ps. 19:14; Matt. 9:4; Luke 1:51).

The word 'heart' in Scripture refers mainly to the whole inner life of a person which functions through the mind.

The theme of deception in the New Testament

A prominent theme in the New Testament is the warning about deception. Jesus warned his disciples (Matt. 7:15–20; 24:4–5, 11, 24), Paul warned the Ephesian elders (Acts 20:28–31), and he frequently referred to the danger in his epistles (e.g. 2 Cor. 11:13–15; 1 Tim. 4:1; 2 Tim. 4:3–4), as did Peter (2 Peter 2:1–3) and John (1 John 4:1).

The danger of deception

THE WARNINGS GIVEN BY OUR LORD
- False prophets and false sheep (Matt. 7:15–20)
- Many deceivers (Matt. 24:4–5, 11, 24)

THE WARNINGS GIVEN BY THE APOSTLE PAUL
- False apostles (2 Cor. 11:13–15)
- False spirits (1 Tim. 4:1)
- False teachers (2 Tim 4:3–4)

THE WARNINGS GIVEN BY THE APOSTLE PETER
- False teachers (2 Peter 2:1–3)

THE WARNINGS GIVEN BY THE APOSTLE JOHN
- False prophets (1 John 4:1)

The fact that there are so many warnings about deception in Scripture clearly indicates that there is a very real danger of being deceived. And being deceived obviously means that a person or teaching is thought to be perfectly valid, biblical, correct and above-board, but it is not, and people are taken in, deceived, misled. No wonder that in Ephesians 6 Paul speaks of the 'wiles' of the devil (v. 11).

A striking aspect of the New Testament's warning concerning deception is the variety of words used. No fewer than ten different words are used to warn about this danger. This reinforces the fact that this is an important subject and represents a very real danger.

The need for discernment

THE WORDS USED FOR DECEPTION

The purpose in studying these words is to illustrate the many different types of deception and to demonstrate how prominent this subject is in the Bible.

- *planaō*: to go astray, to wander, to deceive by leading into error (Matt. 24:4–5, 11, 24)
- *apatē*: deceit or deceitfulness (2 Thes. 2:10)
- *exapateō*: to beguile thoroughly, to deceive wholly (2 Cor. 11:3; Rom. 16:17–18)
- *phrenapataō*: to deceive in one's mind (Titus 1:10)
- *dolos*: primarily a bait or snare, hence craft, deceit, guile (2 Cor. 11:13)
- *methodeias*: craft, deceit, wile (Eph. 4:14; 6:11)
- *goētēs*: primarily a wailer, hence from chanting spells—a wizard, sorcerer, enchanter, cheat, imposter (2 Tim. 3:13)
- *paralogizomai*: to reckon wrongly, hence to reason falsely, or to deceive by false reasoning, to delude (Col. 2:4)
- *deleazō*: to catch by a bait, hence to beguile, to entice (2 Peter 2:14; 2:18)
- *panourgia*: 'all working', hence unscrupulous conduct, craftiness, cunning (2 Cor. 4:2; 11:3)

The command to discern or judge

The fact that discernment is needed is underlined not only by the many references to deception, but also by the clear commands to judge, weigh or consider, for example, 1 John 4:1–3; 1 Thessalonians 5:21.

WORDS ABOUT DISCERNING IN THE NEW TESTAMENT

- *anakrinō*: to distinguish, scrutinize, question, judge closely, investigate, examine (Acts 17:11; 1 Cor. 2:14)
- *diakrinō*: to discriminate, to judge thoroughly, to discern (1 Cor. 6:5; Matt. 16:3)
- *diakrisis*: a thorough judging, the noun of the above (Heb. 5:14)
- *dokimazō*: to test, prove, scrutinize so as to decide, to make proof (1 John 4:1)
- *kritikos*: critic or judge, one fit for or skilled in judging (Heb. 4:12)

Appendix 3

The last things (eschatology)

The return of the Lord Jesus Christ

First Thessalonians is unique among Paul's letters in that it is the only one that contains a reference to the return of Jesus Christ in every chapter.

In chapter 1 the Thessalonians are described as turning to God from idols and waiting for 'His Son from heaven' (1:9–10). Christ's return is linked with deliverance from 'the wrath to come'. The joyful relief and blessedness of that fact will be considerably weakened if we do not have an adequate understanding of God's wrath.

The second chapter closes with Paul's joyful expectation of seeing the Thessalonian believers 'in the presence of our Lord Jesus Christ at His coming' (2:19). The Greek word used here for the return of Christ is *parousia*, his 'presence': clearly a synonym for Christ's return.

The same word is used at 3:13, where the 'presence', or coming, of the Lord Jesus is seen to be 'with all His saints'. He is already present with us now by his Spirit, so this means something more. It indicates the visible presence of Christ in his glorified body.

Chapter 4 contains an extended section of teaching on the return of Christ which is aimed at comforting those who have lost loved ones. Unlike 'others who have no hope', believers are not to be ignorant of the truth that when Christ returns he will bring with him those who 'sleep', an expression to mean 'have died' (4:13–14). The believers who are still alive when Christ returns will 'by no means' precede those who have died (4:15). There will be no advantage in still being alive when Jesus comes again. It will not be possible to miss this glorious event. There will be a word of command, the voice of an archangel and the trumpet of God (4:16). Those believers who have died 'in Christ' will rise from the dead first, and then the living believers will be caught up together with them to meet the Lord in the air. And so we shall be with the Lord for ever (4:16–17). There is no mention of an intervening period such as a millennium. This passage teaches that the return of Christ signals 'the end'. These words should be a comfort to all believers.

Chapter 5 commences with a reminder to the Thessalonians of something they knew very well, namely, that the return of Christ will be sudden and without warning, 'as a thief in the night' (5:2). Sudden destruction will come upon those who are in darkness (5:1–4). Christians, who are sons of light and of the day, should not be taken by surprise, but should be alert, sober and ready (5:5–8). Unlike the unbelievers, Christians will not 'suffer wrath' (v. 9); whether already dead (asleep) or still alive (awake), we shall live with Christ for ever (v. 10). Paul's desire for the Thessalonian believers is that they may be kept blameless until Christ returns (v. 23). That should be our desire also.

The Second Epistle also has a strong emphasis upon the last things, but in this case the teaching is limited to the first two chapters. Chapter 1 declares that those who persecute believers, do not know God and do not obey the gospel of our Lord Jesus Christ will be judged and punished. By contrast, Christ will be glorified in, and admired by, all believers. Chapter 2 majors on the events that will precede Christ's return. Christians are not to be deceived into thinking that the *parousia* has already taken place. Before that great event there will be a falling away among professed believers, and an agent of Satan called 'the man of sin' will make his appearance upon the stage of history.

There is no mention of a millennium in these epistles. The only New Testament book that specifically mentions a millennium is Revelation. That book is difficult to interpret and even John Calvin did not tackle it. How one interprets Revelation affects one's understanding of eschatology. There are four major interpretations of Revelation:

1. 'It (nearly) all happened in the past' (the preterist interpretation).

2. 'It is all happening now' (the historicist interpretation).

3. 'It will all happen in the future' (the futurist interpretation).

4. 'It is the ideas that count' (the idealist interpretation).

A very fine book on eschatology, discussing all the various views, is *The Promise of the Future* by Cornelis P. Venema.[1] He briefly defines the four interpretations of Revelation as follows:

[A] preterist reading of the book says that the events described in its language of vision and prophecy were events occurring or about to occur at the time the book was first written. These events are, from our vantage point, past events, things that have already occurred—hence the term. A futurist reading of the book says that the events described in its prophecy are events yet to occur in the future, primarily in the period just prior to Christ's coming at the end of the age. An historicist reading of the book identifies the events in the visions of Revelation with historical developments throughout the history of the church. An idealist reading of the book says that the visions and prophecy of Revelation refer to events that typify the principles and forces at work in the entire period of history between Christ's first and second comings.[2]

Notes

1 **Cornelis P. Venema,** *The Promise of the Future* (Edinburgh: Banner of Truth, 2000).

2 Ibid. p. 305, n. 1.

The question of alcohol

Should a minister or a missionary, or indeed any Christian, drink alcohol? For missionaries to Muslim countries the answer, perhaps, is clear. Alcohol is forbidden in those lands. The Bible does not appear to give a definite answer at first glance. But there are principles taught in the Bible which are meant to influence our behaviour.

However, before we examine the Scriptures, let us take into account today's situation, for it is very different from Bible times in several respects.

In the first place, as far as beverages containing alcohol are concerned, in Bible times there were basically just wine and a form of beer. Today there are many alcoholic beverages, including very strong spirits, which for many young people are a tempting step down to the abuse of other substances (i.e. stronger drugs). The possibilities of becoming seriously inebriated are very much greater.

Second, modern civilization has produced many more potentially dangerous situations, such as driving motor vehicles and piloting planes. In Bible times, if a man got drunk and mounted his donkey he would have been unlikely to cause a serious accident; but a driver of any motorized vehicle today who is under the influence of alcohol can become guilty of manslaughter within seconds of starting to drive. Today's situation is therefore much more complicated.

Third, science has discovered much more about alcohol and the human body than could have been known in Bible times. In a programme shown on BBC television doctors stated that alcohol can cause many diseases.[1] It is now classified as a drug, and it affects the brain and bodily functions in a variety of ways. It is these practical reasons as well as Bible teaching that should influence our decision in this matter.

Let us also remember that, in Bible times, apart from water, milk and freshly squeezed fruit juice, wine was about the only common beverage available. Water, perhaps, would not always be safe or available, hence Paul's advice to Timothy, who was having stomach trouble, in 1 Timothy 5:23. But it is very important to remember that several ways of preventing grape juice from fermenting were known. The simplest and most common method was simply to boil it. This killed the yeast. If the resulting thickened liquid was then stored in a new wineskin (i.e. one not tainted with yeast cells), it would remain unfermented for a long time. To use it, people would squeeze a portion into a cup and dilute it with water.

Now when we turn to the Bible we must consider the various words used.

Old Testament

There are two Hebrew words used for wine in the Old Testament. The most common is *yayin*. This word is used about 140 times to indicate both fermented and unfermented wine. It is used of fermented wine in such passages as Genesis 9:20–21; 19:32–33; 1 Samuel 25:36–37; Proverbs 23:30–31. The same word is used for the sweet, unfermented juice of the grape. It is also used of the juice as it is pressed from the grape, as, for example, in Isaiah 16:10 and Jeremiah 48:33. Jeremiah refers to juice still in the grape as *yayin*. *The Jewish Encyclopedia* states, 'Fresh wine before fermentation was called *yayin-mi-gat* (wine of the vat).'[2]

The other relevant Hebrew word is *tirosh*, a word meaning 'new wine' or 'harvest wine'. Brown, Driver and Briggs state that *tirosh* means 'fresh or new wine, freshly pressed wine'.[3] *Tirosh* occurs thirty-eight times in the Old Testament. It rarely refers to fermented wine (but see Hosea 4:11), but nearly always to the unfermented juice of the grape, such as the juice that is still in the grapes (Isa. 65:8) or juice from newly harvested grapes (Deut. 11:14; Prov. 3:10; Joel 2:24). The Jewish Encyclopedia states that '"*Tirosh*" includes all kinds of sweet juices and must, and does not include fermented wine'.4

In addition to these two words there is another Hebrew word that occurs twenty-three times in the Old Testament. This is the word *shekar*, usually translated as 'intoxicating drink' (NKJV) or 'beer' (e.g. 1 Sam. 1:15) or 'fermented drink' (NIV; Num. 6:3). This word seems to refer most often to a fermented beverage perhaps made from palm juice, pomegranates, apples or dates.

New Testament

The Greek word translated 'wine' is *oinos*. This can refer both to fermented and to unfermented grape juice. The use of this word to refer to unfermented grape juice is testified to in various pre-Christian and early Christian writers, but it can also be seen within the Bible itself. In the Septuagint (Greek version of the Old Testament) *oinos* is used to translate both *yayin* (a term referring to both fermented and unfermented grape juice) and *tirosh* (unfermented juice). The context normally indicates which is intended, but this is not always the case. So, for example, the oft-quoted 'use a little wine for your stomach's sake' (1 Tim. 5:23) may refer to either.

What about the Lord's Supper? One fact that surprises many people who assume that fermented wine was used in the institution of the Lord's Supper is that nowhere in the New Testament is the term 'wine' used in connection with the Lord's Table! Consistently, when the contents of the cup are referred to, the phrase 'fruit of the vine' is used. Alternatively, the word 'cup' is employed. That could leave the matter undetermined. However, there are other considerations.

The Lord's Supper was instituted when Jesus and his disciples were eating the Passover. The Passover law in Exodus 12:14–20 prohibited the presence and use of *leaven* or *yeast* during Passover week (Exod. 12:15). This is because leaven symbolized corruption and sin (see Matt. 16:6, 12;

1 Cor. 5:7–8). There is an interesting comment in the *Jewish Encyclopedia*:

According to the Synoptic Gospels, it would appear that on the Thursday evening of the last week of his life Jesus with his disciples entered Jerusalem in order to eat the Passover meal with them in the sacred city; if so, the wafer and the wine of ... the communion service then instituted by him as a memorial would be the unleavened bread and the unfermented wine of the Seder service.5

Having established that in the Bible the term 'wine' refers to both fermented and unfermented juice, and that only the context can (normally) tell the reader which is meant, we can now examine some of those passages which clearly refer to fermented drink.

In Genesis 6:9 Noah was noted as a righteous and blameless man, yet at 9:21 he was drunk, incapable, and manifesting uninhibited behaviour.

Genesis 19:30–38 tells of the shameful incident in which Lot's daughters got him drunk and then committed incest with him.

In Genesis 27:25 Jacob was able to deceive Isaac into blessing him instead of Esau, and it seems that wine was involved to help in the deceit.

In Leviticus 10:9 priests were forbidden to drink when on duty, and this was a perpetual statute for all generations.

The Nazirites were to abstain from wine and strong drink.

In Deuteronomy 21:20 rebellion is expressed in gluttony and drunkenness.

In preparation for the birth of her extraordinary son, Samson's mother was commanded not to drink wine (Judg. 13:4, 7, 14).

The first chapter of Esther tells how the king wanted to show off his queen to the assembled nobles. He called for her to come and exhibit herself, but she refused, so he dismissed her. He had been drinking for seven days (Esth. 1:10).

The book of Proverbs, a book of wisdom, has many warnings about drinking. At 4:17 drink is related to violence (don't we know about that today!); at 20:1 wine mocks and brawls, and those who get intoxicated lack wisdom. At 23:21 we are warned that drinking leads to poverty. Verses 29 to 35 of the same chapter are an extended warning about the sorrow, contentions, complaining, wounds, red eyes and unsteadiness caused by drinking fermented wine, with the additional comment that it harms all who drink it and is addictive.

The prophets issue many warnings about strong drink. Isaiah utters woes against those who pursue it (5:11) and those who boast in their ability to drink (5:22). To those who, instead of repenting, are careless and dissolute, he warns that judgement will be inevitable (22:12–14), and he exclaims that 'strong drink is bitter to those who drink it' (24:9). It produces reeling, staggering, confusion, false spirituality and vomit (28:7)! Spiritual blindness, sleepiness and lack of understanding come on those who drink (56:10–12).

Daniel and his companions refused the king's wine, drank water instead and were blessed in their stand (Dan. 1:8–17). Hosea warns that wine takes away the understanding (4:11) and produces sickness (7:5). Joel links wine with injustice and immorality (3:3), while Amos links it with the oppression of the poor and needy (4:1) and lack of concern for God's people (6:6). Habakkuk declares that wine produces proud and haughty behaviour (2:5). There is no doubt at all that the consistent testimony of the Old Testament is that fermented wine is bad news.

In the New Testament, there are various warnings. In Romans 13:13 drunkenness is linked with sexual immorality. The whole of Romans 14 is very pertinent to this matter, but two verses may encapsulate what our attitude should be:

- 'Therefore let us not judge one another anymore, but rather resolve this, not to put a stumbling block or a cause to fall in our brother's way' (14:13).

- 'It is good neither to eat meat nor drink wine nor do anything by which your brother stumbles or is offended or is made weak' (14:21).

Our example is important. Putting this matter in the form of a question, we may ask, 'Does drinking alcohol cause some to stumble or be made weak?' It certainly does. In 1 Corinthians 8 Paul again warns us against using our freedom in a way that causes others to stumble:

- 'But beware lest somehow this liberty of yours become a stumbling block to those who are weak' (8:9).
- 'And because of your knowledge shall the weak brother perish, for whom Christ died? But when you thus sin against the brethren, and wound their weak conscience, you sin against Christ' (8:11–12).

If a minister took just a tiny drink of wine at a wedding or at Christmas, young people, or others, observing would not say, 'The pastor only drinks a tiny amount occasionally', but would simply conclude, 'The pastor drinks.' Thus he could become the ruin of someone else. For this reason alone I have been a lifelong teetotaller.

But there are other considerations. Our bodies are temples of the Holy Spirit (1 Cor. 6:19–20). We should do our utmost to keep them pure, and that surely includes doing nothing that would ruin their health. Alcohol is notorious for the many health problems it causes. So the best plan, it seems to me—because of the many warnings of Scripture, because of the importance of our example, because of modern dangers, and because our bodies are temples of the Holy Spirit—is to avoid it altogether.

Notes

1 'Alcohol: More Harm than Heroin', *Panorama*, BBC 1, 12 October 1987.

2 'Wine' in *The Jewish Encyclopedia*, at: jewishencyclopedia.com; accessed March 2011.

3 **Francis Brown, S. R. Driver** and **Charles A. Briggs**, *A Hebrew and English Lexicon of the Old Testament* (Oxford: Clarendon Press, 1939); accessed at: archive.org/details/hebrewenglishlex00browuoft.

4 'Wine' in *The Jewish Encyclopedia*; accessed March 2011. Other authorities claim, however, that there is little difference between the various words and that all may refer to fermented wine. See, for example, the articles 'Wine and Strong Drink', in **J. D. Douglas,** *The New Bible Dictionary* (London: Inter-Varsity Fellowship, 1962), p. 1331; and 'Wine', in **Geoffrey W. Bromiley, (gen. ed.),** *The International Standard Bible Encyclopedia*, vol. iv (Grand Rapids, MI: Eerdmans, 1988), pp. 1068ff.

5 'Jesus of Nazareth: The Last Supper', *The Jewish Encyclopedia*.

Select bibliography

Brown, Colin, (ed.), *The New International Dictionary of New Testament Theology* (Exeter: Paternoster, 1975–1978)

Bromiley, Geoffrey W., (gen. ed.), *The International Standard Bible Encyclopedia* (Grand Rapids, MI: Eerdmans, 1988)

Bruce, F. F., *1 & 2 Thessalonians*, vol. xxxxv (Word Biblical Commentary; Nashville: Thomas Nelson, 1982)

Chilton, David, *The Days of Vengeance: An Exposition of the Book of Revelation* (Fort Worth: Dominion Press, 1987)

Denney, James, *The Epistles to the Thessalonians* (London: Hodder & Stoughton, 1892)

Douglas, J. D., (organizing ed.), *The New Bible Dictionary* (London: Inter-Varsity Fellowship, 1962)

Elwell, Walter A., (ed.), *Evangelical Dictionary of Biblical Theology* (Grand Rapids, MI: Baker / Carlisle: Paternoster, 1996)

Gill, John, *Exposition of the Old and New Testaments: 1 & 2 Thessalonians* (The Baptist Standard Bearer, 1746–1763; repr. London: Matthew & Leigh, 1810)

Green, Gene L., *The Letters to the Thessalonians* (Grand Rapids, MI: Eerdmans / Leicester: Apollos, 2002)

Grudem, Wayne, *Systematic Theology* (Leicester: Inter-Varsity Press / Grand Rapids, MI: Zondervan, 1994)

Hendriksen, William, *1 & 2 Thessalonians* (London: Banner of Truth, 1972)

Henry, Matthew, *Commentary on the Whole Bible* (PC Study Bible; Seattle, WA: Biblesoft, 2006)

MacArthur, John, Jr., *1 & 2 Thessalonians* (The MacArthur New Testament Commentary; Chicago: Moody, 2002)

Morris, Leon, *The Apostolic Preaching of the Cross* (2nd edn.; London: Tyndale, 1960)

Morris, Leon, *The Cross in the New Testament* (Exeter: Paternoster, n.d.)

Morris, Leon, *The First and Second Epistles to the Thessalonians* (NICNT; Grand Rapids, MI: Eerdmans, 1991)

Stevenson, J., (ed.), *A New Eusebius: Documents Illustrative of the History of the Church to AD 337* (London: SPCK, 1960)

Venema, Cornelis P., *The Promise of the Future* (Edinburgh: Banner of Truth, 2000)

Wanamaker, Charles A., *The Epistles to the Thessalonians* (NICTC; Grand Rapids, MI: Eerdmans / Carlisle: Paternoster, 1990)

About Day One:

Day One's threefold commitment:

- To be faithful to the Bible, God's inerrant, infallible Word;
- To be relevant to our modern generation;
- To be excellent in our publication standards.

I continue to be thankful for the publications of Day One. They are biblical; they have sound theology; and they are relative to the issues at hand. The material is condensed and manageable while, at the same time, being complete—a challenging balance to find. We are happy in our ministry to make use of these excellent publications.

JOHN MACARTHUR, PASTOR-TEACHER, GRACE COMMUNITY CHURCH, CALIFORNIA

It is a great encouragement to see Day One making such excellent progress. Their publications are always biblical, accessible and attractively produced, with no compromise on quality. Long may their progress continue and increase!

JOHN BLANCHARD, AUTHOR, EVANGELIST AND APOLOGIST

Visit our website for more information and to request a free catalogue of our books.

www.dayone.co.uk

Exploring Habakkuk

TIM SHENTON

96PP, PAPERBACK

ISBN 978–1–84625–055–2

Why does a righteous and sovereign God tolerate wrongdoing? How are the divine attributes reconciled with the triumph of the godless? Why do the wicked prosper and rule over the righteous? Why does God raise up 'ruthless and impetuous' nations to execute judgement on his own people? These are some of the questions that perplexed Habakkuk, challenged his faith and caused him to question God's government of the world. These are some of the questions that still perplex Christians today. Tim Shenton helpfully addresses these points in a clear and substantial exposition of the text of Habakkuk.

Tim Shenton is the Head Teacher of St Martin's School and an elder at Lansdowne Baptist Church, Bournemouth. He has written a number of other books, including daily readings for younger readers, a study on revival and is engaged in several writing projects. He and his wife, Pauline, have two daughters.

Habakkuk is the record of a perplexed prophet, unable to comprehend the depth of

Habakkuk
An expositional commentary

Tim Shenton

divine purpose in his day. Written as a dialogue between himself and God, and concluding with a profound expression of worship, this brief book is of great relevance to thoughtful Christians today. We contemplate it and understand the seer's perplexity. Now, to make the book even more accessible to the modern reader, Tim Shenton has provided us with a very helpful commentary on the writings of this man of God. Careful and clear, it is an excellent aid for every believer who would know and love the Lord. Take it and read. And then, bow before the Lord in worship.

—*James Renihan, Dean, Professor of Historical Theology at Westminster Seminary, Institute of Reformed Baptist Studies, Escondido, California*

Exploring Joshua

COLIN N PECKHAM

PAPERBACK, 240 PAGES

ISBN 978–1–846250–93–4

Joshua—what a book! It is a necessary bridge between the Law of Moses and the rest of Israel's history. It magnifies the faithfulness and power of God. It runs from the epic crossing of the Jordan to the final conquest of the land, this being seen as a vivid and graphic picture of claiming our rich inheritance in Christ. It shows that they could only get into the land of victory and fullness through crossing Jordan, the 'river of death', this being a picture of our dying with Christ and rising with him to a new and abundant resurrection life. It reveals the reasons for their failures and shows obedience and faith to be the basis for their victories.

Joshua is a very important book in the canon of Scripture and this devotional commentary merits your attention. It will challenge you with penetrating insights into Scripture and into your own heart. That in essence is its objective—to confront men and women with the necessity of integrity, purity and victory through obedience and faith.

Rev. Dr Colin Neil Peckham was born in South Africa, where he spent ten years in evangelistic ministry and youth work before entering Bible College in Cape Town. He then emigrated to the UK, where he became Principal of the Faith Mission Bible College. He had an extensive preaching ministry and authored several books. He passed away in 2009.

If you are looking for a fast moving, down-to-earth and challenging insight into Joshua, then this is it. Colin Peckham presents a grasp of the book that is easy to take in, particularly the long historical chapters, and manages at the same time to show how the book's message is just as vital for today as it has always been. Buy it, study it and act upon it.
—REV. DR A M ROGER, PRINCIPAL, THE FAITH MISSION BIBLE COLLEGE, EDINBURGH

TIM SHENTON

PAPERBACK, 112 PAGES

ISBN 978–1–846250–87–3

Nahum: Approximately one hundred years after Jonah preached to the citizens of Nineveh to turn 'from their evil ways' and escape imminent judgement, God commissioned Nahum to prophesy the city's complete destruction. At the time of his 'burden', the Assyrian Empire was both strong and wealthy, yet Nahum prophesied that soon the entire kingdom would be crushed forever under the power of God's wrath.

Obadiah: Obadiah's prophecy unveils God's sovereignty over all nations and events, and gives an example of his direct intervention in the political and military affairs of human history. The Sovereign LORD does as he pleases with the powers of heaven and the peoples of the earth. No one can hold back his hand or say to him: 'What have you done?'

Both prophecies are a revelation of God's character and his moral government of the world—a revelation that contains a message of hope, comfort and encouragement for every Christian: 'THE LORD REIGNS FOR EVER'! It matters not how many nations oppose his rule or oppress his people; it makes no difference how many spiritual forces of evil ally themselves for his dethronement, for the Lord's purposes will prevail. All that he has promised will be fulfilled. He is in control. His dominion is an eternal dominion.

Tim Shenton takes us to the most neglected of the Old Testament prophecies, Nahum and Obadiah, and gives us a clear verse-by-verse explanation. Better yet, he consistently shows these little prophecies to have ongoing significance. ... This is a book that provides both understanding of difficult books and comfort for difficult times—and that certainly makes it well worth reading!
—*ROGER ELLSWORTH*

Exploring Haggai

TIM SHENTON

PAPERBACK, 80 PAGES

ISBN 978–1–846250–86–6

A selfish disregard for the purpose of God is all too common among Christian people who live in 'panelled houses' while God's house 'remains a ruin'. As in the days of Haggai, excuses for apathy are shamelessly voiced, blind eyes are turned to the judgements of God, and defiled hearts sink into unfaithfulness. And yet the LORD Almighty remains faithful to his people and true to his word. Through repeated trials he calls the backslider to repentance, with timely encouragements and gracious promises he strengthens the downhearted, and for his own glory he transforms the sins of neglect and ignorance into the servants of his purpose.

With urgency the prophet condemns the wickedness of waiting for the 'right' time when duty calls today, and of lamenting the past— desiring an experience today similar to that of yesterday. And he warns of the grave peril of expecting immediate material results. It is a message that must be taken seriously by the twenty-first century church.

The book of Haggai presents a powerful challenge and provides great encouragement for the church in the twenty-first century. Tim Shenton's lucid exposition of this dynamic book gets to the heart of the prophet's message by carefully explaining and skilfully applying the text. Although this is a short commentary, the author's meticulous research had enabled him to enlighten us with invaluable background information which will sharpen our understanding of its urgency and passion.

—SIMON J ROBINSON, SENIOR PASTOR, WALTON EVANGELICAL CHURCH, CHESTERFIELD, ENGLAND

Exploring Esther
Serving the unseen God

COLIN D JONES

ISBN 978–1–846250–10–1

128PP PAPERBACK

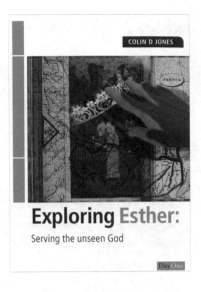

The study of the providence of God is both exciting and profitable, it thrills our hearts as we see the wisdom and power of our Heavenly Father, it strengthens our resolve as we marvel at the sufficiency of his grace and it brings comfort when we do not understand what is happening to us or around us. Esther is all about that marvellous providence. Studying it can deepen our trust, enrich our worship, and intensify our love for our great God. It will reassure us that though we may not always see him he never loses sight of us. The history of Esther is one of the clearest examples of Paul's great assertion in Romans 8:28—'We know that in all things God works for the good of those who love him.'

Colin D Jones has been in the ministry since 1971. He became the Pastor of Three Bridges Free Church, Crawley, in 1996 after 22 years of ministry at Wem Baptist Church, Shropshire. He is a member of the Council of the FIEC. He and his wife, Chris, have four daughters.

Very few modern commentaries on the Book of Esther manage to combine a high view of God's providence and the historicity of the narrative with serious exposition and masses of warm, practical application. This one does.
—JONATHAN STEPHEN, DIRECTOR AFFINITY.